Understanding Post-traumatic Stress

Understanding Post-traumatic Stress

A Psychosocial Perspective on PTSD and Treatment

Stephen Joseph
University of Essex, UK

Ruth Williams
Institute of Psychiatry, London, UK

William Yule
Institute of Psychiatry, London, UK

JOHN WILEY & SONS

Chichester · Weinheim · New York · Brisbane · Singapore · Toronto

Other Wiley Editorial Offices

John Wiley & Sons, Inc., 605 Third Avenue,
New York, NY 10158-0012, USA

VCH Verlagsgesellschaft mbH,
Pappelallee 3, 0-69469 Weinheim, Germany

Jacaranda Wiley Ltd, 33 Park Road, Milton,
Queensland 4064, Australia

John Wiley & Sons (Asia) Pte Ltd, 2 Clementi Loop #02-01,
Jin Xing Distripark, Singapore 129809

John Wiley & Sons (Canada) Ltd, 22 Worcester Road,
Rexdale, Ontario M9W 1L1, Canada

Library of Congress Cataloging-in-Publication Data

Joseph, Stephen.
    Understanding post-traumatic stress: a psychosocial perspective
on PTSD and treatment / Stephen Joseph, Ruth Williams, William Yule.
        p.   cm.
    Includes bibliographical references and index.
    ISBN 0-471-96800-5 (cloth).—ISBN 0-471-96801-3 (pbk.)
    1. Post-traumatic stress disorder.   2. Psychic trauma.
3. Adjustment (Psychology)   I. Williams, Ruth, MA (Oxon), Dip.
Psych.   II. Yule, William.   III. Title.
RC552.P67J67   1997
616.85'21—dc20   96-41655
                                                        CIP

British Library Cataloguing in Publication Data

A catalogue record for this book is available from the British Library

ISBN 0-471-96800-5 (cased)
ISBN 0-471-96801-3 (paper)

Typeset 10/12 pt Plantin from the authors' disks by Vision Typesetting, Manchester
Printed and bound in Great Britain by Bookcraft Ltd, Midsomer Norton, Somerset
This book is printed on acid-free paper responsibly manufactured from sustainable forestation, for which at least two trees are planted for each one used for paper production.

TABLE OF CONTENTS

ABOUT THE AUTHORS

Stephen Joseph is a lecturer in psychology at the University of Essex. Trained in social psychology at the London School of Economics he went on to work with survivors of disaster at the Institute of Psychiatry where he addressed the issues of why some people cope very well with traumatic events while others struggle to come to terms with their experiences. Following this he returned to Ireland to take up a lectureship at the University of Ulster. There he turned his interest to political violence and its consequences before moving back to England in 1994 to take up work at the University of Essex where he has continued to conduct research into post-traumatic stress disorder. He has published articles in *British Journal of Clinical Psychology*, *British Journal of Medical Psychology*, *British Journal of Psychiatry*, *Journal of Child Psychology and Psychiatry*, and *Behaviour Research and Therapy*.

Ruth Williams is a Senior Lecturer in the Psychology Department of the Institute of Psychiatry where she has worked for some 20 years. Her main interests are in Cognitive Therapy and in the application of cognitive-behavioural approaches to general adult problems. She is a founder of the Institute of Psychiatry's well-known post-qualification course in Cognitive-Behavioural Therapy.

William Yule trained as a clinical psychologist at the Institute of Psychiatry and Maudsley Hospital in London where he was for many years head of the clinical psychology services and Professor of Applied Child Psychology. He has published over 300 articles and nine books on a wide range of topics in child psychology. For the past eight years, he has been heavily involved in the study and treatment of PTSD in both adults and children. He has shown that PTSD is both a commoner and more chronic reaction in children and adolescents than had hitherto been suspected. Since the summer of 1993, he has been an adviser to UNICEF on its psychosocial programme for war-effected children in former Yugoslavia and is Technical Director of a major programme to develop services for war-affected children in Mostar, Bosnia. He is a member of the Board of the International Society for Traumatic Stress Studies, and is on the boards of both the Journal of Traumatic Stress and the new electronic journal, *Traumatology*. He was elected Chair of ACCP in June 1996.

I have returned
from a world beyond knowledge
and now must unlearn
for otherwise I clearly see
I can no longer live.

(Charlotte Delbo (1995), *Auschwitz and After*)

PREFACE

The field of traumatic stress research has grown enormously in recent years. So much more is now known about the psychological consequences of traumatic events and their treatment than when we first became involved in this field in the late 1980s. We became involved in the study of traumatic stress following the capsize of the *Herald of Free Enterprise* in 1987 when survivors were referred to the Institute of Psychiatry in London for assessment and treatment. Then, traumatic stress research was still very much in its infancy in Britain. However, the pace of development since then has been remarkable and shows no sign of slowing down. Not everyone who is exposed to trauma goes on to develop severe and chronic psychological problems and it is this observation that has driven our work. Why do some people cope very well with trauma while others struggle a great deal? It is this interest in the individual and in how he or she interrogates and reconstructs his or her memories and past experiences which sums up the character of this book.

The book has been written for undergraduates doing an advanced clinical option, postgraduate clinical psychologists, and practising clinicians who want to understand more about post-traumatic stress and its treatment. Over the years many people have collaborated with us in our work on traumatic stress and many of the ideas in the book have their origins in discussions with them. In particular, we would like to thank Bernice Andrews, Chris Brewin, Sandra Ten Bruggencate, Ed Cairns, Tim Dalgleish, Peter Hodgkinson, Willem Kuyken, Gerry Mulhern, Sian Thrasher, Troy Tranah, Andrew Walker, and Ronnie Wilson. Grateful thanks also to Michael Coombs, Wendy Hudlass, and Mike Shardlow at Wiley. But most of all, our thanks must go to the survivors themselves who have worked with us and have kindly agreed to take part in our research. This book is dedicated to them.

Stephen Joseph
Ruth Williams
William Yule

ACKNOWLEDGEMENTS

The authors are grateful to Yale University Press for permission to reproduce the quotation on p. ix and to Plenum Publishing Corp. for permission to reproduce the quotations from Manton and Talbot (1991) on pages 116 and 117.

Permission has been sought for all the other copyright material that is quoted in the book and acknowledgements are made at appropriate points in the text.

Chapter 1

GENERAL INTRODUCTION

On 21 December 1988, a bomb exploded on board a Pan Am jet flying above Scotland at 31,000 feet on route to JFK at New York from London. Two hundred and fifty-nine passengers and crew were killed as well as eleven people on the ground. The bodies and wreckage were strewn over almost 900 square miles around the town of Lockerbie.

Tragic events such as at Lockerbie can strike at any time and at any place. There is approximately a 1 in 5 million probability of being killed in an air crash. These are good odds. After all, there is a 1 in 10,000 probability of being struck by lightning (Krantz, 1992). Although it is unlikely that you will die in an air crash or be struck by lightning, between 1967 and 1991 there were 7766 disasters world wide involving the death of more than 7 million people and affecting nearly 3 trillion individual lives (International Federation of Red Cross and Red Crescent Societies World Disaster Report, 1993). One survivor of the capsize of the *Herald of Free Enterprise* ferry in 1987, when later asked about her views on life, replied that she now felt that something bad was just waiting around the corner to happen. A fear of future catastrophe is common among survivors of disaster. Fears of future catastrophe constituted an important part of Pauline's problems shown in Case History 1.

Such fears are often based on an overestimation of the probability of such events. However, there is evidence that most people see bad events as more unlikely to happen than they actually are. Most of us live in a bubble of perceived invulnerability to the numerous everyday personal tragedies of car accidents, house fires, muggings, sexual assaults, and illnesses. Increasingly in recent years, psychologists and psychiatrists have come to recognise that such events can have a profound and long-lasting effect on the people involved. Such an example is provided by Henry (see Case History 2).

Although the topic of post-traumatic stress disorders has become popular over the last few years, one of the first people to develop a post-traumatic paradigm was Freud whose original view of neurosis, the 'seduction theory', emphasised the role of actual sexual abuse in the development of later emotional disorders. Freud soon revised this theory because, it has been suggested, the emphasis on sexual abuse was not well received in Vienna and because he found it difficult to accept how widespread sexual abuse might be if his theory were correct. He revised his theory to suggest that the memories of patients

CASE HISTORY 1

Pauline—an unmarried woman aged 22 years, working in marketing for a drug company—was first seen seven months after suffering from an accidental gas poisoning at her home in which two other young people, close friends, were killed. She reported intrusive and distressing recollections of experiences during her period of partial suffocation in the house when she felt trapped and wanted to break a window and also of her time in hospital when she witnessed her friend dying and thought she would die next. Pauline was convinced that something awful was going to happen to herself or to one of her friends in the near future. She reported extreme anxiety in situations involving confinement (queues, trains and the tube) or when driving or being driven (sweating, raised heart rate, hyperventilation). She felt apathetic, feeling there was no point in doing things; she had a sense that she would not live much longer. She also reported signs of general hyperarousal: she had difficult staying asleep, concentration at work was poor, she was always 'on edge' and startled easily. Although she continued working and showed little behavioural avoidance, she reported trying to avoid thoughts and feelings about the tragedy. She distracted herself and feared losing control of her thoughts. She had given up smoking but was abusing alcohol at weekends (up to 15 pints of beer).

Pauline's boyfriend, also a survivor, had also been referred for help but failed to attend. Pauline was very angry about his failure to support her. He refused to talk about the tragedy and seemed dazed. Pauline said that she didn't think he wanted to get better. He had lost two jobs and she had now asked him to leave their house.

CASE HISTORY 2

Henry is a 52-year-old single man who is a political refugee from Pakistan, having suffered imprisonment and torture for political opposition. He had been diagnosed by the psychiatric service as suffering from a chronic depressive illness with marked suicidal ideation, having made at least one suicidal attempt. The diagnosis of a dependent personality disorder had also been made. He had been treated for at least 10 years with antidepressant medication and several hospital admissions without clear benefit, though compliance was thought poor. He had been referred for psychotherapy on two occasions but had not attended beyond a few sessions. He was working as a cleaner for the local council although he has a degree in political sciences, law and industrial relations. He had been accustomed to a life of comfort and status in his own country. He escaped and came to the UK 14 years ago and sought asylum because of death threats. He had left his wife and two children at home and they were now dead. He felt extreme guilt at having escaped and survived them. His previous experience of torture had caused severe damage to his body which had since been reconstructed surgically. Henry was very-selfconscious and aware of the unusual appearance of his face. He was extremely anxious in public places, afraid of being looked at and laughed at and tried to prevent people from seeing his face. He referred to his profound distrust of strangers, as if 'every human being is wicked and cruel'. He reported wandering around in London, 'searching for a moment of calm'. Reported symptoms included tension and difficulty in breathing. As well as extreme sadness at his multiple losses, he reported reliving his torture experiences, nightmares 3–4 times per week and marked sleep disturbance. He was having difficulty concentrating at work and was profoundly alienated from the people he worked with. Henry referred to himself as a 'spoilt child', not able to compromise and accept the reality of his new situation with his social status as the 'lowest member of society'.

seeking treatment may have been fantasies of such events (see Herman, 1992b for an excellent discussion of this 'forgotten history').

THE APPROACH OF THIS BOOK

The approach which we have taken in this book is that post-traumatic stress reactions have multiple causes. By definition, the experience of a traumatic event is the necessary cause. But not all survivors of traumatic events go on to develop severe or chronic distress. So, although the experience of a traumatic event may be a necessary cause, it is not a sufficient cause and various psycho-social factors must either mediate or moderate the effects of traumatic events.

The psychosocial perspective which we have adopted on post-traumatic stress reactions brings together the current thinking in social and cognitive psychology relevant to understanding adaptation to a wide range of life-stressors. It is not just what happens to people that is important, but also what it means to those people in relation to their sense of who they are, the world they live in and what their expectations are for the future. Exposure to traumatic events can challenge the whole meaning of a person's life and his or her sense of purpose. One person might construe an event as a lucky escape from which some benefit has in some way been derived, whereas another person might construe the same event as a catastrophic misfortune which proves that life is meaningless. The effects of the traumatic event on the emotional and behavioural reactions of these two people will invariably be influenced by these different appraisals.

The importance of understanding the role of psychosocial factors in the development of post-traumatic stress reactions is that, unlike the traumatic event itself, they are potentially modifiable and are therefore possible targets for therapeutic intervention. For example, techniques can be aimed at examining the way in which a person makes sense of the experience and how he or she copes with what has happened.

In Chapter 2 we will provide a more detailed description of the psychological reactions experienced by survivors and outline some of the difficulties involved in the psychiatric classification and assessment of trauma-related reactions. Chapter 2 will also provide coverage of the historical development of the diagnostic category of post-traumatic stress disorder (PTSD: APA, 1994). A major issue is whether or not the symptoms outlined as diagnostic of PTSD should be regarded as indicative of abnormal or normal processes. Although PTSD provides a useful framework for conceptualising psychological reactions, our approach has a broader focus that encompasses normal functioning and views the symptoms of PTSD as indicative of unresolved processing of the traumatic event. Measurement is the cornerstone of psychological science and, in Chapter 3, we discuss some of the commonly used instruments as well as some theoretical and practical issues in assessment. In Chapter 4 we will consider the psychological effects of different traumatic events and raise the question of whether all events are interchangeable with regard to their effects or whether different kinds of event lead to variations in symptoms and functional impairment. In Chapter 5 we will outline the main theoretical approaches to understanding post-traumatic stress reactions and present our psychosocial model of adjustment to traumatic stressors. In Chapter 6 we will review the evidence for the role of psychosocial factors and in Chapter 7 we will review what is known about the efficacy of various treatments within a framework derived from our model of psychosocial adjustment. Finally, in Chapter 8, we will summarise the key issues that have emerged and discuss their implications.

Chapter 2

NORMAL AND ABNORMAL
REACTIONS TO TRAUMA

INTRODUCTION

An avalanche in the Italian Alps in 1775 trapped three women in their house for 37 days without open air or daylight and with only minimal nourishment. Looking back at the medical account provided at the time, the authors of a recent report concluded that one of the women developed what might be described today as moderately severe post-traumatic stress disorder (PTSD) with a chronic course of two years (Parry-Jones & Parry-Jones, 1994). Going back another hundred years to 1666, Samuel Pepys's description of his psychological symptoms following the Great Fire of London also corresponds to the description of PTSD (Daly, 1983).

But although psychological suffering in response to traumatic events has always been with us, it wasn't until 1980 that the term PTSD was officially introduced into the psychiatric literature. The term PTSD provided a common language which has succeeded in bringing together research in a wide range of fields under one, unifying, theoretical umbrella. Prior to 1980, the effects of traumatic events on psychological health had been discussed using a variety of different terms. For example, Rape Trauma Syndrome and Combat Stress Reaction (Herman, 1992b). Undoubtedly, the introduction of PTSD has led to more efficient research programmes and consequently better treatment. This chapter will provide an overview of the history of PTSD and some of the issues surrounding this concept.

Key Topics

Historical perspectives
Horowitz's two-factor model
Post-traumatic stress disorder
Course of disorder
Associated symptoms
Children and adolescents
Conclusion

HISTORICAL PERSPECTIVES

The nineteenth century saw the advent of the railway and with it descriptions of post-traumatic stress reactions in relation to railway collisions, e.g., spinal concussion and railway spine (Erichsen, 1866). Since then, the effects of traumatic events on psychological health have been recognised under various names (see Gersons & Carlier, 1992; Trimble, 1981 for reviews); most of these labels have been chosen in relation to combat, e.g., nervous shock (Page, 1885), traumatic neurosis (Oppenheim, 1892), anxiety neurosis (Freud, 1894, 1919), fright neuroses (Kraepelin, 1886), and shell shock (Mott, 1919; South-ward, 1919).

Shell shock is perhaps the most well known of these terms and retains some common currency today when people talk about the effects of traumatic events. Originally it referred to the belief that combat-related disorder was caused by minute brain haemorrhages which resulted from the lodging of shrapnel in the brain during explosions. But the observation that soldiers could develop shell shock even in the absence of explosions led to the belief that shell shock implied weakness of character with the consequence that many soldiers of the First World War, who today would be diagnosed as suffering from PTSD, were executed for cowardice. Fortunately, our understanding of post-traumatic stress reactions has moved beyond this view to recognise that anyone may develop severe and chronic disturbance as a result of traumatic experience—although some people may be more vulnerable or more resistant to the development of disorder.

By the Second World War, further descriptions of post-traumatic stress reactions were provided by psychiatrists. For example, post-trauma-syndrome (Kardiner, 1941), traumatophobia (Rado, 1942), and war neurosis (Grinker & Spiegel, 1943). The clinical descriptions of these terms were remarkably similar to each other as well as to the earlier descriptions provided during the First World War. For example, the post-trauma-syndrome described by Kardiner (1941) included increased feelings of irritability and outbursts of aggression, exaggerated startle response and fixation on the trauma, disrupted personality functioning, and disturbed dreams.

Similar reactions were also being described in adult civilian survivors of traumatic events around this time. For example, Adler (1943), in her most influential study of survivors of Boston's Coconut Grove nightclub fire, made reference to trauma related intrusive thinking, nightmares and insomnia, as well as avoidance behaviours. Other work in the second half of the twentieth century documented increased psychological symptoms in civilian survivors of Hiroshima (Lifton, 1967), natural disasters such as floods (e.g., Abrahams, Price, Whitlock, & Williams, 1976; Bennet, 1970; Logue, Hansen & Struening, 1979; Powell & Penick, 1983; Gleser, Green, & Winget, 1981) and cyclones (e.g., Patrick & Patrick, 1981; Parker, 1977); as well as accidents (e.g., Wilkinson, 1983); combat (e.g., Keane, Zimering, & Caddell, 1985b); rape (e.g.,

Burgess & Holmstrom, 1974a, 1974b, 1978; Steketee & Foa, 1987); child sexual abuse (e.g., Frank & Stewart, 1984), political violence in Northern Ireland (e.g., Lyons, 1974), and other events such as the Three Mile Island incident (e.g., Bromet, Parkinson, Schulberg, Dunn, & Gondek, 1982a).

Many research studies have now also accumulated which show that children and adolescents may also develop post-traumatic stress reactions following various stressors such as witnessing mother's sexual assault (e.g., Pynoos & Nader, 1988); a fatal school shooting (e.g., Schwarz & Kowalski, 1991); a sniper attack (e.g., Pynoos et al., 1987); a concentration camp (e.g., Kinzie, Sack, Angell, et al., 1986); warfare (e.g., Arroyo & Eth, 1985; Saigh, 1989); sexual abuse (e.g., Burgess, Hartman, McCausland, & Powers, 1984; Frederick, 1985b; Kiser et al, 1988; McLeer, Deblinger, Atkins, Foa, & Ralphe, 1988; Wolfe, Gentile, & Wolfe, 1989; Wolfe, Sas & Wekerle, 1994); and boating accidents (e.g., Martini, Ryan, Nakayama, et al., 1990).

However, the literature on the subject of trauma-related reactions lay scattered and lacked a common language until the Vietnam War provided the impetus for the current interest in post-traumatic phenomena (see Figley, 1978) and the introduction of the term post-traumatic stress disorder (PTSD: APA, 1980).

HOROWITZ'S TWO-FACTOR MODEL

The diagnostic specification of PTSD was influenced by Horowitz's (1975, 1976, 1979) work on the phenomenology of trauma-related reactions. Horowitz described reactions to trauma within an information-processing model in which, post-trauma, the person is initially assailed by intrusive and emotionally disturbing memories of the trauma and tends to use avoidant strategies to ward off these distressing thoughts, images, and feelings. Phases of intrusion and avoidance occur as the person attempts to process or 'work through' the experience. We shall consider Horowitz's work in more detail in Chapter 5, but for the moment it is important to note that Horowitz considered reactions to consist of alternating phases of intrusions and avoidance or 'denial' and that these symptom categories constituted the architecture of post-traumatic stress reactions (see Table 2.1). This two-factor model, as it became known, was adopted to a large extent by those preparing the American Psychiatric Association's third edition of the *Diagnostic and Statistical Manual of Mental Disorders* (DSM-III) (APA, 1980) as the framework for the new concept of PTSD.

Table 2.1   Operational definitions of signs and symptoms of intrusion and denial

Signs and symptoms of intrusion:
  pangs of emotion;
  rumination or preoccupation;
  fear of losing bodily control or hyperactivity in any bodily system;
  intrusive ideas in word form;
  difficulty in dispelling ideas;
  hypervigilance;
  re-enactments;
  bad dreams;
  intrusive thoughts or images while trying to sleep; intrusive images;
  startle reactions;
  illusions; and hallucinations.

Signs and symptoms of denial:
  avoidance of associational connections;
  numbness;
  reduced level of feeling responses to other stimuli;
  rigid role adherence;
  loss of reality appropriacy of thought by switching attitudes;
  unrealistic narrowing of attention;
  vagueness;
  inattention;
  inflexibility or constriction of thought;
  loss of train of thought;
  loss of reality appropriacy of thought by sliding meanings;
  memory failure;
  loss of reality appropriacy of thought by use of disavowal;
  warding of reality-orientated thought by use of phantasy.

Adapted from Horowitz (1979).

POST-TRAUMATIC STRESS DISORDER

Diagnostic and Statistical Manual of the American Psychiatric Association

Within the DSM-III criteria for PTSD (see Table 2.2), symptoms were grouped into three sections: (1) re-experiencing of the traumatic event; (2) numbing of responsiveness to or reduced involvement in the external world; and (3) a miscellaneous section which included memory impairment, difficulty concentrating, hyperalertness or an exaggerated startle response. Patients with PTSD were described as psychophysiologically hyperaroused and they showed an intensification of symptoms following exposure to events associated with the trauma.

In addition, DSM-III described three forms of PTSD: acute (the onset of symptoms within six months from the event and a duration of less than six months); chronic (a duration of symptoms for six months or more); and delayed (the onset of symptoms at least six months after the trauma) (APA,

Table 2.2 DSM-III criteria for PTSD

---

1. The existence of a recognizable stressor that would evoke significant symptoms of distress in almost anyone.

2. Re-experiencing of the trauma as evidenced by at least one of the following:
   (a) Recurrent and intrusive recollections of the event.
   (b) Recurrent dreams of the event.
   (c) Sudden acting or feeling as if the traumatic event were re-occurring, because of an association with an environmental or ideational stimulus.

3. Numbing of responsiveness to or reduced involvement with the external world, beginning some time after the trauma, as shown by at least one of the following:
   (a) Markedly diminished interest in one or more significant activities.
   (b) Feeling of detachment or estrangment from others.
   (c) Constricted affect.

4. At least two of the following symptoms that were not present before the trauma:
   (a) Hyperalertness or exaggerated startle response.
   (b) Sleep disturbance.
   (c) Guilt about surviving when others have not, or about behavior required for survival.
   (d) Memory impairment or trouble concentrating.
   (e) Avoidance of activities that arouse recollection of the traumatic event.
   (f) Intensification of symptoms by exposure to events that symbolize or resemble the traumatic event.

Reprinted with permission from the *Diagnostic and Statistical Manual of Mental Disorders*, Third Edition. Copyright 1980 American Psychiatric Association.

1980). These forms of PTSD reflected the clinical experience that there seemed to be no time constraints on the development of PTSD, often taking the form of an immediate reaction, or appearing after weeks, months, or after a period of prolonged incubation, perhaps lasting several years.

What was unique about this disorder was that, with the exception of organic brain syndromes, substance abuse disorders, and puerperal psychosis, the symptoms were thought to arise as the direct result of a psychologically traumatic event (although DSM-III did note that pre-existing psychopathology may increase the likelihood of an individual developing PTSD). The introduction of the diagnostic classification of PTSD was important to the scientific community as it provided the essential constituent for scientific generalisation, a common language with which to describe phenomena, leading to a sharp increase in published work on the topic of post-traumatic stress reactions (Blake, Albano, & Keane, 1992).

However, diagnostic classification is constantly evolving to take account of new knowledge and in 1987 a revised version of the third edition of the *Diagnostic and Statistical Manual* was introduced (DSM-III-R) (APA, 1987) with slight changes to the criteria for the diagnosis of PTSD (see Table 2.3). DSM-III-R asserted that to meet diagnostic criteria, symptoms must usually begin in the immediate aftermath of a traumatic event and last for no less than one month. However, it was also noted that the re-experiencing may not occur for a number of years and that a number of avoidance symptoms may occur

Table 2.3   DSM-III-R criteria for PTSD

A.   The person has experienced an event that is outside the range of usual human experience and that would be markedly distressing to almost anyone, e.g., serious threat to one's life or physical integrity; serious threat or harm to one's children, spouse, or other close relatives and friends; sudden destruction of one's home or community; or seeing another person who has recently been, or is being, seriously injured or killed as the result of an accident or physical violence.

B.   The traumatic event is persistently reexperienced in at least one of the following ways:
   (1)   recurrent and intrusive distressing recollections of the event(in young children, repetitive play in which themes or aspects of the trauma are expressed)
   (2)   recurrent distressing dreams of the event
   (3)   sudden acting or feeling as if the traumatic event were recurring (includes a sense of reliving the experience, illusions, hallucinations, and dissociative [flashback] episodes, even those that occur upon awakening or when intoxicated)
   (4)   intense psychological distress or exposure to events that symbolize or resemble an aspect of the traumatic event, including anniversaries of the trauma

C.   Persistent avoidance of stimuli associated with the trauma or numbing of responsiveness (not present before the trauma), as indicated by at least three of the following:
   (1)   efforts to avoid thoughts or feelings associated with the trauma
   (2)   efforts to avoid activities or situations that arouse recollections of the trauma
   (3)   inability to recall an important aspect of the trauma (psychogenic amnesia)
   (4)   markedly diminished interest in significant activities (in young children, loss of recently acquired developmental skills such as toilet training or language skills)
   (5)   feeling of detachment or estrangement from others
   (6)   restricted range of affect, e.g., unable to have loving feelings
   (7)   sense of a foreshortened future, e.g., child does not expect to have a career, marriage, or children, or a long life

D.   Persistent symptoms of increased arousal (not present before the trauma), as indicated by at least two of the following:
   (1)   difficulty falling or staying asleep
   (2)   irritability or outbursts of anger
   (3)   difficulty concentrating
   (4)   hypervigilance
   (5)   exaggerated startle response
   (6)   physiologic reactivity at exposure to events that symbolize or resemble an aspect of the traumatic event (e.g., a woman who was raped in an elevator breaks out in a sweat when entering any elevator)

E.   Duration of the disturbance (symptoms in B, C, and D) of at least one month.

Specify delayed onset if the onset of symptoms was at least six months after the trauma.

Reprinted with permission from the *Diagnostic and Statistical Manual of Mental Disorders*, Revised Third Edition. Copyright 1987 American Psychiatric Association.

throughout this period of delayed onset. As with DSM-III, in the DSM-III-R system there were also three sections of symptoms: re-experiencing, avoidance, and hyperarousal. However, the re-experiencing section now included distress caused by re-exposure to trauma-relevant stimuli which had been included in DSM-III's miscellaneous section. This was an important shift in thinking which recognised that re-experiencing was often accompanied by strong emotional responses. Similarly, the numbing section now included efforts to avoid thoughts, feelings, and activities associated with the trauma from DSM-III's miscellaneous section. This, too, was important in recognising that avoidance reactions can take many forms. These changes illustrate how diagnostic criteria are constantly evolving as more becomes known about the phenomenology of a disorder. In this case, the changes in criteria reflected the view that symptoms could be grouped into two main clusters, intrusions and denials, as proposed by Horowitz; although some symptoms of PTSD, i.e., difficulty falling or staying asleep and difficulty concentrating, remained outside of the two-factor model despite these symptoms being viewed by Horowitz as indicators of intrusion and denials respectively. Another change in the diagnostic criteria between DSM-III and DSM-III-R was the omission of survivor guilt. Although guilt is commonly observed in survivors of traumatic events (Raphael, 1986), its specificity is likely to be low in the presence of bereavement or major depression where guilt is also common (March, 1990).

The role of prior psychopathology

Both DSM-III and DSM-III-R represented an important shift in understanding from previous editions of the DSM which had emphasised the role of prior psychopathology in understanding emotional reactions to trauma. The DSM-I (APA, 1952) contained the diagnosis 'gross stress reaction' which, although characterised by an individual's exposure to extreme emotional and physical stress, was thought to diminish rather rapidly unless maintained by premorbid personality traits. Similarly, in the DSM-II (APA, 1968) the category of 'gross stress reaction' was deleted and trauma-related stress was considered only in the context of adult adjustment reactions where a diagnosis of 'transient situational disturbance' could be given. As the name of this reaction implies, stress responses were thought of as time-limited phenomena with prolonged responses to stress having their roots in early individual history and personality. A role for early individual history and personality has, however, been reintroduced in DSM-IV (APA, 1994). An example which illustrates the role of early experiences is given by Mary in Case History 3.

Here it could be possible that Mary's early established belief in physical injury as a consequence of sexual abuse had led her to catastrophise physical symptoms as indicative of extreme pathology. Also her distrust of others had led to multiple investigations despite nothing being found. Her experience of an extremely unpleasant muscular reaction, together with her mother's attribu-

CASE HISTORY 3

Mary is a 28-year-old single Afro-Caribbean woman, born in Jamaica. She lives with her mother and is unemployed. She was seen only after the encouragement of her boyfriend, four years after having experienced an adverse reaction to medication while a patient in hospital. She reported that nightmares began three days after the experience. She reported that in her dream her body is arching up and she cannot breathe. She calls a nurse's name and asks for water and says that she does not want to die. She believes she cannot move and that she is about to die. In consequence she is afraid to sleep at night and tries to stay awake. She also experiences intrusive thoughts about the experience while awake. She sees images of the nurse, of a doctor and hears her mother's voice saying that she will die or be paralysed. These memories are also triggered by coming to the clinic, reading in the newspaper about medical mistakes and watching TV programmes about hospitals. She attempts to avoid such thoughts and feelings. She does not talk about her experiences because she does not want to burden others. In particular she avoids the hospital where she was taken and the area immediately around it. She has lost interest in former interests. She has given up her psychology course, she rarely goes out socially and does not want to be with people.

Mary has a lengthy medical history dating from the age of 15 years when she was referred for psychiatric assessment and found to be depressed with behavioural disturbances. She subsequently underwent numerous physical investigations for abdominal pain, 'fits', respiratory symptoms and menstrual irregularities and migraine. She has had three laparoscopies with no major abnormalities found. A previous muscular dystonic reaction to Maxilon, an anti-emetic had been observed. Four years ago a psychologist obtained a history of repeated sexual abuse at the age of 11 years committed by her step-father. Mary is reported to have believed that she suffered internal physical damage during this forced intercourse. Currently, Mary was being treated for migraine and arthritic knees.

---

tions, was sufficient to make Mary reach the traumatic conclusion that she was dying—a conclusion which was unable to check out with others. Hence previous psychological problems may interact with severity of an event in accounting for individual variation—a point we shall return to later.

As well as containing the diagnostic criteria for PTSD (see Table 2.4), DSM-IV reintroduced the category of acute stress disorder (see Table 2.5). Acute stress disorder is specified as lasting for a minimum of two days and a maximum of four weeks in contrast to PTSD which has a specified duration criteria of at least one month. Survivors must have had the symptoms for at least this amount of time to meet the criteria for diagnosis. The main change in DSM-IV, however, was the shift in thinking regarding Criterion A (the criterion for assessing whether or not the person has been exposed to a traumatic event).

What is a traumatic event?

The example of Mary may lead us to question the definition of 'trauma'. Despite the attempt in previous editions of DSM to define traumatic events

Table 2.4 DSM-IV Criteria for PTSD

A. The person has been exposed to a traumatic event in which both the following were present:
  (1) The person experienced, witnessed, or was confronted with an event or events that involved actual or threatened death or serious injury, or a threat to the physical integrity of self or others.
  (2) The person's response involved fear, helplessness, or horror. *Note:* In children, this may be expressed instead by disorganised or agitated behaviour.

B. The traumatic event is persistently re-experienced in one (or more) of the following ways:
  (1) Recurrent and intrusive distressing recollections of the event, including images, thoughts, or perceptions. *Note:* In young children, repetitive play may occur in which themes or aspects of the trauma are expressed.
  (2) Recurrent distressing dreams of the event. *Note:* In children, there may be frightening dreams without recognisable content.
  (3) Acting or feeling as if the traumatic event were recurring (includes a sense of reliving the experience, illusions, hallucinations, and dissociative flashback episodes, including those that occur on awakening or when intoxicated). *Note:* In young children, trauma-specific re-enactment may occur.
  (4) Intense psychological distress at exposure to internal or external cues that symbolise or resemble an aspect of the traumatic event.
  (5) Physiological reactivity on exposure to internal or external cues that symbolise or resemble an aspect of the traumatic event.

C. Persistent avoidance of stimuli associated with the trauma and numbing of general responsiveness (not present before the trauma), as indicated by three (or more) of the following:
  (1) Efforts to avoid thoughts, feelings, or conversations associated with the trauma.
  (2) Efforts to avoid activities, places, or people that arouse recollections of the trauma.
  (3) Inability to recall an important aspect of the trauma.
  (4) Markedly diminished interest or participation in significant activities.
  (5) Feeling of detachment or estrangement from others.
  (6) Restricted range of affect (e.g., unable to have loving feelings).
  (7) Sense of foreshortened future (e.g., does not expect to have a career, marriage, children, or a normal life span).

D. Persistent symptoms of increased arousal (not present before the trauma) as indicated by two (or more) of the following:
  (1) Difficulty falling or staying asleep.
  (2) Irritability or outbursts of anger.
  (3) Difficulty concentrating.
  (4) Hypervigilance.
  (5) Exaggerated startle response.

E. Duration of the disturbance (symptoms in criteria B, C, and D) is more than one month.

F. The disturbance causes clinically significant distress or impairment in social, occupational, or other important areas of functioning.

Specify if:
  Acute: if duration of symptoms is less that three months.
  Chronic: if duration of symptoms is three months or more.

Specify if:
  With delayed onset: if onset of symptoms is at least six months after the stressor.

Reprinted with permission from the *Diagnostic and Statistical Manual of Mental Disorders*, Fourth Edition. Copyright 1994 American Psychiatric Association.

Table 2.5 DSM-IV criteria for Acute Stress Disorder

A. The person has been exposed to a traumatic event in which both of the following were present:
  (1) The person experienced, witnessed, or was confronted with an event or events that involved actual or threatened death or serious injury, or a threat to the physical integrity of self or others.
  (2) The person's response involved fear, helplessness, or horror.

B. Either while experiencing or after experiencing the distressing event, the individual has three (or more) of the following dissociative symptoms:

  (1) A subjective sense of numbing, detachment, or absence of emotional responsiveness.
  (2) A reduction in awareness of his or her surroundings (e.g., 'being in a daze').
  (3) Derealisation.
  (4) Depersonalisation.
  (5) Dissociative amnesia (i.e., inability to recall an important aspect of the trauma).

C. The traumatic event is persistently re-experienced in at least one of the following ways: recurrent images, thoughts, dreams, illusions, flashback episodes, or a sense of reliving the experience; or distress on exposure to reminders of the traumatic event.

D. Marked avoidance of stimuli that arouse recollections of the trauma (e.g., thoughts, feelings, conversations, activities, places, people).

E. Marked symptoms of anxiety or increased arousal (e.g., difficulty sleeping, irritability, poor concentration, hypervigilance, exaggerated startle response, motor restlessness).

F. The disturbance causes clinically significant distress or impairment in social, occupational, or other important areas of functioning or impairs the individual's ability to pursue some necessary task, such as obtaining necessary assistance or mobilising personal resources by telling family members about the traumatic experience.

G. The disturbance lasts for a minimum of two days and a maximum of four weeks and occurs within four weeks of the traumatic event.

H. The disturbance is not due to the direct physiological effects of a substance (e.g., a drug of abuse, a medication) or a general medical condition, is not better accounted for by Brief Psychotic Disorder, and is not merely an exacerbation of a preexisting Axis I or Axis II disorder.

objectively as events outside the range of usual human experience (see Tables 2.2 and 2.3), the question of what actually constitutes a traumatic event has proved to be a definitional quagmire. But it is a question of considerable importance because, by definition, criterion A has traditionally served as the gatekeeper to the diagnosis of PTSD.

  . . . If a person does not meet the required definition of a stressful event, it matters little whether all the other criteria are met because the person cannot be diagnosed with PTSD. If Criterion A is loosely defined and over inclusive, then the prevalence of PTSD is likely to increase, whereas a restrictive definition will reduce its prevalence. (Davidson & Foa, 1991, p. 346).

Some events, such as an aeroplane disaster or ferry sinking, were clearly understood to fulfil criterion A as specified in DSM-III and DSM-III-R. However, there remained much debate on whether other events, such as the death of a spouse through cancer, met the criterion (Baum, 1987; March, 1993). If a person can develop all the emotional and behavioural symptoms of PTSD without having experienced an event outside the range of usual human experience, then it could be argued that the definition of what constitutes a traumatic event must change. It was argued that what was important was how the person perceived the event and thus that criterion A should include reference to subjective factors. Clearly, what is traumatic to one person may not be so to another. But others argued that by broadening the definition to include subjective factors, criterion A would become all but abolished so that trauma was defined in terms of its effects. In response, it was argued that previous definitions, despite attempting to define the event objectively, implied subjective perception as well as objective environmental factors, anyway. For example, judgements of unusualness of the event, the chief criterion in DSM-III and DSM-III-R, were necessarily based on the clinicians assessment of what the average person in similar circumstances and with similar sociocultural values would experience (see March, 1993).

In response to these arguments, the authors of the DSM-IV reformulated criterion A (of both Acute Stress Disorder and PTSD) to include: (1) exposure to a traumatic event coupled with (2) the person's reaction to it (see Tables 2.4 and 2.5). The inclusion of subjective factors into criterion A of DSM-IV was an important theoretical shift, one which is central to the model of psychosocial adaptation which we shall describe in Chapter 5.

International Classification of Diseases

As already noted, the APA's classification system provided researchers with the common language with which to facilitate research throughout the world on PTSD. Following this lead, the World Health Organisation (WHO) also included the category of PTSD within the most recent edition of the International Classification of Diseases, ICD-10 (WHO, 1993).

Prior to this, ICD-9 (WHO, 1978) acknowledged two diagnoses to cover the emotional problems which follow trauma. The first was 'Acute Reaction to Stress'. This was defined as a very transient disorder of any severity and nature, which occurred in individuals without any apparent mental disorder in response to exceptional physical or mental stress, such as disaster or combat, and which was thought to subside usually within hours or days. In addition to this diagnosis, there was 'Adjustment Reaction' which was defined as a mild or transient disorder lasting longer than an acute stress reaction and which occur-

Table 2.6   ICD-10 criteria for acute stress reaction

There must be an immediate and clear temporal connection between the impact of an exceptional stressor and the onset of symptoms; onset is usually within a few minutes, if not immediate. In addition, the symptoms:

(a)   show a mixed and usually changing picture; in addition to the initial state of 'daze', depression, anxiety, anger, despair, overactivity, and withdrawal may all be seen, but no one type of symptoms predominates for long;

(b)   resolve rapidly (within a few hours at the most) in those cases where removal from the stressful environment is possible; in cases where the stress continues or cannot by its nature be reversed, the symptoms usually begin to diminish after 24–48 hours and are usually minimal after about three days.

This diagnosis should not be used to cover sudden exacerbations of symptoms in individuals already showing symptoms that fulfil the criteria of any other psychiatric disorder, except for those in F60 (personality disorders). However, a history of previous psychiatric disorder does not invalidate the use of this diagnosis.

Includes: acute crisis reaction
            combat fatigue
            crisis state
            psychic shock

red in individuals of any age without any apparent pre-existing psychopathology. Such disorder was thought to be often relatively circumscribed or situation specific and usually closely related in time and content to stressors such as bereavement, or separation.

ICD-10 introduced the new category of 'reaction to severe stress and adjustment disorders'. As with the APA system, the experience of a traumatic event is thought to be a necessary aetiological factor in the disorders contained within this category. Within this category, ICD-10 considers three diagnoses: (1) acute stress reaction, (2) post-traumatic stress disorder, and (3) adjustment disorder.

Acute stress reaction (see Table 2.6) describes a transient disorder which develops in an individual without any other apparent mental disorder in response to exceptional physical and/or mental stress. Symptoms are thought to appear usually within minutes of the impact of the stressful stimulus and, often, to disappear within hours. Notably, symptoms, expected to last no longer than 2–3 days at the most, include an initial state of 'daze' with some constriction of the field of consciousness and narrowing of attention, inability to comprehend stimuli, and disorientation. Autonomic signs of panic anxiety (tachycardia, sweating, flushing) are commonly present. With regard to the stressor itself, ICD-10 notes that the stressor may be an overwhelming traumatic experience involving serious threat to the security or physical integrity of the individual or of a loved one (e.g., natural catastrophe, accident, battle, criminal assault, rape), or an unusually sudden and threatening change in the social position and/or network of the individual, such as multiple bereavement or domestic fire. The risk of this disorder developing is increased if physical exhaustion or

Table 2.7 ICD-10 criteria for Post-traumatic Stress Disorder

This disorder should not generally be diagnosed unless there is evidence that it arose within six months of a traumatic event of exceptional severity. A 'probable' diagnosis might still be possible if the delay between the event and the onset was longer than six months, provided that the clinical manifestations are typical and no alternative identification of the disorder (e.g., as an anxiety or obsessive–compulsive disorder or depressive episode) is plausible. In addition to evidence of trauma, there must be a repetitive, intrusive recollection or re-enactment of the event in memories, daytime imagery, or dreams. Conspicuous emotional detachment, numbing of feeling, and avoidance of stimuli that might arouse recollection of the trauma are often present but are not essential for the diagnosis. The autonomic disturbances, mood disorder, and behavioural abnormalities all contribute to the diagnosis but are not of prime importance.

The late chronic sequelae of devastating stress, i.e., those manifest decades after the stressful experience, should be classified under F62.0.

Includes:traumatic neurosis.

organic factors (e.g., in the elderly) are also present. Individual vulnerability and coping capacity play a role in the occurrence and severity of acute stress reactions, as evidenced by the fact that not all people exposed to exceptional stress develop the disorder.

The diagnostic criteria of post-traumatic stress disorder outlined by the WHO (see Table 2.7) are similar to those of the APA and involve the identification of a threatening event which is thought to be necessary in the onset of disorder, although the approach to making the diagnosis is very different. As with the APA system, it is recognised that other factors, such as pre-existing disorder, may play a role in the aetiology of PTSD, but they are not thought to be either necessary or sufficient. Symptoms are thought to arise as a delayed and/or protracted response to a stressful event or situation (either short- or long-lasting) that is exceptionally threatening or catastrophic and which is likely to cause pervasive distress in almost anyone (e.g., natural or man-made disaster, combat, serious accident, witnessing the violent death of others, or being the victim of torture, terrorism, rape, or other crime). Predisposing factors such as personality traits (e.g., compulsive, asthenic) or previous history of neurotic illness may lower the threshold for the development of the syndrome or aggravate its course, but they are neither necessary nor sufficient to explain its occurrence. Typical symptoms include episodes of repeated reliving of the trauma in intrusive memories or 'flashbacks' or dreams, which occur against the persisting background of a sense of 'numbness' and emotional blunting, detachment from other people, unresponsiveness to surroundings, anhedonia, and avoidance of activities and situations reminiscent of the trauma. Commonly, there is fear and avoidance of cues that remind the sufferer of the original trauma. Rarely, there may be dramatic, acute bursts of fear, panic or aggression, triggered by stimuli arousing a sudden recollection and/or re-enactment of the trauma or of the original reaction to it. There is usually a

Table 2.8   ICD-10 criteria for adjustment disorders

Diagnosis depends on a careful evaluation of the relationship between:
(a)   form, content, and severity of symptoms;
(b)   previous history and personality; and
(c)   stressful event, situation, or life crisis.

The presence of this third factor should be clearly established and there should be strong, though perhaps presumptive, evidence that the disorder would not have arisen without it. If the stressor is relatively minor, or if a temporal connection (less than three months) cannot be demonstrated, the disorder should be classified elsewhere, according to its presenting features.

Includes: culture shock
         grief reaction
         hospitalism in children.

Excludes: separation anxiety disorder of childhood (F93.0).

If the criteria for adjustment disorder are satisfied, the clinical form or predominant features can be specified by a fifth character:

F43.20   *Brief depressive reaction*
A transient, mild depressive state of duration not exceeding 1 month.

F43.21   *Prolonged depressive reaction*
A mild depressive state occurring in response to a prolonged exposure to a stressful situation but of duration not exceeding 2 years.

F43.22   *Mixed anxiety and depressive reaction*
Both anxiety and depressive symptoms are prominent, but at levels no greater than specified in mixed anxiety and depressive disorder (F41.2) or other mixed anxiety disorder (F41.3).

F43.23   *With predominant disturbance of other emotions*
The symptoms are usually of several types of emotion, such as anxiety, depression, worry, tensions, and anger. Symptoms of anxiety and depression may fulfil the criteria for mixed anxiety and depressive disorder (F41.2) or other mixed anxiety disorder (F41.3), but they are not so predominant that other more specific depressive or anxiety disorders can be diagnosed. This category should also be used for reactions in children in which regressive behaviour such as bed-wetting or thumb-sucking are also present.

F43.24   *With predominant disturbance of conduct*
The main disturbance is one involving conduct, e.g., an adolescent grief reaction resulting in aggressive or dissocial behaviour.

F43.25   *With mixed disturbance of emotions and conduct*
Both emotional symptoms and disturbance of conduct are prominent features.

F43.28   *With other specified predominant symptoms*

state of autonomic hyperarousal with hypervigilance, an enhanced startle reaction, and insomnia. Anxiety and depression are commonly associated with the above symptoms and signs, and suicidal ideation may be present. Excessive use of alcohol or drugs may also be a complicating factor. The onset follows the trauma with a latency period which may range from a few weeks to months (but rarely exceeds six months). The course is thought to be fluctuating but recovery can be expected in the majority of cases. In a small proportion of patients, the ICD-10 notes, the condition may show a chronic course over many years and a transition into an enduring personality change.

The category of 'Adjustment disorders' (see Table 2.8) refers to states of subjective and emotional disturbance which arise in the period of adaptation to a significant life change or to the consequences of a stressful event. ICD-10 also notes that the stressor involved may have affected the person's social network through, for example, bereavement. Although it is assumed that the condition would not have arisen without the stressor, what differentiates this category from that of post-traumatic stress disorder is the acknowledgement of the role of individual difference variables. Symptoms are thought to include depressed mood, anxiety, worry, a feeling of inability to cope, plan ahead, or continue in the present situation, and some degree of disability in the performance of daily routine. With adolescents, conduct disorders are thought to be an associated feature and in children, regressive behaviour such as thumb sucking may be part of the symptom pattern. The onset is usually within one month of the occurrence of the stressful event and the duration of symptoms does not usually exceed six months, except in the case of prolonged depressive reaction where the duration is not thought to exceed two years.

The importance of the ICD-10, in contrast to that of the DSM-III-R, was that it drew attention to the varieties of stress response and the relative roles of the traumatic event and psychosocial factors. With regard to PTSD, however, the major difference between the WHO and APA systems is that ICD-10 states that symptoms of emotional numbing are not necessary for the diagnosis of PTSD—although emotional numbing is viewed as a frequent accompaniment to the disorder.

It is the re-experiencing symptoms which are the hallmark signs of PTSD. (Symptoms in common to each of our three case examples so far.) In particular, sleep disturbances have been characterised as a hallmark of PTSD (Ross, Ball, Sullivan, & Caroff, 1989) and, along with nightmares, are referred to frequently in the PTSD literature (e.g., Glaubman, Mikulincer, Porat, Wasserman, & Birger, 1990; Hefez, Metz, & Lavie, 1987; Inman, Silver, & Doghramji, 1990; Lavie, Hefez, Halperin, & Enoch, 1979; Marshall, 1975; Mellman, Kulick-Bell, Ashlock, & Nolan, 1995; Rosen, Reynolds, Yeager, Houck, & Hurwitz, 1991; van der Kolk, Blitz, Burr, Sherry, & Hartmann, 1984a).

COURSE OF DISORDER

Understandably, the very long-term effects of traumatic events are not as well documented as the shorter term effects. However, the evidence beginning to accumulate does suggest that, for survivors of some events, the effects can be very long-lasting. Holen (1991), for example, found that some survivors of an oil rig collapse in the North Sea continued to show psychological problems eight years after the event. PTSD has been reported 14 years on in 17% of survivors of the Buffalo Creek disaster (Green et al., 1990a). Some events appear to be particularly likely to lead to long-term distress. Kilpatrick, Saunders, Veronen, Best, & Von (1987) reported that almost 17% of their sample of women met full PTSD criteria 17 years after a sexual assault. Longer-term studies have shown PTSD up to 40 years later in Second World War combat veterans and POWs (Davidson, Kudler, Saunders, & Smith, 1990; Hierholzer, Munson, Peabody, & Rosenberg, 1992; Kluznik, Speed, Van Valkenburg, & Magraw, 1986; Rosen, Fields, Hand, Falsettie, & Van Kammen, 1989; Speed, Engdahl, Schwartz, & Eberly, 1989; Spiro, Schnurr, & Aldwin, 1994; Zeiss & Dickman, 1989) and Jewish survivors of the Holocaust (Krystal, 1970; Kuch & Cox, 1992).

Although these data suggest that PTSD can continue many years after an event, survivors often report only being intermittently troubled by their symptoms (Zeiss & Dickman, 1989) and PTSD can have a varied course (Blank, 1993). Evidence for this comes chiefly from McFarlane (1988b) who assessed over 300 firefighters for psychiatric 'caseness' using the General Health Questionnaire at 4, 11, and 29 months after the event (see Box 2.1). McFarlane identified eight patterns of response: (1) 50% fell into the no-disorder group (i.e., not reaching caseness at any of the three time points); (2) 9% fell into the acute group (i.e., reaching caseness at 4 months but not at 11 or 29 months); (3) 10% were identified as persistent and chronic (i.e., reaching caseness at all three time points); (4) 6% fell into the resolved chronic group (i.e., reaching caseness at 4 and 11 months but not at 29 months); (5) 5% fell into the recurrent group (i.e., reaching caseness at 4 and 29 months but not at 11 months); (6) 3% fell into the persistent delayed onset group (i.e., not reaching caseness at 4 months but reaching caseness at 11 and 29 months); (7) 5% fell into the 11 month delayed onset group (i.e., not reaching caseness at 4 or 29 months but reaching caseness at 11 months); and (8) 11% fell into the 29 month delayed onset group (i.e., not reaching caseness at 4 or 11 months but only at 29 months).

ASSOCIATED SYMPTOMS

The diagnosis of PTSD represents only a circumscribed set of symptoms experienced by survivors of traumatic events. As well as enduring personality changes, which Horowitz (1986a, 1986b) refers to as post-traumatic character disorder, many studies of survivors report high levels of both anxiety and depressive symptoms in association with PTSD. Such an example is provided by Sarah (see Case History 4)

Sarah suffered multiple losses as a consequence of the accident, her injuries

---

Box 2.1 Assessment of psychological health using the GHQ

The General Health Questionnaire was originally designed as a screening instrument with the general population. However, it has been used satisfactorily with disaster victims in a number of studies (e.g., Joseph et al., 1993g; Parker, 1977; McFarlane, 1988a, 1988b, 1989, 1992a), railway accidents (Karlehagen et al., 1993; Malt et al., 1993) and has been extensively employed in the population surveys conducted in Northern Ireland to assess the effects of political violence (Cairns & Wilson, 1989). There are several versions of this instrument available ranging from the short 12 item version to the 60-item version (Goldberg, 1972, 1978; Goldberg & Hillier, 1979; Goldberg & Williams, 1988). However, it is the 28-item version (Goldberg & Hillier, 1979) which has generally been adopted as the GHQ-28 consists of four subscales: somatic symptoms, anxiety and insomnia, social dysfunction, and severe depression. However, several studies have used the 12-item General Health Questionnaire (Goldberg, 1972) which, despite its brevity, has been found to be a valid measure of psychiatric impairment (Henderson, Byrne, & Duncan-Jones, 1981; Tennant, 1977) with a 90% specificity and a 78% sensitivity of PTSD using a structured interview (McFarlane, 1986b). Using this questionnaire patients can be grouped into those scoring above or below a certain cutoff point; depending on the version used, those scoring above the cutoff point are classified as cases. Other general self-report measures which have been used include the 90-item Symptom Checklist (SCL-90: Derogatis, 1977, 1983). The SCL-90 has been used extensively in the work by Baum and his colleagues on residents living near Three Mile Island (e.g., Baum, Gatchel, & Schaeffer, 1983b; Davidson, Weiss, O'Keefe, & Baum, 1991).

---

and her prolonged period of immobility: her job, her financial security, her plans for the future, her relationship, her independence and her very personality. Sarah blamed herself for the feelings of grief and rage she felt, was unable to express these feeings and remained psychologically stuck in a chronic depression.

McFarlane and Papay (1992) investigated multiple diagnoses in the victims of a natural disaster. Over 450 firefighters who had been exposed to the bush fire that devastated large areas of southeastern Australia in 1983 were screened using the General Health Questionnaire at 4, 11, and 29 months subsequent to the event (see Box 2.1).

On the basis of these data, a high-risk group of 147 firefighters were interviewed using a standard interview schedule—the Diagnostic Interview Schedule (DIS: Robins & Helzer, 1985) at 42 months to examine the prevalence of PTSD as well as affective and anxiety disorders. PTSD was the most common disorder (18%) followed by major depression (10%). Only 23% of the 70 subjects who had developed PTSD did not attract a further diagnosis, usually of major depression. McFarlane and Papay's data are particularly important because theirs was a community sample and thus the coexistence of disorders was not simply a consequence of treatment-seeking or some other factor. Of course it may be that exposure to bushfire is particularly depressogenic. The generalisability of these data needs to be established. However, other research

CASE HISTORY 4

Sarah, a 34-year-old woman, of Afro-Caribbean background, was seen three years after a major car accident in which she was the passenger and suffered multiple and serious fractures requiring long periods of hospitalisation. Indeed, Sarah still suffered considerable pain, was badly scarred and walked with difficulty and with a stick. She was still awaiting further surgery on her wrist and leg and was involved in a claim for financial compensation. She was unable to work, was relying upon benefits and was forced to live at home with her parents. She expressed extreme frustration at her necessary dependency and loss of control over her life.

Sarah spoke about her memories of the accident in a flat, unemotional voice and generally presented herself as cheerful and outgoing. But she reported recurrent intrusive memories of the accident and of her experiences in hospital. She felt she was much more anxious than before the accident, especially when being reminded of the accident (e.g., a film depicting a car crash on TV) or in situations such as walking down the street alone. She was phobic of travelling by bus, train, and tube and extremely reluctant to go outside alone. She was particularly concerned with the probability of further accidents, with meeting people and having to talk about her difficulties and being vulnerable in a public place. She reported making efforts to shut off distressing memories using music as a distractor.

Notably, Sarah spoke of herself as a changed person: formerly carefree and independent, she reported feeling insignificant, without purpose, and uncertain of her changed identity. Before the accident she had been a professional athlete and involved in fashion design, intending to set up her own business. It was clear that her whole world had changed dramatically. She was now largely confined to her parents' home, inactive, unable to see friends and overcome with sadness and irritation. She felt guilty about her feelings.

suggests that depression is also common among survivors of other events. For example, North, Smith, and Spitznagel (1994) also report that the most frequent additional post-disaster diagnosis in survivors of a mass shooting was major depression, which was present in 35% of women and 25% of men. Furthermore, Loughrey, Bell, Kee, Roddy, and Curran (1988) investigated the incidence of PTSD among 499 people exposed to various types of civilian trauma in Northern Ireland, finding that out of those who developed PTSD, 35% showed a diagnosis of depression compared to 12% of those not suffering from PTSD. In addition, co-morbidity appeared to be an important predictor of chronic PTSD.

Substance abuse

There have been many reports of increased substance use in survivors of traumatic events, particularly in combat veterans (Jelinek & Williams, 1984; Lacoursiere, Godfrey, & Ruby, 1980; Penk et al., 1981; Solomon, Mikulincer, & Kotler, 1987b) where substance abuse is a common co-diagnosis along with depression and anxiety (Davidson & Foa, 1991). In one study of 40 Vietnam veterans with PTSD, it was found that 63% reported heavy and often abusive alcohol consumption (Keane, Caddell, Martin, Zimering, & Fairbank, 1983).

In a larger study of 268 Vietnam veterans, Roth (1986) found that almost half of the combat veterans with stress disorders were heavy drinkers and that over half used drugs other than alcohol. Friedman and colleagues surveyed a large sample of veterans who had applied for outpatient services. Of those diagnosed as suffering from PTSD, 19% were also diagnosed with current alcohol abuse or dependence (Friedman et al., 1987). In another study, it was found that of 440 veterans suffering from PTSD, 22% had a current diagnosis of alcohol abuse or dependence and 6% as suffering from drug abuse or dependence (Kulka et al., 1990). What is particularly interesting, however, is that when past history was investigated, Kulka et al. (1990) found that 75% of these same veterans could have been diagnosed as alcohol abusing or dependent and 23% drug abusing or dependent prior to the war.

But although substance abuse seems to be particularly prevalent among combat veterans, it is not confined to this population, and it has also been reported in survivors of sexual assault and child sexual abuse (Yeary, 1982) as well as survivors of disaster (Abrahams et al., 1976; Logue et al., 1979; Gleser et al., 1981; Goenjian, 1993).

In our 30-month follow up of the survivors of the *Herald of Free Enterprise* (Joseph, Yule, Williams, & Hodgkinson, 1993f) several questions were asked about changes in substance use. Respondents were asked to rate whether they had used alcohol, cigarettes, sleeping tablets, antidepressants, and tranquillisers more than they usually did. We found that retrospective ratings for the six months immediately following the disaster showed that 73% reported that their alcohol consumption had increased; 44% that their cigarette consumption had increased; 40% that their use of sleeping tablets had increased; 28% that their use of antidepressants had increased; and 21% that their use of tranquillisers had increased. What was interesting was that although all ratings of use had significantly decreased at 30 months after the event, compared to the retrospective ratings for the first six months, many were still using alcohol and cigarettes at an increased level suggesting that, for some survivors at least, the increased use of cigarettes and alcohol may become stable and long-term habits. An interesting example of alcohol abuse in an adult survivor of childhood abuse is provided by Rose (see Case History 5).

As well as presenting serious health risks, alcohol problems may have serious effects on other areas of a person's life. For example, with Vietnam veterans there is evidence that alcohol abuse, along with other factors such as low levels of social support, may lead to later homelessness (Rosenheck & Fontana, 1994).

Cognitive impairment

There is evidence suggesting that impairment of memory and cognition are major characteristics of PTSD. Wilkinson (1983), in his report on survivors of the Hyatt Regency Hotel skywalk collapse, found that 44% of his 102 subjects

CASE HISTORY 5

Rose, a 70-year-old retired teacher, was referred because of fears of driving and of travelling by train. These problems dated from having suffered a fracture of the right humerus six months before. Rose was also reported to be drinking heavily and she had been previously suspended from work suspected of being intoxicated while on duty although, on inquiry, she had been cleared of this misdemeanour. A year ago she had been referred to two services for alcohol abuse but had not been engaged. Rose described the fracture as having been subjectively 'traumatic'. She had broken her arm in a fall at home alone. She had not sought help. She couldn't see how she could manage travelling and she didn't want to go to hospital fearing she 'wouldn't come home again.' (She had always had a horror of anaesthesia.) She couldn't undress herself and sat on the floor all night, fearful of looking at her arm and hoping that the swelling would go down. Eventually she called the doctor. In retrospect she thought she could have killed herself. Rose thought she had been drinking too much since the death of her mother, five years previously, also after a fall. Rose continued to think of her a great deal, to blame herself for not doing more for her mother. She also recounted an upsetting experience at the funeral when she was informed that her mother's body had not been in the chapel of rest as she had expected. All of these events had culminated in Rose being on leave from work for a prolonged period, being confined to the home, being dependent upon others and having difficulty coping with everyday tasks. On her expected return to work she felt vulnerable to another adverse experience and feared an assault on the train. This fear resulted in avoidance and finally in her taking retirement. Without the structure and meaning her work gave her, Rose felt more depressed and pitied herself, leading her to feel she deserved a drink. She had no plans for the future, she tended to procrastinate in day-to-day tasks and had little contact with others. After some sessions in therapy, Rose began to telephone in distress, often in an intoxicated state and disclosed that she had been assaulted by a man in childhood who tried to strangle her and subsequently killed himself. This experience had never been discussed and had given her a sense of guilt and responsibility.

---

had difficulty concentrating and 27% had memory difficulties. A more recent study that has evaluated the cognitive deficits in PTSD patients by means of objective tests, such as the Wechsler Adult Intelligence Scale, reports evidence that patients with PTSD have substantial impairment of cognitive functioning (Gil, Calev, Greenberg, Kugelmass, & Lerer, 1990). Gil et al. (1990) argue that their results are consistent with the view that PTSD patients have a generalised cognitive deficit similar to that encountered in other psychiatric disorders such as depression and schizophrenia. However, they do suggest that the deficits observed are likely to be a secondary consequence of general psychiatric symptomatology rather than a primary feature of the disorder. Other more recent work has documented autobiographical memory disturbance in PTSD patients (McNally, Lasko, Macklin, & Pitman, 1995). A complex example of severe PTSD where cognitive impairment was important is provided by Mark (see Case History 6).

CASE HISTORY 6

Mark is a 60-year-old single man of Jamaican origin who was first seen for assessment in connection with his compensation claim seven months after experiencing an objectively minor road traffic accident in which he was the driver. Mark had suffered injury to his neck in the accident, was phobic of driving and was unable to work as a lorry driver. He worried about his financial security and had exhausted his savings. Mark experienced intrusive imagery of the accident, in which he had thought he might be killed, and also disturbing related images of his own death and of his own grave and tombstone. He was seriously depressed, believing himself to be useless and his life over. He had withdrawn from social activities and his cohabitee of some years had left unable to tolerate his disturbed sleeping pattern, lack of affection, and irritability. Mark complained particularly of difficulties in concentration and claimed only to be able to maintain concentration for about five minutes. He reported going into another room in his house and being unable to remember the reason. He attempted to read and do puzzles but lost concentration easily. In therapy, he benefited from behavioural work to lift his mood but he was unable to remember and utilise the simple principles and was extremely vulnerable to relapse. Four years prior to the accident Mark had suffered a left cerebral infarction.

Physical health

As well as psychological problems, there is evidence that there may also be physical health consequences of exposure to traumatic events. Although operational definitions of physical health vary from study to study, research has shown that trauma is associated with declines in subjective health ratings (Logue et al., 1979; Melick, 1978; Price, 1978), an increased use of medical services (Abrahams et al., 1976; Bennet, 1970; Price, 1978), and the development of a wide variety of physical health conditions, including tiredness, headaches, chest pains, gastrointestinal disorders, cardiovascular disorders, renal disorders, respiratory diseases, and infectious diseases as well as impairments in the immune system (Abrahams et al., 1976; Clayer, Bookless-Pratz, & Harris, 1985; Logue et al., 1979; McFarlane, Atchison, Rafalowicz, & Papay, 1994; Price, 1978; Raphael, 1986; Solomon et al., 1987b).

Social relationships

Exposure to traumatic events may also have a number of effects on social relationships. Evidence for this is provided by McFarlane (1987) who reported longitudinal data on the impact of the 1983 Australian bushfire on the patterns of social interaction in the families involved. A group of 183 disaster-affected families were compared with 497 families who had not been exposed to the disaster. At both 8 and 26 months after the event, the interaction in the disaster-affected families was characterised by increased levels of irritability, fighting, withdrawal, and decreased enjoyment from shared activities. Furthermore, a substantial proportion of the variance of irritable distress could be

---

CASE HISTORY 7

Frank is a 55-year-old married man who was self-employed before his involvement in a major shipping disaster. Frank had a particularly miraculous escape, having been in the lower side of the ship at the moment of capsize. His wife, Maureen, was also a vicarious victim because she had been intended to make the crossing herself and had been prevented by a bout of 'flu. Before the disaster, Maureen had also run a small business of her own. Frank had travelled a good deal, so to some extent their lives had been independent. Frank had physical injuries as well as severe PTSD following the disaster. Being self-employed, his business fell apart, Frank was virtually housebound and Maureen was unable to continue with her business. The couple began to suffer financially and Frank's rage at the injustice of these events was a prominent component of his post-trauma reaction. His rage was compounded by the discovery of a pronounced visual field defect on one examination which placed his driving licence in jeopardy. The couple began to drink heavily and Frank admitted to hitting his wife. Part of their frequent rows stemmed from Frank's inability to understand Maureen's problems when, from his point of view, she had nothing to do with the tragedy. He had no interest in sexual relations and Maureen felt bitter and depressed about her perceived rejection by him. The couple were referred for conjoint therapy but Frank refused and filed for divorce.

---

accounted for by disaster-related variables which suggested that the event played an important aetiological role in the increase of irritable distress. These data provide evidence in a civilian population that there is a relationship between exposure to traumatic events and poorer subsequent interpersonal functioning. Other evidence is provided by Goenjian (1993) who has also noted the increased prevalence of marital discord, intrafamilial and interpersonal violence in civilian survivors of the Armenia earthquake. Data with male Vietnam veterans also shows that PTSD is associated with increased social maladjustment (Kulka et al., 1990). An example of interpersonal problems is provided by Frank (see Case History 7).

CHILDREN AND ADOLESCENTS

Although less is known of the manifestations of post-traumatic stress reactions in children and adolescents compared to adults, their reactions are now explicitly considered in the diagnostic criteria for PTSD (APA, 1994). DSM-IV emphasises repetitive play and trauma-specific re-enactment as well as distressing dreams in children (see Table 2.4). However, up until relatively recently there were few studies on the effects of traumatic events on children (see Yule, 1990, 1991). In part, this was because of the difficulty in conducting adequate studies of the immediate aftermath of traumatic events, but also because adults are often very protective towards children and are often unwilling to acknowledge what children may have suffered. Consequently, adults may deny that children have major psychological sequelae that warrant investigation (Yule & Williams, 1990). Thus, there were fewer systematic studies of the effects of major trauma on children and many of the earlier published ones suffered from major methodological weaknesses (Garmezy, 1986). For example, Garmezy and Rutter (1985) summed up the findings from published studies concluding that

> ... behavioural disturbances appear to be less intense than might have been anticipated; a majority of children show a moderate amount of fear and anxiety but this subsides; regressive behaviour marked by clinging to parents and heightened dependency on adults appears and then moderately mild sleep disturbance persists for several months; a later less severe stressor such as a storm may lead to a temporary increase in emotional distress, although this is variable; enuresis occurs in some cases, while hypersensitivity to loud noises may be evident in others. (Garmezy & Rutter, 1985, p. 162)

In their view, severe acute stressors, such as major disasters, resulted in socially handicapping emotional disorders in some children, but in the majority of those cases, the disturbances were short lived. Because children tend not to show amnesia for the event, nor to show 'psychic numbing' or intrusive flashbacks, they argued that there was no need for a specific diagnostic category for children parallel to PTSD in adults.

However, more recent research has questioned this view (e.g., McNally, 1993; Yule, 1990, 1991). Yule (1991) has noted that the evidence reviewed by Garmezy and Rutter (1985) rarely dealt with the aftermath of major civilian disasters in which the children have been exposed to life-threatening events. Other evidence suggests that children, like adults, may experience severe and chronic post-traumatic reactions. Yule (1991) concludes that up to 30–50% of children may experience significant impairment following major disaster. As with adults, Yule (1991) also notes that bereavement reactions will complicate the presenting picture of symptoms. What is interesting, however, is that children's symptoms are almost identical with those recognised by the American Psychiatric Association as comprising PTSD (see Case History 8).

This case illustrates the low priority too often given to dealing with the emotional sequelae of road traffic accidents. It is probable that Hazel's reactions were potentiated by the facts that one brother had been killed in a previous road accident and a sister had been badly injured in another. None of these pertinent details had been picked up at the time. Then, the school, while sympathetic, did nothing to arrange help. It was only after medico-legal assessment that help was eventually arranged. Some three to four years of unnecessary suffering was the result.

Another example is given by Alison (Case History 9). This case illustrates the acute reaction to a traumatic event in a child and how prompt intervention may have prevented a full-blown PTSD developing. A single case like this can never prove that the natural course of recovery would not have been as dramatic, but

CASE HISTORY 8

Hazel (15) was crossing the road at a pedestrian-controlled crossing with members of her family. A bus was stopped as she walked past it, the next she recalls was being on the ground with her mother screaming and other people rushing around her. She was taken to the Casualty Department of the local hospital where she was found to have various sprains, bruises, and cuts, but was discharged home. She was not offered any counselling for herself. Treatment was suggested when she was assessed a year later for medico-legal purposes, but it was a further year before she was referred for treatment.

In the five years since the accident, Hazel had changed. She avoided all reminders of the accident and especially avoided crossing the road at that crossing, despite its being the most convenient for many journeys. She could not watch the television news for fear she would see an accident. She could not talk about it to friends or family, and would start crying when it was mentioned. She had always regarded herself as a strong, self-reliant person, but said of the accident, 'That's one of the things that makes me angry. Every other bit of my life, I'm in control. But that bit, *it* is in control.' In fact, she had developed a very strong sense of anger towards the van driver as he had overtaken the bus at the crossing and hit her.

She still thought about the accident all the time and that still upset her. When these thoughts came into her mind, she would try to make herself not think about them, but this rarely worked. She had had bad dreams about it initially, but these had stopped over the years. She worried that a similar accident might happen to other members of her family, as it had in the past.

When the accident first happened, she had just been settling in to her secondary school. She had been a bright pupil, interested in everything. She became lethargic with no interest in anything, staying indoors a lot and rarely going out. Her sleep suffered badly and even at the time of treatment, it would often be 2 a.m. before she got off to sleep. She still has problems concentrating and also complains of having a poor memory.

On the Impact of Event Scale, she scored 55. She scored 14 on the Birleson Depression Scale, but only 4 on the Children's Manifest Anxiety Scale. She was taken on for treatment and while this was complicated by illness and death in the immediate family, she made slow but steady progress and was able to return to leading a full and active life.

This case illustrates the low priority too often given to dealing with the emotional sequelae of road traffic accidents. It is probable that Hazel's reactions reflected the fact that one brother had been killed in a previous RTA and a sister had been badly injured in yet another one. None of this had been picked up by those dealing with her. Then, the school, while sympathetic, did nothing to arrange help and it was only after a medico-legal assessment that help was eventually arranged. Some three to four years of unnecessary suffering was the result.

---

given the very high scores on the Impact of Event Scale, it is unlikely that the stress reaction would have resolved spontaneously as quickly.

It is on the basis of many cases like these that we would argue that children and adolescents are at risk of PTSD following exposure to a traumatic event. Generally, the reactions of children share the same thematic content as for adults (Weiss, 1993b) (see Table 2.9).

CASE HISTORY 9

Alison (12) was on her way home from school. She was late for her train and as she ran down the stairs to the platform, she saw it pulling away. Then she saw an old man fall under the wheels of the train and she recoiled in horror as she saw his decapitated head roll along the track. She fled home in terror and was crying inconsolably.

She was seen in a specialist clinic a few days later, having been referred by the railways counselling service. She had not attended school for a few days and then only went if taken by car, a considerable imposition for her parents. She had become very clingy, from being a very confident, outgoing girl. She had to sleep in her mother's bed at night for comfort and security. She had recurring, intrusive images and thoughts about the decapitated head, and thought that it moved and talked to her. She tried unsuccessfully to push these thoughts and images from consciousness. She was avoiding travelling by train. She had great difficulty sleeping, difficulty in concentrating at school and was much more alert to dangers around her as well as being much more jumpy when there were unexpected noises.

It turned out that she thought that the man may have committed suicide and she was angry at him for doing so when she saw it. On investigation, it transpired that the elderly man's clothing had got trapped in the train door and he was dragged under the wheels. It was an accident. The dilemma was whether to tell Alison that it was an accident and thereby confirm any fears that travelling by train was dangerous, or let her continue to believe he had killed himself. It was decided to tell her the truth.

At the initial interview, it was explained to her that she was experiencing a normal, if distressing, reaction to an abnormal event. She was not going mad. Advice was given about managing the distress and a month later things had got much better. Alison was again able to travel to school by train and the intrusive images had all but stopped. Her scores on various questionnaires confirmed this improvement:

	Referral	One month later
Impact of Events	49	26
Depression	12	3
Anxiety	17	2

This case illustrates the acute reaction to a traumatic event and how prompt intervention may have prevented a full-blown PTSD developing. A single case like this can never prove that the natural course of recovery would not have been as dramatic, but given the very high scores on the Impact of Event Scale, it is unlikely that the stress reaction would have resolved spontaneously as quickly.

The case also illustrates a fine diagnostic point. As Alison was first assessed within a week of the trauma, then she is not eligible to receive a diagnosis of PTSD since symptoms must have been present for at least four weeks. Thus, one cannot claimed to have 'cured' a disorder that technically was not present. At least she satisfied the criteria for a diagnosis of 'Acute Stress Reaction'.

A Broader Syndrome Continuous with Normal Behaviour

Traumatic events act as a powerful trigger to the onset of depressive and anxiety disorders as well as PTSD. As our examples have shown, a survivor of a traumatic event with only the symptoms of PTSD would be an exception. McFarlane and Papay (1992) note that in the published studies examining co-morbidity, more than 80% of subjects with PTSD appear to have another disorder, although what this is seems to depend on the population studied.

Table 2.9   Common reactions of children after exposure to trauma

- Not wanting to sleep alone, wanting to sleep with parents.
- Being afraid of things that are reminders of the trauma, as in an earthquake, loud noises or feeling buildings shake with passing traffic.
- Crying and fearful clinging—being worried about where parents are.
- Unusual aches and pains; headaches, tummyaches.
- Regressive behaviours—that is, going back to habits that had been overcome like thumb-sucking, bed-wetting, 'babytalk'.
- Play that is aggressive or re-creates the disaster.
- Being confused about what the trauma is and what it means.
- Being worried and/or confused about death.
- Trouble concentrating and doing work in school.
- Worries about their own parents' or siblings' and friends' safety.
- Shame or guilt about things they did or didn't do.
- Worry about the future—'if I grow up'.
- Worry about how parents have reacted to the trauma.

Reproduced, with permission, from Weiss (1993b, p. 19).

Most survivors diagnosed with PTSD will have a range of depressive and anxious reactions whether or not they meet the full criteria to receive a secondary diagnosis. The menu for the diagnostic category of PTSD may simply describe a circumscribed set of symptoms that form part of a broader syndrome that sits astride other major diagnostic groupings. The general exclusion of anxious and depressive symptoms from the criteria for PTSD, McFarlane and Papay (1992) argue, has been significantly determined by the preponderant view that PTSD symptoms are organised around the two-factor model of intrusive and avoidant phenomena.

Negative emotional states (e.g., rage, anger, guilt, shame) are common. Feelings of guilt and shame have been documented in many populations which have been studied. For example, in our 30-month follow up of survivors of the *Herald of Free Enterprise* disaster we were interested in the levels and patterns of guilt and shame. It was found that over half of our sample of 73 survivors felt guilt for being alive when so many died; approximately one-third said that they felt guilty about things they did; and two-thirds said that they felt guilty about things they failed to do. In addition, almost one-third said that they felt they had let themselves down during the disaster; and almost half said that they felt they had let others down (Joseph, Hodgkinson, Yule, & Williams, 1993b).

As well as guilt and shame, there may be intense feelings of rage and anger. Such negative emotional states are distressing and can lead to destructive behaviours, such as substance abuse, in an attempt to dull or block them.

Although it is helpful for communication purposes (arguably one of the principle scientific functions of diagnosis) to classify people into those with and without PTSD, in reality, survivors suffer from a wide range of emotional and behavioural reactions which might be envisaged as continuous with normal emotional and behavioural reactions. We consider that the diagnostic classification of PTSD has been important in providing a common language for the scientific community but, in reality, people's reactions to severe life-stressors can be viewed as ranging along a continuum of adaptation. Work akin to that of Kendall (1976), who investigated the distribution of 'neurotic' and 'endogenous' symptoms finding no 'point of rarity' that would distinguish two syndromes, needs to be done to further establish our view.

Another role of diagnostic classification, reinforced by the needs of courts of law, is to draw a line across this continuum to separate those survivors who are distressed and dysfunctional and 'psychiatrically damaged' from those who are not. Post-traumatic stress reactions follow particular events, although not all people who are exposed to an event will go on to develop severe and chronic problems. The reactions have a recognisable form and early course. However, as we have seen it is a changeable function of classificatory practice whether these reactions are called a 'psychiatric disorder' or not, and these practices may be influenced by factors other than scientific understanding of 'illnesses'. For example, Norris (1992), in an epidemiological study, noted that the rates of PTSD would double if the avoidance criterion were to use a cut-off of two symptoms rather than three. Such a change could have significant implications for compensation judgements and for the planning of services.

Although statistical evidence supports the existence of a constellation of cognitive, emotional, and behavioural phenomena similar to those contained within the diagnostic category of PTSD (e.g., Keane, Wolfe, & Taylor, 1987), there remains debate over whether or not PTSD merits its status as a discrete disorder rather than being considered an amalgam of other disorders. PTSD is at present classified as an anxiety disorder. Certainly it has much in common with panic disorder, phobic anxiety, generalised anxiety disorder (GAD), and obsessive-compulsive disorder (OCD) (Davidson & Foa, 1991). But PTSD also has much in common with mood disorders, and depression would seem to be a common feature. Many of the characteristics of PTSD also invite its consideration as a dissociative disorder (Spiegel, 1988). Complete amnesia, but, more often, partial amnesia of the event (particularly of the reactive feelings) has been noted in combat veterans (Silver, 1984). Psychogenic amnesia and flashbacks may also be considered as dissociative symptoms.

It can be concluded that the range of reactions following exposure to a traumatic event is wide. Exposure to trauma may have a variety of cognitive, emotional, behavioural, and social consequences as well as impaired physical health. Of course, epidemiological findings about reactions to traumatic events are dependent on the criteria used in the assessment of those reactions. PTSD is a syndrome that sits astride other major diagnostic groupings such as anxiety and depression and there remains much debate over the phenomenology of the reactions experienced by survivors of traumatic events.

We would encourage a wider psychosocial perspective to be taken which emphasises the survivor's overall subjective well-being. The literature has focused on pathological adjustment and testifies to the severity and chronicity of distress often experienced by survivors of traumatic events. But there are often positive psychological reactions following trauma such as an increased ability to appreciate life and to show more compassion towards others (Collins, Taylor, & Skokan, 1990; Lehman et al., 1993; Taylor, Lichtman, & Wood, 1984; Zeidner & Ben-Zur, 1994).

With a sample of 35 adult survivors of the *Jupiter* cruise ship, we found that most agreed that they no longer took life for granted (94%), valued their relationships more (91%), valued other people more (88%), felt more experienced about life (83%), and no longer took people or things for granted (91%). A large number also agreed that they tried to live life to the full now (71%), were more understanding and tolerant (71%), and looked upon each day as a bonus (77%). Just over half said that they had a greater faith in human nature (54%) and were more determined to succeed in life (50%). Just under half agreed that they no longer worry about death (44%).

However, greater endorsement of these items were not associated with lower symptom scores as was predicted, instead we found a trend contrary to what we had predicted for those endorsing these beliefs to have higher intrusive and avoidant symptoms (Joseph, Williams, & Yule, 1993c). This might reflect the need for meaning that survivors have, the most distressed having the greatest need to find meaning. It might also be that positive responses such as these are symptomatic of distress at the time of assessment but would predict lower distress later on.

CONCLUSION

Although clinicians working with survivors will conduct standardised interviews based on either the APA or WHO systems, these systems have provided only a temporary gold standard because of the changing criteria within and across each system. For example, it is possible that someone suffering from excessive guilt and who would have fulfilled the DSM-III criteria in 1980 would not have fulfilled the DSM-III-R criteria in 1987. Alternatively, someone suffering from distressing intrusive recollections might fulfil the ICD-10 (WHO, 1993) criteria but not the DSM-IV criteria if they did not also present with symptoms of emotional numbing and avoidance. Nevertheless, such problems are not unusual within the psychiatric literature. For example, even the validity of the concept of schizophrenia remains in question (Boyle, 1990) and it is likely that the concept of PTSD will continue to evolve as more about the phenomenology of reactions to extreme stress becomes understood. Furthermore, the fact of frequent psychiatric co-morbidity raises the question of what exactly researchers and clinicians should be trying to assess. The overlap with other and more generally recognised depressive and anxiety disorders highlights the need for specificity in the classification of PTSD. But although a circumscribed menu of symptoms is a requirement of psychiatric classification, in reality, the range of post-traumatic stress reactions is wide. Thus, on the one hand, psychiatric classification requires that the menu of symptoms be fairly circumscribed to avoid overlap with other disorders, but on the other, there is a need for an extended menu of symptoms that recognises the wide range of trauma-related reactions.

SUMMARY POINTS

1. The problems in psychological functioning that people often experience following exposure to traumatic events have a recognisable form and early course. The hallmark symptoms are intrusive thoughts, feelings, and images. The term PTSD was first introduced into the clinical literature by the American Psychiatric Association in 1980 (APA, 1980) in an attempt to describe the clinical characteristics exhibited by survivors of traumatic events.

2. Although there have been several revisions to the criteria necessary for the diagnosis of PTSD since 1980, much debate remains over the architecture of PTSD symptomatology and in particular the definition of trauma. Recent theoretical work emphasises the role of subjective perception in the development of trauma-related disorder.

3. The diagnosis of PTSD is often accompanied by other related disorders as well as a wide range of cognitive, emotional and behavioural problems. Research suggests that depression is the major co-diagnosis. A broader perspective on symptoms which recognises the multifaceted nature of post-traumatic stress reactions is encouraged.

4. The reactions of children and adolescents to trauma are similar to those of adults. Post-traumatic stress disorder has been reported in children and adolescents following a wide range of different events.

5. Finally, a perspective which views symptoms of PTSD as continuous with symptoms of normal adaptation is advocated.

Chapter 3

ASSESSMENT AND MEASUREMENT

Reliable and valid measurement is the cornerstone of psychological science. Since the original formulation of PTSD in DSM-III (APA, 1980) there has been much interest in standardised measurement of PTSD (e.g., Allen, 1994; Ollendick & Hoffman, 1982; Litz, Penk, Gerardi, & Keane, 1992). The range of psychological reactions that people experience after trauma is wide and, as we have seen, includes not only the symptoms necessary for the diagnosis of PTSD but also those of depression, anxiety, as well as problems in cognitive and social functioning. The clinician working with survivors of traumatic events is faced with the task of collecting relevant information about the patient in an attempt to understand what the problem areas are and of formulating the case with a view to deciding upon a treatment plan. The clinician will probably also assess the client at several stages during the course of treatment to see how he or she is responding to the treatment and again at the end of treatment to determine whether it has been effective. Research scientists may want to pool the information collected by many clinicians to find out in a more systematic and controlled way the most effective methods of treatment. Alternatively, they may want to conduct surveys of groups of survivors to find out about the effects of a particular event or to run experiments to find out how survivors react to certain stimuli. In all of these cases, the reliability and validity of the assessments will determine the value of the research. Most of the assessment techniques used with survivors of traumatic events are either based on data obtained from interviews or from self-report questionnaires.

Key Topics

Interviews
Self-report
Associated symptoms
Children and adolescents
Issues and recommendations
Conclusion

INTERVIEWS

Several standard structured psychiatric interview schedules now include questions to assess PTSD symptoms (see Watson, 1990 for a review), e.g., the Diagnostic Interview Schedule (DIS: Robins & Helzer, 1985) and the Structured Clinical Interview (SCID: Spitzer, Williams, & Gibbon, 1987). These interview schedules are fairly lengthy and are used by clinicians to assess for various psychiatric disorders. Other interview schedules have been developed solely for the assessment of PTSD. To illustrate the format of interview schedules, as well as some theoretical issues concerning the nature of disorder and its assessment, we will consider two of the most recently developed tools, the PTSD Interview (PTSD-I: Watson, Juba, Manifold, Kucala, & Anderson, 1991a) and the Clinician-Administered Post-Traumatic Stress Disorder Scale (CAPS: Blake, Weathers, Nagy, et al., 1990).

The PTSD Interview (PTSD-I: Watson et al., 1991a) asks whether the interviewee has experienced an unusual, extremely distressful event (the DSM-III/III-R definition of trauma). This question is then followed by a request for details and reflects section A of the DSM manual criteria. Seventeen items follow which closely reflect the symptoms of PTSD as described by DSM-III-R, each of which is answered on a 7-point Likert scale that ranges from 'no; never' to 'extremely; always'. Respondents provide a verbal response which is recorded by the examiner. This provides information on the frequency of symptoms. A score of 4 ('somewhat; commonly') is considered sufficient to meet the relevant DSM criteria. This provides information on whether or not the person qualifies for a diagnosis of PTSD. Two additional questions are asked to determine whether the section E requirement of a duration of at least one month has been met. The authors report very high test–retest reliability and internal reliability for the PTSD-I.

PTSD, as defined by DSM, is a disorder which a person either has or does not have. Although this is how psychiatric classification works, there is much debate in the field of abnormal psychology over whether disorder should be viewed in this way or whether abnormal behaviour should be viewed as continuous with normal behaviour. The reader will note that the PTSD-I can be used to make a diagnosis of disorder (i.e., answers of somewhat/commonly or above to all of the questions) or to provide a continuous score of symptom frequency.

The Clinician-Administered Post-Traumatic Stress Disorder Scale (CAPS: Blake, Weathers, Nagy, et al., 1990a) also consists of 17 questions based on DSM-III-R which are administered by the clinician. The CAPS assesses both lifetime and present presence of PTSD as well as both the frequency and intensity of PTSD symptoms. Using clinicians' diagnosis, it has been found to have good agreement with clinical diagnosis and convergent validity with self-report scales of PTSD symptomatology (e.g., Hovens et al., 1994b). Hovens et al. (1994b) conclude that the CAPS appears to be an adequate instrument for the assessment of PTSD and there is now a version developed for use with children. Both instruments are based on diagnostic criteria that have now been revised (APA, 1994). It is inevitable, given the time it takes to conduct and publish research, that assessment procedures will tend to be one step behind the latest thinking in classification. Like the PTSD-I, the CAPS yields both dichotomous diagnostic information about PTSD and continuous symptom scores. However, with regard to continuous scores, the CAPS distinguishes between the frequency and the intensity of symptoms. For example, one person may have slightly upsetting nightmares several times a month whereas another person may have extremely upsetting nightmares several times a month, but if only the frequency of nightmares is assessed, both individuals would receive the same score. It may be useful to take into account both the frequency and intensity of symptoms separately.

If one accepts a continuity between normal and pathological states, interviews that simply dichotomise survivors into those who qualify for a diagnosis and those who do not provide less information than those that provide an indication of the intensity of the person's emotional experiences and the relative position of this person's symptoms compared to other people's. Many people will not meet the full criteria for PTSD but they may be just as impaired in functioning and require the same level of care as those who do. These people might be said to have partial PTSD or subthreshold PTSD (Blank, 1993; Carlier & Gersons, 1995).

SELF-REPORT

Due to practical constraints in research, self-report scales are widely used. The PTSD Inventory (Solomon, Weisenberg, Schwarzwald, & Mikulincer, 1987c) is a self-report scale originally based on DSM-III criteria, but it has since been revised following publication of DSM-III-R (Solomon et al., 1993a). The questionnaire consists of 17 statements corresponding to the 17 PTSD symptoms listed in DSM-III-R and has been shown to have a satisfactory internal reliability (Cronbach's alpha = 0.86) and convergent validity with the SCID.

The Mississippi Scale for combat related PTSD (M-PTSD) is a 35-item self-report Likert scale developed by Keane, Caddell, and Taylor (1988) and is one of the most widely used measures for veterans seeking treatment. Items were derived from the original DSM-III criteria to provide a measure of combat-related PTSD. Ratings are made for each item on a 5-point Likert scale and are summated to provide a continuous measure of PTSD symptom severity ranging from 35 to 175. The M-PTSD assesses the standard PTSD symptoms as well as the associated features of depression, substance abuse, and suicidal tendencies. With a sample of 362 male Vietnam veterans who had sought professional help, Keane et al. (1988) found the scale to have satisfactory internal reliability (Cronbach's alpha = 0.94) and test–retest reliability over a one-week period ($r = 0.97$).

Other data have confirmed the reliability and validity of the M-PTSD (Hyer, Davis, Boudewyns, & Woods, 1991; McFall, Smith, MacKay, & Tarver, 1990a; McFall, Smith, Roszell, Tarver, & Malas, 1990b) and the M-PTSD has been used in numerous studies (e.g., King, King, Gudanowski, & Vreven, 1995; Marmar et al., 1994; McNally, Lasko, Macklin, & Pitman, 1995) and translated into several languages (e.g., Hovens & van der Ploeg, 1993). Using a cutoff score of 107 (Keane, Caddell, & Taylor, 1988), the M-PTSD had a sensitivity (i.e, true positives/true positives + false negatives) of 93% in identifying PTSD patients and a specificity (i.e., true negatives/true negatives + false positives) of 88% in discriminating them from substance-abusing controls patients. Keane et al. (1988) note, however, that the cutoff score may vary with the populations studied.

The Penn Inventory is a 26-item self-report inventory which provides a continuous measure of the degree, frequency, and intensity of PTSD symptomatology (Hammarberg, 1992). Developed on the basis of DSM-III-R criteria, the Penn Inventory was validated on both survivors of civilian trauma and Vietnam veterans and it showed satisfactory internal reliability (Cronbach's alpha = 0.94) and test–retest reliability ($r = 0.96$) as well as convergent validity with other scales.

There are two major approaches to the development of self-report measures. First, the development of new tests for assessing PTSD symptoms, and second, the study of existing tests and their usefulness in diagnosing PTSD. The Mississippi Scale, the Penn Inventory, and the PTSD Inventory are examples of the first approach and are based on the DSM criteria. However, much work has also been concerned with the latter approach using the Minnesota Multiphasic Personality Inventory.

Minnesota Multiphasic Personality Inventory

The Minnesota Multiphasic Personality Inventory (MMPI) has been widely used in the assessment of PTSD. This is an interesting approach as it is informative about the wider phenomenology of post-traumatic stress reactions. The MMPI is the most widely used personality self-report inventory in the USA (Colligan & Offord, 1992) and consists of 550 self-statements which are rated as true or false. The items in the MMPI make up 10 clinical scales: hypochondriasis, depression, conversion hysteria, psychopathic deviate, masculinity–feminity, paranoia, psychasthenia, schizophrenia, hypomania, and social introversion. Studies have shown that PTSD patients show general elevation on many or all subscales (Fairbank, Keane, & Malloy, 1983b; Foy, Sipprelle, Rueger, & Carroll, 1984; Silver & Salamone-Genovese, 1991) but also that some survivor groups may have particular profiles. To illustrate, it has been found that substance-abuse veterans with PTSD showed MMPI elevations on the psychopathic, paranoia, and social introversion scales (Roberts,

Penk, Robinowitz, & Patterson, 1982) whereas sexual-abuse survivors have MMPI elevations on the psychopathic deviate and schizophrenia scales (Belkin, Greene, Rodrigue, & Boggs, 1994).

Although such data are informative, the MMPI was developed long before the recognition of PTSD and other research has attempted to develop a PTSD scale on the basis of the MMPI items. Keane, Malloy, and Fairbank (1984) compared PTSD patients with non-PTSD patients on each of the 550 MMPI items. On the basis of these data, Keane et al. (1984) developed a 49-item MMPI-PTSD subscale (PK-MMPI) which differentiated the two groups. Although the PK-MMPI has been used in numerous studies (e.g., Marmar et al., 1994) and there is some evidence for its reliability and validity (Burke & Mayer, 1985; Gerardi, Keane, & Penk, 1989; Watson, 1990), overall the evidence is mixed (Denny, Robinowitz, & Penk, 1987) and it has been suggested that some caution might be employed in its use due to low diagnostic accuracy (Silver & Salamone-Genovese, 1991) and a tendency to identify false positives. False positives refer to those people diagnosed as suffering from the disorder when they are not. This is a problem to a greater or lesser extent with all assessment techniques which aim to classify people into groups which correspond to other external criteria, in this case, the DSM criteria for PTSD. Furthermore, these data have been collected with Vietnam veterans and there is a need to validate the PK-MMPI with survivors of civilian trauma (McCaffrey, Hickling, & Marrazo, 1989).

Although the PK-MMPI has been widely used and is popular among clinicians in the USA because of their familiarity with the MMPI, the main limitation of the PK-MMPI is that the MMPI was designed before PTSD was first defined by the APA (1980) and therefore does not include items that might be thought of as directly testing for all of the core PTSD criteria. Moody and Kish (1989) have suggested that the PK-MMPI measures general psychological maladjustment and dysphoric feelings rather than any specific syndrome.

However, a new version of the MMPI has recently been introduced, the MMPI-2 (Butcher, 1990). Several changes have been made to the PK-MMPI resulting in the PK-MMPI-2 (Lyons & Keane, 1992). The MMPI-2 also includes a new PTSD scale, the PS-MMPI-2 (Schlenger & Kulka, 1989). This is a 60-item scale with 46 items taken from the PK-MMPI with 14 new items which have been shown to discriminate for PTSD. However, the properties of these newer scales await further research.

Multifactorial Assessment

Although PTSD as a disorder consists of groupings of symptoms characterised as re-experiencing, denial, and hyperarousal, most of the instruments we have reviewed are not usually used to yield separate scores for these groupings but instead either a dichotomous assessment of whether or not the person fulfils the diagnostic criteria for PTSD or a continuous score of PTSD intensity.

A further consideration in assessment is whether to treat PTSD symptoms as a homogeneous or a heterogeneous grouping of symptoms. For example, it might be that a person scoring high on re-experiencing symptoms and low on avoidance symptoms may yield the same score as someone scoring moderately high on both re-experiencing and avoidance. Both individuals would, however, receive the same score if the symptoms are simply summated to give a total score which would hide the psychologically significant differences in the presenting symptoms of these two people. Adopting Horowitz's perspective on post-traumatic stress reactions as alternating between intrusions and denials the description of survivors in terms of these two dimensions would seem to be a minimum requirement.

Impact of Event Scale

One of the most widely used instruments worldwide for the assessment of post-traumatic phenomena has been the Impact of Event Scale (IES: Horowitz, Wilner, & Alvarez, 1979). The IES is a self-report measure which was developed on the basis of Horowitz's two-factor theory that can be anchored to any specific life event and taps: (1) intrusively experienced ideas, images, feelings and dreams, and (2) the avoidance of ideas, feelings, or situations. The items on the IES were developed from statements most frequently used to describe episodes of distress by people who had experienced recent life-events and was initially tested on 66 individuals admitted to an outpatient clinic for the treatment of stress-response syndromes, about half of whom had experienced bereavement. The remainder had personal injuries resulting from road accidents, violence, illness, or surgery. Horowitz et al. (1979) report satisfactory internal reliability (Cronbach's alpha = 0.78 for intrusion and 0.82 for avoidance) and test–retest reliability ($r = 0.89$ for intrusion and 0.79 for avoidance). In addition, other research has largely confirmed these findings and the separate factors of intrusion and avoidance (Joseph, Williams, Yule, & Walker, 1992b; Joseph, Yule, Williams, & Hodgkinson, 1993g; Schwarzwald, Solomon, Weisenberg, & Mikulincer, 1987; Zilberg, Weiss, & Horowitz, 1982). The IES correlates well with other PTSD measures (Kulka et al., 1990; Schlenger et al., 1992; Weisenberg, Solomon, Schwarzwald, & Mikulincer, 1987) and has been used in numerous studies with victims of sexual abuse (e.g., Rowan, Foy, Rodriguez, & Ryan, 1993), battered women (e.g., Houskamp & Foy, 1991), train drivers following railway accidents (Malt et al., 1993; Karlehagen et al., 1993) and translated into many languages including Hebrew (Schwarzwald et al., 1987), and Dutch (Brom, Kleber, & Defares, 1986). The IES is most useful because it can be anchored to any life-event making data comparable across studies. In addition, the IES provides a continuous score for both the intrusion and avoidance subscales making it useful for correlational studies. However, the IES was developed to test Horowitz's two-factor structure of post-traumatic stress reactions and does not assess the full range of symptoms associated with PTSD.

Analysis of PTSD symptoms, however, does not usually show a clear structure corresponding to the DSM groupings of intrusions, denials, and hyperarousal raising the question of whether these groupings provide the best description of the architecture of post-traumatic stress reactions. Principal component analysis of the M-PTSD identified six factors (Keane, Caddell & Taylor, 1988) labelled as: 'intrusive memories and depression', 'interpersonal adjustment problems', 'liability of affect and memory', 'rumination features', 'other interpersonal difficulties', and 'sleep problems'. The last four factors were, however, defined by fewer than four items which, Keane et al. (1988) note, raises questions about the reliability of their measurement. Other research has, however, suggested a three-factor structure to the M-PTSD: intrusive re-experiencing; numbing-avoidance and anger; lability and social alienation (McFall et al., 1990a). The architecture of PTSD symptoms is an issue that we will return to in Chapter 8.

Assessment can often be very time consuming and researchers and clinicians have also been interested in devising short scales that can assess for PTSD. For example, Hyer et al. (1991) identify a subset of 10 items that can be used in short screening batteries (Miss-10). Two groups of Vietnam veterans were used and all had been treated on a specialised PTSD unit subsequent to a series of screenings that confirmed PTSD. The first group of 52 veterans were administered the Mississippi Scale twice, on entry and at six weeks. The test–retest reliability was found to be 0.64, and the internal reliability was high at both times (Cronbach's alpha = 0.91 and 0.94 respectively). The second group consisted of 95 veterans who were administered the measure on entry only. Again, internal reliability was high (Cronbach's alpha = 0.92). Hyer et al. (1991) also inspected individual item correlations with the overall scale to identify 10 items with a good test–retest reliability (0.66), and high internal reliability (Cronbach's alpha = 0.94 and 0.96 respectively). For the 95 veterans, internal reliability was high for the Miss-10 (Cronbach's alpha = 0.85) and correlated highly with the total Mississippi Scale ($r = 0.95$). Other variations of the M-PTSD have included a version designed to assess symptoms in female veterans of operation 'Desert Storm' (Wolfe, Brown, & Buscela, 1992) as well as a civilian version (Kulka et al., 1990).

Dissociative Experiences Scale

Investigators are becoming increasingly interested in the dissociation component of PTSD. The Dissociative Experiences Scale (Bernstein & Putnam, 1986) is a 28-item self-report measure of trait dissociation. The scale assesses absorption, depersonalization and derealization, and amnesic experiences. A shorter measure which can be easily included as part of a battery of different measures is the Peritraumatic Dissociative Experiences Questionnaire

(Marmar et al., 1994). This is an 8-item interview based questionnaire for assessing retrospective reports of depersonalization, derealization, amnesia, out of body experience, and altered time perception. Internal reliability was found to be satisfactory (Cronbach's alpha = 0.80) and convergent validity found with other measures of post-traumatic functioning. Dissociation appears to be a particular feature of sexual abuse and forms one component of the Trauma Symptom Checklist (TSC: Briere & Runtz, 1989). Briere and Runtz (1989) report that the TSC has satisfactory internal reliability and that it was able to classify 79% of women as to whether or not they had a history of CSA. Other research points to the validity of the TSC as a measure of the consequences of sexual trauma (Gold, Milan, Mayall, & Johnson, 1994).

Several other self-rating scales have been developed recently to assess PTSD. For example, the Self-Rating Inventory for Posttraumatic Stress (SIP: Hovens et al., 1994a) is a 47-item questionnaire reflecting DSM-III-R criteria and associated features. Although the SIP appears to have excellent reliability and validity it remains to be investigated with an English-speaking population.

Other researchers have developed scales for use following specific events. For example, Zeidner and Ben-Zur (1994) constructed a 6-item scale to assess post-traumatic symptoms following the Gulf War and the SCUD missile attacks on Israel. Subjects rated the frequency (1 = not at all to 5 = almost all the time) of each item: (1) nightmares about missile attacks, (2) attempts to escape or avoid things or people which bring back memories of the crisis period, (3) heightened sensitivity to rooms/places which served as sealed shelters during the war, (4) recurring intrusive thoughts about the crisis, (5) heightened sensitivity to events which occurred during the war, and (6) active attempts at avoiding information relating to events during the war.

ASSOCIATED SYMPTOMS

The General Health Questionnaire has been widely used in traumatic stress research (see Box 2.1) as a measure of global dysfunction. The Beck Depression Inventory (BDI: Beck, 1967), and the State-Trait Anxiety Inventory (STAI: Spielberger, Gorsuch, & Lushene, 1970) are also widely used and well-validated measures which have received some attention in the growing PTSD literature. For example, Fairbank et al. (1983a) reported that PTSD Vietnam veteran's BDI scores were higher than both psychiatric and healthy combat control subjects, and that their STAI scores were significantly higher than those of healthy combat control subjects. In addition, Orr et al. (1990) found Vietnam veterans diagnosed as suffering from PTSD scored higher on the BDI and STAI than healthy combat control subjects. These findings provide psychometric support for PTSD's reported co-morbidity with major depression and anxiety disorders. The BDI and the STAI have been used in numerous other studies (e.g., Basoglu & Paker, 1995; Joseph, Yule, & Williams, 1994; McNally, Lasko, Macklin, & Pitman, 1995).

However, although self-report measures of anxiety and depression, such as the BDI and the STAI, are thought to tap distinct constructs, scores on the BDI and the STAI have been found to be strongly correlated (e.g., Joseph, Yule, & Williams, 1995a) questioning this distinction. This is echoed within the psychometric literature where it has actually proved difficult to distinguish the constructs of anxiety and depression (Feldman, 1993). There is growing evidence for a tripartite model of depression and anxiety that divides symptoms into three groups: manifestations of anhedonia specific to depression, somatic arousal unique to anxiety, and symptoms of general distress that are largely non-specific (Clark & Watson, 1991; Watson & Clark, 1984; Watson et al., 1995b; Watson et al., 1995a).

Depending on the nature of the event, many survivors may also be bereaved and investigators will often want to measure grief reactions. One commonly used scale is the Texas Inventory of Grief (TIG: Faschingbauer, Devaul, & Zisook, 1977) although several versions of this scale now exist (see Hodgkinson, Joseph, Yule, & Williams, 1995).

CHILDREN AND ADOLESCENTS

As with adults, assessment of children and adolescents can be through interview or self-report measures. However, assessment with these age groups has received less attention than adults (McNally, 1991). The Post-Traumatic Stress Disorder Reaction Index is a 20-item structured interview based on DSM-III criteria for assessing childhood PTSD (Frederick, 1985a). It has also been validated with adults (Frederick, 1987) and a translated version has been used by Goenjian and colleagues in their study of the effects of the Armenia earthquake (Goenjian, 1993; Goenjian et al., 1994; Pynoos et al., 1993) and found to be a valid index in evaluating PTSD (Goenjian et al., 1994). It is therefore a useful instrument for studies which wish to compare the responses of children and adults and is suitable for use cross-culturally.

Often parents or teachers are called upon to make ratings of children's behaviour. Several scales designed for this purpose are available. For example, the Behaviour Problem Checklist (Quay & Peterson, 1979), the Child Behaviour Checklist (Achenbach & Edelbrock, 1983), and the Rutter parent and teacher rating scales (Goodman, 1994; Rutter, 1967). However, these parent or teacher scales may underestimate the level of distress experienced by the child (Terr, 1985; Yule & Williams, 1990), possibly because of the tendency for adults to underestimate children's emotional distress but also because the scales do not contain items sensitive to traumatic stress reactions. In addition, children are often afraid of admitting how they feel to anyone. Each child may feel that he or she is either unusual or will be teased by others. For these reasons, both adult report data as well as self-report measures are recommended (Saigh, 1989). Various self-report measures have been employed to assess post-traumatic stress reactions, depression, anxiety, fears, and the consequences of sexual abuse. Often self-reports may reveal differences between PTSD positive and PTSD negative groups where parent reports do not (Wolfe, Sas, & Wekerle, 1994) although Wolfe, Gentile, & Wolfe (1989) have emphasised that the right questions must be asked of children if they are to report on their subjective state.

Impact of Event Scale

Although originally developed for use with adults, the Impact of Event Scale (IES: Horowitz, Wilner, & Alvarez, 1979) has been used successfully with children (e.g., Joseph, Brewin, Yule, & Williams, 1993a; Marmar et al., 1994; Yule, Udwin, & Murdoch, 1990b) and has been described as probably the best questionnaire available for evaluating childhood PTSD (McNally, 1991). It has been used with children who survived the *Herald of Free Enterprise* disaster (Yule & Williams, 1990) and children who survived the capsize of the *Jupiter* cruise ship (Yule, Ten Brugencate, & Joseph, 1994; Yule & Udwin, 1991; Yule et al., 1990b). Yule and Williams (1990) reported that children as young as 8 years found the scale to be generally meaningful and relevant to their experiences although more recent work has identified some items as too difficult and a shorter version of the scale for children has been developed (Dyregrov & Yule, 1995a, 1995b).

But, as with adults, the range of symptomatology reported by children and adolescents following trauma is wide and other self-report scales that have been employed with child survivors are the Birleson Depression Scale (Birleson, 1981) and the Revised Children's Manifest Anxiety Scale (Reynolds & Richmond, 1978). Yule and Udwin (1991) were able to contact 24 teenage girls 10 days after the sinking of the *Jupiter* cruise ship. During a debriefing session, all 24 completed the Impact of Event Scale, the Birelson Depression Scale, and the Revised Children's Manifest Anxiety Scale. On the basis of their scores on these measures at 10 days after the sinking, 10 girls aged 14 years were judged to be at high risk of developing problems. When help was offered on an individual or group basis (and without disclosing which girls were considered to be at high risk,) 8 of the 10 high-risk group came forward for help on the first day. The other two attended the second meeting. Only five others ever attended any group meeting. This was, Yule and Udwin (1991) note, a highly significant relationship between scores on the screening scales and later help seeking. They concluded that this battery of measures showed considerable promise in identifying those children who are most in need of help after a disaster.

Fear Survey Schedule

In another study, Yule, Udwin and Murdoch (1990b) asked the same 24 girls (and three control groups) to complete the Revised Fear Survey Schedule for Children (Ollendick, 1983). In the affected school, three subgroups of girls were distinguished: those who went on the cruise and were traumatised, those who had wanted to go but could not get a place, and those who showed no interest in going in the first place. However, this latter group could not be considered as an unaffected control group as the whole school was badly affected by the aftermath of the disaster. Accordingly, fourth-year girls in a nearby school also completed the fear schedule. The fear survey items were rated as being related to the events on the cruise or not. There was agreement among the authors that 11 items were related and 33 were unrelated. It was found that there were no differences across the four exposure groups on unrelated fears (e.g., spiders). In contrast, on related fears (e.g., drowning), only the girls who experienced the traumatic events showed a significant increase in reported fears. On this basis, this self-report measure may also have potential as a valuable screening instrument, but only when items specific to the event are used.

Sexual Abuse

Other self-report measures which have been used include the Children's Depression Inventory (Kovacs, 1983) as well as specific measures such as the Sexual Abuse Fear Evaluation (Wolfe & Wolfe, 1986; Wolfe et al., 1989, 1994). This is a 27-item scale that is embedded within the Fear Survey Schedule for Children—Revised (Ollendick, 1983) to assess fears related to events and situations that sexually abused children report as more distressing. Several studies have found that scores on standardised self-report measures of depression or anxiety may not be elevated although scores on measures such as the Sexual Abuse Fear Evaluation are (see Wolfe et al., 1994). For this reason, other measures such as the Child Sexual Behaviour Inventory (CITES: Friedrich et al., 1992) and the Children's Impact of Traumatic Events (Wolfe, Wolfe, Gentile, & LaRose, 1986) may be useful in the assessment of sexual abuse. The CITES, since revised (CITES-R: Wolfe, Gentile, Michienzi, et al., 1991), has 78 questions and can be either used as a self-report or administered as an interview. The CITES-R has four subscales: PTSD (intrusive thoughts, avoidance, hyperarousal, sexual anxiety); social reactions (negative reactions from others, social support); abuse attributions (self-blame, guilt, empowerment, vulnerability, dangerous world); and eroticism. McNally (1991), in his review of children's measures, notes that the CITES-R cannot be used to provide a PTSD diagnosis because it fails to assess the full range of symptoms.

However, the use of self-report scales or clinical interviews is not always possible with children and it may be necessary to use some other form of assessment. For example, Gleser, Green, & Winget (1981) report data using the Psychiatric evaluation Form (PEF: Endicott & Spitzer, 1972) completed by the research team on the basis of psychiatric reports from lawsuit proceedings. Fears are thought to be common. Dollinger, O'Donnell and Staley (1984) studied the effects of a lightening strike on 27 soccer players and two spectators all aged 10 to 13 years. All had been knocked flat by the lightening strike in which one boy was killed and six required immediate medical treatment. The survivors later completed the Louisville Fear Survey for Children, 104 items rated on 5-point scales. The investigators found that the children on the soccer field showed more fear of storms than did matched controls, and these fears were more intense. But also, it was found that responses showed a clear generalisation gradient with fears of storms being strongest, followed by fears relating to sleep, noise, disasters, death, and dying while there was no effect on fears of people or embarrassment. Similar findings are reported by Yule et al. (1990b) with children who survived the *Jupiter* sinking. Recent evidence also suggests that infants and young children (i.e., less that 4 years of age) can develop post-traumatic disorders after traumatic events, although it does not seem that they exhibit symptoms in a way that can be diagnosed by DSM-IV criteria but instead require more behaviourally anchored and developmentally sensitive criteria (Scheeringa, Zeanah, Drell, & Larrieu, 1995).

ISSUES AND RECOMMENDATIONS

Although cutoff scores are often proposed for self-report scales so that they can be used diagnostically, the use of cutoff scores reflects a dichotomous categorisation and there will often be very little difference between those respondents scoring just below the cutoff point and those scoring just above the cutoff point. Furthermore, appropriate cutoff points will vary with the population under study (Watson, 1990). Recommended cutoff points for classification should be used with great caution.

A further limitation of the various self-report measures is the possibility that respondents can easily fake psychopathology. This has been demonstrated in studies with the IES (Lees-Haley, 1990) although other work using the MMPI has suggested that when asked to fake symptoms, respondents will tend to overendorse PTSD symptoms (Fairbank, McCaffrey, & Keane, 1985). The possibility of factitious presentations (Lacoursiere, 1993) has prompted researchers to find other objective methods of assessment. In addition to clinical interviews and self-report instruments, there has been some interest in the development of psychophysiological measures of PTSD. This refers to the assessment of autonomic activity when survivors are re-exposed to traumatic stimuli. In an early study, Blanchard, Kolb, Pallmeyer, and Gerardi (1982) found that heart rate, skin conductance, and electromyography responses to combat stimuli discriminated PTSD patients from normal control subjects.

More recently, Blanchard, Kolb, Gerardi, Ryan, and Pallmeyer (1986) proposed that heart rate reactivity to combat stimuli could serve as a marker for PTSD because it accurately classified 88% of PTSD patients. In addition, the use of cognitive and neuropsychological measures also appear to be promising (Wolfe & Charney, 1991).

Changes in Outlook

Generally the literature has focused on pathological adjustment and testifies to the severity and chronicity of distress often experienced by survivors of traumatic events. But there are often positive psychological reactions following trauma such as an increased ability to appreciate life and to show more compassion towards others (Collins, Taylor, & Skokan, 1990; Lehman et al., 1993; Taylor, Lichtman, & Wood, 1984; Zeidner & Ben-Zur, 1994). One self-report instrument that has been designed to assess both negative and positive trauma-related reactions is the Changes in Outlook Questionnaire (Joseph, Williams, & Yule, 1993c). This is a 26-item self-report measure (see Figure 3.1) that contains two scales tapping positive changes (e.g., I value my relationships much more now) as well as negative changes (e.g., I have very little trust in other people now). Many people who are involved in disaster and who are not identified as overtly suffering from severe psychological disturbance can undergo major changes in their approach to life and we would argue that, at present, disaster research is constrained by its focus on psychopathological responses. It is through the assessment of both positive and negative responses that it should become possible to identify more accurately those at risk of long-term disturbance.

Assessment of Psychosocial Factors

Although exposure to a traumatic event is a necessary aetiological factor in the development of PTSD, exposure would not appear to be sufficient and reactions to trauma are thought to be multiply determined. For this reason some researchers have advocated an assessment procedure compatible with research and clinical purposes. For example, Freedy, Kilpatrick, and Resnick (1993) outline an assessment instrument that they have used with survivors of Hurricane Hugo. This includes questions on pre-disaster factors, within-disaster factors, post-disaster factors as well as mental health outcome. Various self-report instruments exist for the measurement of coping resources and behaviour (e.g., Carver, Scheier, & Weintraub, 1989; Folkman, Lazarus, Dunkel-Schetter, DeLongis, & Gruen, 1986a; Hobfoll, Lilly, & Jackson, 1991; Matheny, Curlette, Aycock, Pugh, & Taylor, 1987; Matheny, Aycock, Curlette, & Junker, 1993; Muris, van Zuuren, de Jong, de Beurs, & Hanewald, 1994; Tobin, Holroyd, Reynolds, & Wigal, 1989), social support (Joseph, Andrews, Williams, & Yule, 1992a; Power, 1988; Sarason, Levine, Basham, &

Each of the following statements have been made by survivors of disaster at some time. Please read each one and indicate, by circling one of the numbers next to it, how much you agree or disagree with it at the present time:
1 = Strongly disagree; 2 = Disagree; 3 = Disagree a little; 4 = Agree a little;
5 = Agree; 6 = Strongly agree

1.	I don't take life for granted any more	1	2	3	4	5	6
2.	I value my relationships much more now...	1	2	3	4	5	6
3.	I feel more experienced about life now...	1	2	3	4	5	6
4.	I don't worry about death at all any more...	1	2	3	4	5	6
5.	I live everyday to the full now............	1	2	3	4	5	6
6.	I look upon each day as a bonus.........	1	2	3	4	5	6
7.	I'm a more understanding and tolerant person now.........................	1	2	3	4	5	6
8.	I have greater faith in human nature now...	1	2	3	4	5	6
9.	I no longer take people or things for granted...	1	2	3	4	5	6
10.	I value other people more now..........	1	2	3	4	5	6
11.	I am more determined to succeed in life now...	1	2	3	4	5	6
12.	I don't look forward to the future any more...	1	2	3	4	5	6
13.	My life has no meaning any more......	1	2	3	4	5	6
14.	I no longer feel able to cope with things...	1	2	3	4	5	6
15.	I fear death very much now..............	1	2	3	4	5	6
16.	I feel as if something bad is just waiting around the corner to happen.	1	2	3	4	5	6
17.	I desperately wish I could turn the clock back to before it happened.......	1	2	3	4	5	6
18.	I sometimes think it's not worth being a good person.................................	1	2	3	4	5	6
19.	I have very little trust in other people now...	1	2	3	4	5	6
20.	I feel very much as if I'm in limbo.......	1	2	3	4	5	6
21.	I have very little trust in myself now...	1	2	3	4	5	6
22.	I feel harder towards other people.....	1	2	3	4	5	6
23.	I am less tolerant of others now.........	1	2	3	4	5	6
24.	I am much less able to communicate with other people...........................	1	2	3	4	5	6
25.	Nothing makes me happy any more...	1	2	3	4	5	6
26.	I feel as if I'm dead from the neck downwards.....................................	1	2	3	4	5	6

N.B. Items 1 to 11 are summated to give a total score for the positive response scale. Items 12 to 26 are summated to give a total score for the negative response scale.

Figure 3.1   Changes in Outlook Questionnaire

Sarason, 1983; Sarason, Shearin, Pierce, & Sarason, 1987), attributional style and locus of control (e.g., Peterson et al., 1982; Rotter, 1966) and life-events (e.g., Brugha, Bebbington, Tennant, & Hurry, 1985; Paykel, 1983; Sarason, Johnson, & Siegal, 1978; Smith, 1992; Zuckerman, Oliver, Hollingsworth, & Austrin, 1986).

CONCLUSION

A large number of operational definitions for the assessment of trauma-related reactions have appeared. These definitions can be grouped into either (1) highly structured interviews, or (2) self-report symptomatology measures. The use of structured interviews and self-report rating scales not only assist in making a diagnosis, but also allow quantification and reduce the subjectivity inherent in clinical judgements of the severity of what are private phenomena. However, regardless of the individual reliability and validity of the various assessment tools, researchers have advocated the use of multiple assessment measures prior to conferring the diagnosis of PTSD (Denny, Robinowitz, & Penk, 1987; Malloy, Fairbank, & Keane, 1983; Keane, Caddell, & Taylor, 1988; Wolfe & Keane, 1993). Included in such an approach is an emphasis on the clinical interview, self-report instruments, and psychophysiological assessment. The range of psychological problems experienced by survivors is wide and includes not only the symptoms of PTSD but also those of depression and anxiety as well as difficulties in social functioning and substance abuse. On this basis, a multimethod approach to assessment is encouraged, one that includes not only pathological outcomes but an evaluation of the person's attitudes towards life.

SUMMARY POINTS

1. Several standardised interview schedules have been developed on the basis of the DSM criteria. However, there remains some debate on how best to conceptualise reactions to extreme stressors and measures will all need to be updated and validated with respect to DSM-IV criteria.
2. Self-report questionnaires have been developed on the basis of psychometric evidence. There have been two approaches to the development of self-report measures: first, the development of new tests for assessing PTSD; second, the study of existing tests and their usefulness in diagnosing PTSD. The MMPI has received much attention.
3. Adults often appear to underestimate children's reactions and therefore self-report measures are especially valuable when working with children. Several measures that have been developed that focus on child sexual abuse, and appear promising.

4. Other work has shown that survivors often experience both negative and positive reactions and there is a need also to ask about other changes that survivors may experience. There is some evidence that positive existential changes in outlook are common following some events and that survivors may sometimes report that the experience of the traumatic event has been in some way beneficial to them.

Chapter 4

TYPES OF TRAUMA: FROM NATURAL DISASTER TO POLITICAL VIOLENCE

INTRODUCTION

Earlier definitions of what constitutes a traumatic event emphasised unusual experiences (APA, 1980), i.e., mass transportation disasters. But this definition was fraught with problems (see Davidson & Foa, 1991) and it became clear that what was needed was an indication of the tendency of the stressor to produce psychological problems rather than attempt to define a trauma by its frequency. As our cases have shown, the individual experience of an event as traumatic may be highly idiosyncratic. This chapter, however, will review the types of event that have usually been found to produce post-traumatic stress reactions. Over the last 15 years there has been an explosion in research on the psychological effects of various traumatic events. Typical PTSD-inducing events are generally outside of individual control, unpredictable, involve the potential for physical injury or death, and possess the capacity to elicit affect-laden visual imagery (see March, 1993). However, there is tremendous variability in the prevalence of disorder found between studies of different events (Rubonis & Bickman, 1991) raising the question of whether different events lead to different rates of disorder and different symptoms.

Key Topics

Epidemiological findings
Natural disaster
Technological disaster
Combat
Criminal victimisation
Sexual assault
Childhood sexual abuse
Political violence
Refugees
Event factors
Conclusion

EPIDEMIOLOGICAL FINDINGS

Estimates of psychological impairment in the first year following natural disaster reported in the review by Raphael (1986) range from around 20% in survivors of Cyclone Tracy (Parker, 1977) to around 50% in survivors of the Xenia Tornado (Taylor, Ross, & Quarantelli, 1976) demonstrating the variability in prevalence rates between studies. The incidence of psychological impairment in any population exposed to a traumatic event is expected to be a function of the intensity of the event. But if we want to compare the incidence rates between different events it is necessary that each of the studies uses the same methods of assessing psychological impairment. Most of the studies reviewed by Raphael, however, were conducted before the introduction of PTSD and investigated the prevalence of distress using different measures. So, the results are a function of the measurement tools used as well as the actual differences that might exist between populations, making it difficult to reach meaningful conclusions about which events are the most distressing. But with the introduction of the diagnostic category of PTSD investigators have increasingly been working under the same conceptual umbrella using compatible measures of impairment allowing for generalisations to be made about which events are most likely to lead to high levels of impairment.

NATURAL DISASTERS

Epidemiological findings suggest that events involving death and destruction on a massive scale are especially likely to lead to psychological problems. In 1985 a volcanic explosion in Columbia destroyed the small town of Armero killing 80% of its 30,000 inhabitants. Seven months after the incident, a sample of 200 adult survivors were screened for evidence of psychological impairment using a self-report questionnaire. Fifty-five per cent were found, on the basis of their scores on the questionnaire, to be severely distressed (Lima, Pai, Santacruz, & Lozano, 1987). In a two-year follow up study, Lima, Pai, Lozano, and Santacruz (1991) report data on a representative sample of 40 people who were included in their 1987 study. Interestingly, at two years using the same self-report questionnaire, they identified 78% as emotionally distressed. Contrary to what one might have expected, these findings indicate an increase rather than a decrease in distress over time. Lima et al. (1991) suggest that this may, at least in part, be due to the adverse environmental conditions experienced by survivors subsequently, such as poor housing and unemployment. However, the authors also note that a small number of survivors showed no evidence of emotional distress during the first two years, raising the question of what makes some individuals emotionally resilient. In a further study Lima et al. (1993) found that 30% of survivors were emotionally distressed at five years. This study makes some interesting points that illustrate very well the usefulness of the psychosocial approach to understanding post-traumatic stress reactions. In particular, the fact that distress might actually be maintained or exacerbated by other post-trauma psychosocial stressors such as poor housing conditions demonstrates that psychological impairment following exposure to trauma is a function of factors which may or may not be a function of the traumatic event itself. This is another reason why even when apparently similar events are compared the prevalence rates can vary widely. For example, studies of the psychological effects of earthquakes have yielded mixed findings, some studies indicating that the psychological effects are often mild and transient (e.g., Popovic & Petrovic, 1964; Takuma, 1978; Tierney, 1985), whereas others have showed more severe and long-lasting effects (e.g., Carr, 1991; Galante & Foa, 1986; Lima et al., 1989; Maj et al., 1989; Bourque, Aneshensel, & Goltz, 1991). The fact that different assessment measures were used across these studies confounds the picture even further.

However, one finding that is largely consistent, although it might be argued that it does not take a psychologist to tell us, is that those events involving widespread death and destruction are associated with the most severe and long-lasting psychological symptomatology. For example, De La Fuente (1990) reported that over 30% of the survivors of the 1985 earthquakes in Mexico displayed PTSD. Work with almost 600 adult survivors of the 1988 Armenia earthquake found a PTSD prevalence rate of 74% at 3 to 6 months (Goenjian, 1993). In further studies, Goenjian and colleagues present evidence that the frequency and severity of post-traumatic stress reactions remained high at one and a half years in adults (Goenjian et al., 1994) and children (Pynoos et al., 1993).

Other work by Galante and Foa (1986) of children badly traumatised by the massive earthquakes in a remote mountainous region of central Italy in November 1980 also shows that the effects on children can be severe and long-lasting. But other research on natural disasters with lower death rates suggests that although symptoms may persist for as long as three to five years, most abate in about 18 months (Cook & Bickman, 1990; Krause, 1987; Phifer & Norris, 1989; Shore, Tatum, & Vollmer, 1986; Steinglass & Gerrity, 1990). This finding that symptoms abate in around 18 months would also seem to be true of children (Vogel & Vernberg, 1993).

TECHNOLOGICAL DISASTER

Green and her colleagues have conducted a most impressive series of studies on adult and child survivors of the Buffalo Creek dam collapse in which 125 people were killed and the community destroyed. They followed a group of survivors from 2 to 14 years following the event (Gleser, Green, & Winget, 1981; Green et al., 1990a). At 14 years, they found that 28% of the adult sample had PTSD whereas a comparison group had a rate of 8%. Green et al.,

(1994) conducted a 17-year follow-up of 99 of the 207 children who survived the Buffalo Creek disaster in 1972. In contrast to the earlier findings with adults, their results with children showed little evidence of psychiatric impairment. Green et al. (1994) conclude that '. . . some optimism is warranted with regard to long-term recovery in children exposed to severe events' (p. 78). Although these data are encouraging, work with children and adolescents who survived the sinking of the *Herald of Free Enterprise* ferry in 1987 has found severe distress at 12–15 months and six years post-disaster, suggesting that in the short term at least there may be serious problems (Yule & Williams, 1990).

Interestingly, technological accidents, such as Three Mile Island, have been found to be associated with long-term effects up to six years later in adults (Baum, 1990; Baum & Fleming, 1993; Baum, Fleming, & Singer, 1983a; Baum, Gatchel, & Schaeffer, 1983b; Davidson, Fleming, & Baum, 1986) despite the fact that the Three Mile Island nuclear incident involved no apparent physical damage to people or property. Handford et al. (1983) conducted a study at one and a half years on thirty-five 5 to 19 years olds living within 30 miles of the Three Mile plant. Unlike the work with adults they did not find evidence of increased impairment. There were no cases of PTSD, two children received a diagnosis of anxiety disorder, one, dysthymic disorder, and one, conduct disorder. This rate represents an incidence consistent with what might be expected in the general population. But as discussed in Chapter 3 it may be that these data under-represent the level of distress through the use of parents' ratings of their children's symptoms. Alternatively, since there were no signs of the effects of radiation, the children may have been less frightened by this event in the first place.

Natural versus Technological Disaster

Green and Lindy (1994), in a brief review of the literature on the psychological outcomes following disaster, conclude that it is difficult to distinguish natural and technological disasters from each other in terms of their early impact, but that the persistence of responses may differentiate the two and that the effects of natural disasters seem to be no longer detectable after two years. This may be the case for natural disasters with very limited death and destruction, but for those events involving widespread destruction and death the effects would seem to be extremely severe and it might be that these events have very long-term effects although no evidence is yet available to confirm this. However, the long-term effects of technological disasters are documented and it might be suggested that the fact that technology is involved makes these events particularly traumatic as, unlike acts of God, they may have been avoidable accidents caused by human negligence.

As we shall discuss in Chapter 6, the fact of human involvement in traumatic events can have important implications for how the event is understood, leading to very strong emotions, i.e., anger, rage, guilt, shame, which serve to impede emotional processing. It has been argued that human-caused events such as combat, criminal victimisation, and sexual assault where there is a clear intention to harm appear to have the most severe and chronic effects of all.

COMBAT

Compared to all other events, the effects of war have been particularly well documented. Kulka et al. (1990) have presented data from the National Vietnam Veterans Readjustment Study (NVVRS). This is a comprehensive and rigorous study of the prevalence of PTSD and other psychological problems in readjusting to civilian life among Vietnam veterans. The NVVRS was a national epidemiological study involving face-to-face interviews. NVVRS estimated that 15% of all male Vietnam veterans were current cases of PTSD, 15 or more years after service. This represents about 479,000 of the estimated 3.14 million men who served in Vietnam. Among veteran women, current PTSD prevalence is estimated to be 8.5% of the approximately 7,200 women who served. In addition, NVVRS estimate that approximately one-third of male and one-fourth of women veterans have had PTSD at some time in their lives (Kulka et al., 1990; Schlenger et al., 1992). The NVVRS study indicates that nearly half a million Vietnam veterans are current cases of PTSD. In addition to these analyses, Kulka et al. (1990) also estimated the prevalence of partial PTSD, a subdiagnostic constellation of symptoms, finding lifetime and current prevalence to be 22.5% and 11.1% for male theatre veterans and 21.2% and 7.8% for female theatre veterans, respectively. Together, full and partial prevalence estimates for lifetime PTSD suggest that half of all male (53.4%) and almost half of all female (48.1%) Vietnam veterans have experienced clinically significant symptomatology.

Although the data are sparse, high prevalence rates have also been reported for British servicemen who served in the Falklands War (O'Brien & Hughes, 1991; Orner, Lynch, & Seed, 1993). Five years after the war, O'Brien and Hughes (1991) compared a unit of 64 soldiers who had fought in the 1982 Falklands conflict with a matched unit of 64 who had remained on home duties. O'Brien and Hughes (1991) found a higher reported rate of self-reported symptoms in the veteran group and 22% reported symptoms fulfilling the diagnostic criteria of PTSD, suggesting that in the wider population of Falklands veterans many may be seriously affected five years later.

CRIMINAL VICTIMISATION

In an American survey, it was estimated that the prevalence of civilian trauma and crime-related PTSD was around 1% in the general population (Helzer, Robins, & McEvoy, 1987). There is evidence from a variety of studies that the experience of criminal victimisation is associated with poorer mental health (Kilpatrick, Saunders, Veronen, Best, & Von, 1987; Resnick, Kilpatrick, Dansky, Saunders, & Best, 1993; Sorenson & Golding, 1990). The immediate aftermath of crime can be particularly distressing. Davis and Friedman (1985) in a study of victims of burglary, robbery, and assault found that 45% of victims were experiencing distress 1–3 weeks after the incident, and if sleeping disorders were included, this rose to 75%.

Crime involving random violence can be particularly distressing. Several studies have been carried out following multiple shooting events. Following one shooting which took place in a McDonald's restaurant in San Ysidro killing 21 people and injuring 15, it was found that nearly a third of the community surveyed reported that they were seriously affected by the incident. Those who reported having family or friends involved in the incident were the most likely to exhibit PTSD symptoms (Hough et al., 1990). In another study of a multiple shooting in a small Arkansas town, 80% exhibited some symptoms of PTSD (North, Smith, McCool, & Shea, 1989). A later study by North, Smith, and Spitznagel (1994) investigated the emotional reactions of people after a gunman mounted a firearm assault for almost 15 minutes on a crowd of nearly 150 civilians in a cafeteria in Texas. Twenty-four of those present were killed and many others were wounded. Initially, the gunman drove his truck through the window of the restaurant injuring several people. Then he walked around the room systematically shooting his victims, mainly women, at point-blank range. The police arrived within 15 minutes and cornered the gunman who then shot himself dead. Interviews were carried out within 6–8 weeks with those present. Overall, nearly all had some symptoms of PTSD and 20% of men and 36% of women met the full criteria for PTSD. Other research has shown PTSD symptoms in children at one month (Pynoos & Nader, 1988) and at 14 months (Nader, Pynoos, Fairbanks, & Frederick, 1990) following a fatal sniper shooting in a Californian school. Other research has reported a 19% prevalence rate of PTSD in children after a mass shooting incident at a school (Schwarz & Kowalski, 1991).

Solomon and Horn (1986), in their study of police officers following postshooting incidents, found that 37% of victims experienced a mild reaction, 35% moderate, and 28% severe distress. Similarly, Gersons (1989) investigated the degree and intensity of post-traumatic reactions in 37 police officers of the Amsterdam police force who were involved in serious shooting incidents in the period between 1977 and 1984. In these seven years 62 officers were involved in a shooting incident that involved injury. Gersons (1989) was able to obtain an interview with 37 of these officers. It was not known if this sample was representative of the whole group. Out of the 37, only 3 were found to be symptom free, 17 suffered from some PTSD symptoms, and 17 fulfilled PTSD criteria. Gersons reports that none had looked for help or treatment from doctors, psychologists, or social workers within the police force. It was suggested that this was because of police culture in which officers do not generally complain about psychological issues or discuss emotional reactions. Duckworth (1986) found that 35% of a sample of the police officers involved with the Bradford football club fire were suffering from PTSD, and a further 21% met three of the four DSM-III criteria for PTSD.

SEXUAL ASSAULT

A survey of over 4000 American women found that one-third had experienced a crime such as physical or sexual assault (Resnick et al., 1993). For those exposed to such events, PTSD is a likely outcome. Kilpatrick, Saunders, Veronen, Best, & Von (1987) found a 75% lifetime prevalence rate of exposure to a variety of crimes in a community sample of women. Furthermore, 27.8% of those women exposed to any crime acquired lifetime PTSD. In addition, Kilpatrick et al. (1987) found that there was an overall rate of sexual assault of around 50% and a rate of approximately 20% for completed rape (see also Koss, 1993). The crime of rape was associated with a lifetime PTSD prevalence rate of 57.1%. This and other evidence suggests that rape is one of the most traumatic events and produces rates of PTSD higher than that produced by other events (Breslau, Davis, Andreski, & Peterson, 1991; Kilpatrick et al., 1989; Norris, 1992). Other survey work indicates that over 30% of all rape victims may develop PTSD at some time in their lives (National Victims Center, 1992). Resnick, Veronen, Saunders, Kilpatrick, and Cornelison (1989) found that 76% of rape victims met the diagnostic criteria for PTSD at some point within a year of the assault. Similarly, high rates have been reported by others (Crummier & Green, 1991).

In a prospective study by Rothbaum, Foa, Riggs, Murdock, and Walsh (1992), 64 women who had been subjected to rape or attempted rape were interviewed within a month of the event. Further interviews were conducted weekly over 12 weeks during which time the women completed a variety of self-report measures of psychiatric symptoms. Women who had a prior history of mental disorder were excluded from the study. Most of the remaining women were black, unmarried, and of low income and had been referred by the police. Rothbaum et al. (1992) found that although the incidence of PTSD decreased over the 12 weeks, at the initial interview 94% of the women met the symptomatic criteria for PTSD. By assessment 4, when the DSM-III-R duration criterion of one-month was met, the incidence of PTSD was 65%, and by assessment 12 the incidence of PTSD was 47%.

In addition, there is evidence that women who have experienced sexual assault are likely to suffer from a range of psychological problems including anxiety and fear (Calhoun, Atkeson, & Resick, 1982; Ellis, Atkeson, & Calhoun, 1981; Kilpatrick, Resick, & Veronen, 1981; Kimerling & Calhoun, 1994), depression (Atkeson, Calhoun, Resick, & Ellis, 1982; Frank, Turner, & Duffy, 1979; Kilpatrick, Veronen, & Resick, 1979; Kimerling & Calhoun,

1994), sexual dysfunction (Becker, Skinner, Abel, & Treacy, 1982; Orlando & Koss, 1983), and problems in social adjustment (Kilpatrick et al., 1979; Resick, Calhoun, Atkeson, & Ellis, 1982).

CHILDHOOD SEXUAL ABUSE

Terr (1991) has delineated two classes of trauma that may lead to the development of PTSD. First, Type I trauma involves single traumatic events that are sudden and unexpected. Examples of such an event would be involvement in a road traffic accident or being a victim of criminal or sexual assault.

Type II trauma, on the other hand, involves repeated exposure to a traumatic event that may be predictable and expected. For example, this might include repetitive and prolonged physical or sexual abuse. PTSD, as outlined by the APA and the WHO, is largely concerned with survivors of Type I trauma. Evidence has begun to accumulate, however, for another more complex form of PTSD in survivors of Type II trauma. It has been noted that the problems that occur in child abuse victims reflect a different emphasis from the DSM classification for PTSD (Herman, 1992a; Terr, 1991). A recent review of the evidence for the existence of a complex form of PTSD concludes that there is

> . . . unsystematised but extensive empirical support for the concept of a complex post-traumatic syndrome in survivors of prolonged, repeated victimisation. This previously undefined syndrome may coexist with simple PTSD, but extends beyond it. The syndrome is characterised by enduring personality changes, and high risk for repeated harm, either self-inflicted or at the hands of others. (Herman, 1992a, p. 387)

Herman (1992a) goes on to say that patients suffering from this risk being misdiagnosed as having personality disorders.

A personality disorder refers to pervasive, enduring, inflexible, and distressing patterns of thought and behaviour that deviate from social norms. DSM-IV (APA, 1994) distinguishes between 10 personality disorders grouped into three clusters: (1) paranoid, schizoid, and schizotypal personality disorders characterised by eccentric behaviours; (2) antisocial, borderline, histrionic, and narcissistic personality disorders characterised by dramatic, emotional, or erratic behaviours; and (3) avoidant, dependent, and obsessive-compulsive personality disorders characterised by fearful or anxious behaviours.

Borderline personality disorder, in particular, has been discussed in relation to early trauma and studies show a heightened prevalence of childhood physical and sexual abuse among people with this disorder (Beitchman, Zucker, Hood, DaCosta, & Cassavia, 1992; Browne & Finkelhor, 1986; Finkelhor, 1990; Marcus, 1989). Adults with borderline personality disorder display a pervasive pattern of instability in interpersonal relationships, sexual dysfunction, poor self-image, mood shifts, impulsivity, and destructive behaviour reminiscent of the character Alex Forrest in the film 'Fatal Attraction'.

A wide variety of short- and long-term consequences of child sexual abuse (CSA) have been described (Browne & Finkelhor, 1986; Finkelhor, 1990) and a recent national survey of over 2500 Americans has indicated that 27% of women and 16% of men report CSA experiences (Finkelhor, Hotaling, Lewis, & Smith, 1990). Furthermore, there is evidence that the experience of CSA is associated with the development of PTSD (Burgess et al., 1984; Frederick, 1985b; McLeer et al., 1988; Wolfe, Gentile, & Wolfe, 1989; Wolfe, Sas, & Wekerle, 1994) and related symptoms.

Sexually abused female children may exhibit a wide range of dissociative symptoms and autodestructive behaviours. Increased aggression, feelings of fear, anger, guilt, shame, as well as eating and sleeping disturbances, inappropriate sexual behaviour, truancy from school, are all common in childhood sexual abuse. Women who have been sexually abused as children are more likely to suffer social and interpersonal difficulties in adult life (Browne & Finkelhor, 1986; Mullen, Martin, Anderson, Romans, & Herbison, 1994) as well as inappropriate sexual behaviour and sexual dysfunction and self-harming behaviour. Feelings of isolation, depression, anxiety, low self-esteem, as well as substance abuse have also been shown to be related to early abuse.

Although most of the research into sexual abuse has been with women, recent reports into the sexual abuse of men as children have also suggested that there may be similar problems in long-term functioning (Lisak, 1994; Lisak & Luster, 1994; Schulte, Dinwiddie, Pribor, & Yutzy, 1995). As with women, the evidence suggests that men who have been sexually abused as children may show disturbed attitudes towards sexuality, producing difficulties ranging from fear of sexual contact to a tendency to engage in frequent brief sexual encounters. Mood disorders, anxiety disorder, and substance-use disorders are common and victims often appear to meet criteria for many different psychiatric disorders.

POLITICAL VIOLENCE

For over 25 years Northern Ireland has been exposed to civil disturbance in which over 3000 people have died and over 100,000 people have been injured out of a total population of around only 1.5 million. Since the beginning of the conflict, researchers have been interested in its possible psychological effects (Fraser, 1971). An early study by Lyons (1974) of 100 people who had been directly involved in a bomb explosion found that in the majority of cases there was evidence for affective disturbance, most commonly anxiety with various phobic symptoms. Depression, often with irritability, was also frequently reported. Some PTSD symptoms such as exaggerated startle responses to loud noises were also reported.

In a subsequent study, Hadden, Rutherford and Merret (1978) investigated 1532 patients admitted to the accident and emergency unit of a Belfast hospital because of involvement in a bomb explosion. They found that 50% had sustained 'psychological shock'. Although studies such as that by Fraser (1971), Lyons (1974), and Hadden et al. (1978) were conducted before the introduction of PTSD, more recent data confirms that PTSD may be a consequence of exposure to such violence (Kee, Bell, Loughrey, Roddy, & Curran, 1987). In one study it was found that 50% of a sample assessed following the Enniskillen bombing satisfied the DSM-III criteria for PTSD (Curran, Bell, Loughrey, Roddy, & Rocke, 1988). However, other prevalence estimates have been found to be lower. For example, Loughrey, Bell, Kee, Roddy, & Curran (1988) investigated the incidence of PTSD among 499 people exposed to various types of civilian trauma in Northern Ireland finding that 23% had developed PTSD.

Other work which has been carried out in Northern Ireland have been community-based surveys which have shown that most people in Northern Ireland were not suffering from severe psychological problems (Cairns & Wilson, 1984, 1985, 1989). This might seem surprising given the relentless violence in that society. But it should be noted that for most people in Northern Ireland the political violence was not something that they were directly exposed to. A study of the emotional reactions of civilians resident in Israel during the Persian Gulf War and the SCUD missile attacks was conducted by Zeidner and Ben-Zur (1994) who gathered data on a sample of over 800 adults about three months following the June 1991 cease fire. They found that the effects of the war were weak and in keeping with an 'evaporation model' of stress response (Worthington, 1977). One explanation for this, Zeidner and Ben-Zur suggest, is that the Israeli people have over the years experienced many past traumas including the holocaust and the Israel–Arab conflict. Such an explanation might also apply to the findings of Cairns and Wilson that the people of Northern Ireland appeared to suffer little residual effects of the violence.

REFUGEES

Psychiatric problems have long been documented in refugees (Eitinger, 1959) and evidence suggests that disturbance is not only influenced by migration and subsequent adjustment but also by pre-migration factors such as torture and imprisonment (Westermeyer, Vang, & Neider, 1983). Arroyo and Eth (1985) interviewed 30 central American refugees under the age of 17 years who had been exposed to war before arrival in the United States finding that 10 met diagnostic criteria for PTSD while 9 met criteria for adjustment disorder. Kinzie et al. (1986) interviewed 40 children four years after they had been imprisoned in Cambodian concentration camps where they had undergone starvation, beatings and witnessed the death of others. Twenty met APA criteria for PTSD, 17 of whom had concurrent depressive disorder. Students who had fled Cambodia before Pol Pot came to power received no diagnoses, leading the authors to conclude that their findings did not appear to be a result of migration but of pre-migration factors.

EVENT FACTORS

Although there is evidence throughout the epidemiological literature that bereavement is associated with more severe and chronic disturbance (e.g., Gleser et al., 1981; Goenjian et al., 1994; Singh & Raphael, 1981; Solkoff, Gray, & Keill, 1986; Green, Grace, Lindy, Titchener, & Lindy, 1983; Murphy, 1986; Shore et al., 1986), and generally the higher the rate of death, the higher the later psychological disturbance, these factors alone do not account for the individual differences in reactions among any group of survivors or between groups of survivors.

Various researchers have tried to identify what it is about traumatic events that is most distressing and much research has accumulated showing that the extent of personal injury as well as the degree of life-threat also influence the course of symptomatology in combat veterans (e.g., Breslau & Davis, 1987; Card, 1987; Fontana, Rosenheck, & Brett, 1992; Foy, Resnick, Sipprelle, & Carroll, 1987; Frye & Stockton, 1982; Helzer et al., 1987; Orner, Lynch & Seed, 1993; Solkoff et al., 1986; Yehuda, Southwick, & Giller, 1992) as well as in civilian survivors of a variety of events (e.g., Cluss, Boughton, Frank, Stewart, & West, 1983; Ellis et al., 1981; Green et al., 1983; Gleser et al., 1981; Helzer et al., 1987; Kilpatrick et al., 1989; Maida, Gordon, Steinberg, & Gordon, 1989; Parker, 1977; Resnick, Kilpatrick, Best, & Crummier, 1992; Shore et al., 1986; Smith et al., 1986; Weisaeth, 1983; Western & Milne, 1979).

It would seem that some events can be so traumatic, i.e., involve a high degree of life-threat and personal injury, that almost everyone who is exposed will develop PTSD. For example, Kilpatrick et al. (1989) found that for those women who had experienced rape, life-threat, and physical injury, 80% went on to develop PTSD. The prevalence of disorder thus depends on the nature and intensity of the experience. For example, Helzer et al. (1987) reported a prevalence rate of about 3.5% in Vietnam veterans who were not wounded in battle compared to about 20% in veterans who were. Card (1987) found that 19% of all veterans, and 27% of veterans exposed to heavy combat suffered from PTSD. Even higher estimates have been made for those who were exposed to particularly heavy combat. Foy et al. (1987) observed that 25–30% of low-combat-exposed subjects in their clinical samples met full DSM-III criteria for PTSD, and 70% of their high-combat-exposed subjects were diagnosed as having PTSD. Foy et al. (1987) observe that being wounded, involvement in the deaths of non-combatants, and exposure to atrocities are critical elements in the development of PTSD in combat veterans. With over 5000 veterans from the Second World War, Korea, and Vietnam, it has been shown that symptoms are more severe the more intense the traumatic exposure is, and that responsibility for killing another human being or having been a target of killing are associated with emotional distress (Fontana & Rosenheck, 1994a). The role of combat exposure has received much attention and other research has shown that Second World War veterans exposed to moderate or heavy combat had 13.3 times greater risk of PTSD symptoms measured 45 years later compared with non-combat veterans (Spiro, Schnurr, & Aldwin, 1994).

Intensity of exposure has been defined in a variety of different ways in the above studies. One other factor, however, which appears to be a common defining criterion is that of witnessing death and exposure to the grotesque. Solkoff et al. (1986) found that the stressor variable accounting for most of the variance in PTSD symptoms in survivors of Vietnam was exposure to death and injury. They found support for the hypothesis that PTSD patients would have experienced more intense combat and would have been involved with more death and killing than controls. PTSD subjects were found to perceive themselves as having been closer to personal death and the death of others. They reported more personal involvement in killing, more friends killed, and that they were more likely to have observed their death. PTSD subjects were also in combat for a longer time and more frequently sustained injuries. Witnessing death has also been found to affect children adversely, even as young as 5 years (Malmquist, 1986).

Furthermore, Lund, Foy, Sipprelle, and Strachan (1984) suggested that stress may build cumulatively through exposure to a traumatic event. Lund et al. (1984) employed a Guttman scaling technique to construct a measure of trauma in the Vietnam War. Developed from dichotomous questions about traumatic events, the scale was associated with PTSD symptoms confirming their prediction that stress may build cumulatively. Events involving repeated and prolonged exposure may be most harmful. For example, the duration and frequency of child sexual abuse have been shown to be associated with PTSD diagnostic status (Rowan, Foy, Rodriguez, & Ryan, 1993). In a survey of over 3000 Los Angeles community residents it was found that criminal victimisation was associated with increased thoughts of suicide and depression. Furthermore, those people reporting two or more victimising experiences were more likely to suffer depression than those people reporting only one such event (Sorenson & Golding, 1990).

However, although much of this work has attempted to demonstrate the dose–response relationship, it is difficult to find indices of objective exposure and invariably much of the work has had to rely on the subjective assessment of exposure variables, such as retrospectively assessed perceived life-threat. From this evidence, it is impossible to untangle the effects of objective and subjective factors. However, there is other work which has demonstrated an objective exposure–response relationship. In his study of the aftermath of a paint factory ire, Weisaeth (1983) showed that those workers nearest the centre of the explosion suffered most post-traumatic distress; those furthest from it suffered he least. Similarly, poorer psychological health was demonstrated in Three Mile Island residents living within 5 miles of the plant compared to those living urther away within three months of the leak (Bromet, Parkinson, Schulberg, Dunn, & Gondek, 1982a). Furthermore, Baum, Gatchel, and Schaeffer (1983b) evaluated the psychophysiological impact on residents one year after he Three Mile Island accident compared to people living near an undamaged power plant, people living near a traditional coal-fired power plant, and people iving in an area more than 20 miles from any power plant. Results indicated hat residents of the Three Mile Island area exhibited more self-reported symptoms of stress as measured by the Beck Depression Inventory and the 90-item Symptom Checklist.

In a similar study by Davidson, Weiss, O'Keffe, and Baum (1991) 70 esidents of the Three Mile Island accident area were compared to a control group of 29 subjects who lived some 80 miles southwest of Three Mile Island. All subjects were randomly selected and completed the 90-item Symptom Checklist (Derogatis, 1977). The results of this study suggested that accident area residents continued to exhibit more symptoms of chronic anxiety and omatic complaints than controls even after six years. In addition, measures of heart rate and blood pressure were obtained and it was found that for Three Mile Island residents, both measures were elevated relative to controls.

Similarly, Realmuto, Wagner, and Bartholow (1991) investigated the impact of a gasline explosion in a small midwestern suburban city in 1986 which caused the death of a mother and her daughter and severely injured one other person as well as causing much damage to private property. Thirteen months after the explosion, 3 of the 24 people living at the disaster site satisfied diagnostic criteria for PTSD whereas no subject within the control site was similarly affected. The two groups differed significantly on the mean number of PTSD symptoms reported, those from the disaster site exhibiting the most symptoms. These differences were particularly pronounced on avoidance symptoms, amnesia, disinterest, and detachment. These symptoms were not seen in the control group. The symptom of difficulty sleeping was the most accurate of the PTSD symptom list in identifying a disaster victim.

A higher PTSD prevalence rate was reported for adult and children survivors who lived in cities closer to the epicentre of the Armenian earthquake (Goenian, 1993; Goenjian et al., 1994; Pynoos et al., 1993). Interviews with survivors of the Armenia earthquake revealed that the worst experiences were seeing mutilated corpses, hearing the screams of people in agony trapped in the rubble, and seeing the expressions on people's faces as they searched for loved ones (Goenjian et al., 1994).

Pynoos and Nader (1988) demonstrated that following a fatal sniper shooting of children in a Californian school, children trapped in the playground had he strongest post-traumatic reactions, with those not attending school that day showing the least. Of those attending, nearly 40% of the 9-year-old children were found to have moderate to severe PTSD approximately one month after the event. Fourteen months later, Nader et al. (1990) report that 74% of the most severely exposed children in the playground still reported moderate to severe levels of PTSD.

In addition to the objective severity of the event, current thinking on the coping process emphasises the role of stimulus appraisal (e.g., Folkman, 1984; Folkman & Lazarus, 1980, 1985, 1988; Folkman, Lazarus, Dunkel-Schetter, DeLongis, & Gruen, 1986a; Folkman, Lazarus, Gruen, & DeLongis, 1986b; Lazarus, 1966; Lazarus & Folkman, 1984). Lazarus and his colleagues distinguish between primary appraisal, the assessment of the stressor, from secondary appraisal, the estimation of personal resources to deal with the stressor. The choice of coping strategy, they argue, results from these appraisals. The idiosyncratic way in which events can be appraised is illustrated by Pynoos and Nader (1988) who reported that although the psychological effects appeared to be a function of objective exposure to the sniper shooting, there were individual differences. They provide an example of one boy who had left school early that day leaving his sister in the playground and who went on to develop a severe reaction to the event. Although some experiences are particularly likely to give rise to PTSD, this study illustrates the necessity to take into account individual differences in the appraisal of the stressor and what it represents to the person. Speculatively, the reactions of this boy, for example, might have resulted from a self-appraisal that he had let his sister down.

Other appraisals might be less concerned with personal culpability. Yule, Udwin, and Murdoch (1990b) found that within one school that had sent a party of children on the *Jupiter* cruise, children who had wanted to go on the cruise but failed to get a place showed scores on depression and anxiety that were intermediate between controls and the victims. A similar finding was reported by Fraser (1971) who examined psychiatric admission rates and outpatient referrals in Belfast during 1969 when street riots where at their peak. He divided the city into three areas: (1) where the worst violence had occurred, (2) where signs of tension were present, but violence was not widespread; and (3) the remainder of the city. He found no evidence for increased admissions or referrals in the area of worst violence compared to the rest of the city. However, in the intermediate area, an increase was noted in referrals of male psychotics and male neurotics leading him to conclude that stress reactions were highest in areas which were under threat of attack.

In another study, Cairns and Wilson (1984) investigated reactions of Northern Irish residents in two towns. Both towns were similar in most respects except that one had suffered considerably more violence than the other. It was found that those who lived in the more violent town had higher symptom scores. Also, regardless of which town they lived in, those who perceived their town to have experienced a good deal of violence scored higher than those who perceived their town to have experienced little or no violence. This study demonstrates the main effects of both objective and subjective factors. But those who both lived in the violent town and perceived most violence had considerably higher symptom scores than the other groups.

However, the exposure variables which may predict the onset of disorder are not necessarily those which predict the severity or chronicity of symptoms. For example, Green, Grace, Lindy, and Gleser (1990b) examined the impact of a variety of specific war stressor experiences on the development and chronicity of the PTSD syndrome in a large sample of Vietnam veterans. They addressed a broader range of stressors than are typically explored. In terms of predicting type and persistence of symptoms, there was some differentiation among the stressors studied. Extent of injury, loss, life threat, and injuring or killing Vietnamese predicted developing PTSD symptoms at some point in time, but not maintaining symptoms over many years which was predicted by exposure to grotesque death and special assignment. Fontana and Rosenheck (1994a) report that for war veterans, responsibility for killing another human being is the single most pervasive, traumatic experience of war. Having been a target of killing and having participated in abusive violence were also found to be associated with greater emotional distress.

Although some studies have not found exposure to predict outcome and have emphasised prior vulnerability factors, the bulk of the evidence suggests that the intensity of exposure (both objectively and subjectively assessed) is associated with poorer outcome, at least for the relatively short periods after the event that have usually been studied. Goenjian et al. (1994), in their study of the Armenia earthquake, suggest that at very high levels of exposure most individuals will develop post-traumatic reactions regardless of premorbid vulnerabilities. What this literature seems to suggest is that as the objective (insofar as they can be measured) intensity (whatever that means precisely) of an event increases, so does the likelihood of psychological problems, which should then be viewed as *normal functions of adaptation*. Events involving massive death and destruction, human intention, life-threat and personal injury, are likely to give rise to post-traumatic stress reactions. But despite the fact that some events may be so overwhelming that nearly all will develop post-traumatic stress reactions, most events that are commonly associated with PTSD do not affect the total population in this way. Indeed, post-traumatic stress reactions have been documented following a variety of other stressors which are not generally associated with PTSD, for example, difficult child birth (Ballard, Stanley, & Brockington, 1995). Ballard et al present four case studies of women with a symptom profile suggestive of PTSD. To illustrate, one women, with no history of psychiatric illness, underwent emergency caesarean section. The epidural was not fully effective and she experienced excruciating pain during the operation which took 10 minutes. Afterwards, she experienced nightmares and would re-experience the operation along with intense physiological reactions.

Also, although the evidence is less clear cut, it has been suggested that some events lead to a different pattern of disorder. Severe depressive reactions such as suicidal thoughts and violence towards the self are particularly common in war veterans (e.g., Fontana & Rosenheck, 1994a), rape victims and child sexual abuse victims (e.g., Steketee and Foa, 1987) suggesting that the experience of traumatic events involving human intention may be particularly depressogenic.

Providing an estimate of impairment within any population of survivors is complicated by the fact that the rate of disorder may not be uniformly spread across the population. For example, in a study of over 500 community survivors of the Mt St Helen's volcano, Shore et al. (1986) found that 11% of men compared to 21% of women exposed to high levels of trauma developed either depression, anxiety, or PTSD within the first two years. Natural disasters such as the Mt St Helen's volcano affect whole communities and it is possible to investigate the differential incidence rate among men and women. Some events, however, are more likely to happen to women than men, i.e., sexual assault, whereas other events are more likely to happen to men than women, i.e., combat, making it difficult to compare between events. A different incidence of impairment between sexual assault and combat may reflect the differences in these events or it may be that one group is more vulnerable than the other. Other group differences such as socio-economic status may also be important. Ideally epidemiological studies into the effects of traumatic events should use compatible measures and report the prevalence rate of impairment for various social groupings separately.

CONCLUSION

In this chapter we have reviewed the typical events which have been found to lead to post-traumatic stress reactions. There is evidence that different events may lead to different levels of disorder and different patterns of disorder. But despite the vast amount of research, the evidence does remain relatively sparse due to the methodological difficulties inherent in trauma-related research. For example, difference in the populations studied, the measures used, and the time frames of investigation make it difficult to compare and contrast data across studies. Estimates of PTSD prevalence vary from study to study. Few epidemiological studies have been able to survey total populations and what knowledge we have is based on partial samples which may overestimate or underestimate the level of distress. Although epidemiological work should aim to survey all the survivors of a traumatic event, this is an ideal difficult to achieve as survivors may be geographically scattered, hard to contact, or reluctant to take part in research. Where PTSD is concerned, severe dysfunction is characterised by avoidant behaviour. It is possible, therefore, that much of the research evidence underestimates the levels of distress in disaster populations as the most severely affected may also be the people most likely not to seek professional help or take part in surveys. This is particularly a problem for research that relies on self-identification such as in the case of sexual assault. The issue of representativeness is particularly at question in studies where survivors have been obtained through referral via solicitors dealing with litigation. McFarlane (1986a,b) has argued for the importance of studying individuals who present unsolicited for treatment. He argues that the study of compensation litigants complicates the naturalistic assessment of psychological problems since individual attitudes towards the reporting of symptoms may be affected. Nevertheless, the effects of compensation seeking is an interesting area of investigation in its own right and should be studied.

In conclusion, it would seem that post-traumatic reactions characterise an expected response and normal response to certain traumatic events. Some events, such as rape, will frequently result in predictable distressing responses that meet the diagnostic criteria for PTSD. However, it is also possible that PTSD may appear to be a less normal or expected reaction following other types of events which, on the face of it, do not seem traumatic but can be revealed as being subjectively so when individual experiences and perceptions are taken into account. Clearly, the event is the necessary aetiological factor for the onset of PTSD. However, it would not appear to be sufficient and so there is a need to identify the other factors that may contribute to the development of symptoms.

SUMMARY POINTS

1. Typical PTSD-inducing events are generally perceived as being outside individual control and usually involve the potential for physical injury or death as well as possessing the capacity to elicit affect-laden visual imagery.

2. For most events symptoms of PTSD appear to diminish by around 18 months although for other events there may be very long-lasting effects. Events involving massive death and destruction as well as human agency seem particularly likely to have chronic effects. The long-term effects of the Vietnam War have been well documented.

3. Prolonged repeated trauma can result in deep-seated personality changes and the term post-traumatic character disorder has been suggested. Events such as repeated child sexual abuse seem to be most likely to effect personality development in adverse ways.

4. Although some events such as rape seem particularly likely to lead to post-traumatic stress reactions, other events such as difficult childbirth which are unlikely to lead to post-traumatic stress reactions will nevertheless have severe and long-lasting effects for some individuals.

Chapter 5

THEORETICAL PARADIGMS AND PERSPECTIVES

INTRODUCTION

If we are to be able to help survivors of traumatic events who are suffering from some form of post-traumatic stress reaction, a theoretical model explaining onset and maintenance will be called for. In this chapter we will discuss the main theoretical perspectives which have been applied to understanding post-traumatic stress reactions. As we have seen in Chapter 4, survivors of different events may have different symptoms; some survivors will be more affected than others, and some will remain affected for considerably longer than others. Various theoretical paradigms have been applied to understanding post-traumatic stress reactions but each model is only partially successful so that it has become increasingly clear to us that an integrative approach is necessary to account for the full range of reactions experienced by survivors.

Key Topics

Emotional processing
Conditioning theory
Learned helplessness
Information processing
Social-cognitive perspectives
Towards an integrative psychosocial model
Conclusion

EMOTIONAL PROCESSING

Rachman's (1980) concept of 'emotional processing' provides a useful theoretical framework for conceptualising the psychological reactions of survivors. In a discussion which aimed to link a variety of phenomena such as reactions to disturbing events, nightmares, obsessions and abnormal grief, Rachman suggested that emotional processing results in emotional reactions being 'absorbed' so that exposure to the problematic cue no longer elicits a strong

Table 5.1   Indices of unsatisfactory emotional processing

Direct signs
    Test probes elicit disturbances
    Obsessions
    Disturbing dreams
    Unpleasant intrusive thoughts
    Inappropriate expressions of emotion
    Behavioural disruptions
    Pressure of talk
    Hallucinations
    Return of fear

Indirect signs
    Subjective distress
    Fatigue
    Insomnia
    Anorexia
    Inability to direct constructive thoughts
    Preoccupations
    Restlessness
    Irritability
    Resistance to distraction

Reproduced, with some adaptation, from Rachman (1980) with kind permission from Elsevier Science Ltd, The Boulevard, Langford Lane, Kidlington OX5 1GB, UK.

emotional reaction. He outlines several direct and indirect signs of unsatisfactory emotional processing, many of which are diagnostic criteria for PTSD (see Table 5.1).

> Broadly, successful processing can be gauged from the person's ability to talk about, see, listen to or be reminded of the emotional events without experiencing distress or disruptions. (Rachman, 1980, p. 52).

Rachman points to various factors which give rise to difficulties in emotional processing: these are stimulus factors, personality factors, state factors, and associated activity factors. For example, if the stimulus is predictable, controllable, the person is high in self-efficacy, in a relaxed state at the time, and increases his or her sense of control through associated activity, the person might avoid difficulties in emotional processing. In contrast, if the stimulus is sudden, intense, dangerous, uncontrollable, unpredictable, the person is high on neuroticism, in a state of fatigue, and there are concurrent stressors and the person has a need to suppress appropriate emotional expression, emotional processing will be impeded. Factors thought to promote satisfactory emotional processing are, engaged exposure, sense of control, and relevant conversation. Those likely to impede processing are an avoidance of the disturbing situation, refusal or inability to talk about them, and absence of perceived control.

We have found Rachman's concept of emotional processing to be extremely useful in our thinking. Although his thinking gives emphasis to stimulus characteristics rather than appraisal, Rachman's theory provides a useful conceptual umbrella which links neurotic phenomena previously unrelated which might usefully be thought of as direct and indirect signs of incomplete emotional processing. Post-traumatic stress reactions are therefore seen as indicative of a process which is incomplete.

Goal of Theory

The goal of any theory is to explain: (1) the constellation of reactions that arise following traumatic events; (2) the individual differences in reactions; and (3) the course of those reactions over time. Rachman's theory allows us to understand the constellation of reactions as signs of incomplete emotional processing, as opposed to an abnormal process, and helps to account for individual differences in severity and chronicity of these reactions by reference to the various factors found to promote or impede emotional processing. Although Rachman's work provides the framework for the development of a theory of adaptation to post-traumatic stress, his theory is largely descriptive and a theoretical perspective needs also to explain the mechanisms that are involved.

CONDITIONING THEORY

One of the earliest paradigms to be applied to understanding reactions to traumatic events was that of learning theory. Post-traumatic reactions were viewed as a result of classical conditioning at the time of the trauma. The conditioned links between fear and traumatic stimuli, including those that resemble the trauma, are maintained through the individual's avoidance of memories and situations that elicit them. This theoretical explanation is similar to that given for the development of phobias although higher order conditioning is also invoked to explain the generalised overarousal seen in PTSD.

While helpful in giving an account of mechanisms related to fear maintenance, the theory gives no explanation of the differences between phobias and PTSD nor does it give any explanation of the wide range of other emotional states and problems often found in PTSD.

LEARNED HELPLESSNESS

Signalling the entry of cognitive-behavioural models of emotional disorder into clinical psychology and building upon the principles of operant conditioning, the theory of 'learned helplessness' was developed by Seligman and his colleagues to explain the reactions of animals that had been exposed to extreme stressors such as electric shocks (Overmier & Seligman, 1967; Seligman, 1975; Seligman & Maier, 1967). For example, it was shown that when dogs were immobilised and given inescapable electric shocks, they exhibited a later marked impairment in learning a response which would terminate the shock. Demonstrations of learned helplessness have often used a paradigm in which one animal was yoked to another. Both animals received exactly the same aversive stimulus, but the second animal was able to terminate the stimulus by making an operant response, at which time the first animal's aversive stimulus was also terminated, irrespective of its own response. In this relationship, the first animal has no control, and learns that there is a lack of contingency between what it does and the termination of the aversive stimulus. This intervening belief that action is futile thus accounts for impairments character-ised by, first, a failure to initiate escape responses (motivational deficit); sec-ond, an inability to profit from an occasionally successful escape response (cognitive deficit); and, third, a passive acceptance of the shock (emotional deficit). Together these deficits constitute the learned helplessness syndrome. Learned helplessness was originally offered as a model for depression (Selig-man, 1975) but more recently has been suggested as analogous to PTSD (e.g., Kolb, 1987; van der Kolk, 1983, 1987; van der Kolk et al., 1984b). This dual explanation is interesting in view of the observed overlap in symptoms already discussed. It has been proposed that the similarity between the reactions of animals exposed to uncontrollable and unpredictable events and human sur-vivors of traumatic events may reflect a common biochemical aetiology.

An animal model of PTSD holds considerable theoretical intrigue and van der Kolk and his colleagues (van der Kolk, Boyd, Krystal, & Greenberg, 1984b) have formulated a biochemical model to explain development of PTSD symptoms in humans. This model is based upon the neurochemical alterations that are known to occur in animals exposed to inescapable shock. They argue that traumatic events and associated stimuli may cause profound cat-echolamine depletion similar to the norepinephrine depletion found in animals suffering from learned helplessness and that this might account for such symptoms as loss of motivation. Their model also provides some evidence for a human equivalent of the stress-induced analgesia seen in animals. It is known that some traumatised individuals voluntarily re-expose themselves to trauma-associated stimuli, and then subjectively report a rather paradoxical sense of calm. Van der Kolk and his colleagues suggest that this is due to endorphin release. Cessation of exposure will be followed by physiological hyperactivity and symptoms of opiate withdrawal, but this in turn is modified by re-exposure to the trauma. Furthermore, van der Kolk and his colleagues have pointed out the striking similarities between the symptoms of hyperalertness, anxiety, in-somnia, emotional lability, uncontrollable anger, and the almost identical symptoms of opiate withdrawal syndrome. But although the learned helpless-ness paradigm provides a useful framework for understanding a wider range of reactions and complements the classical conditioning perspective, together

these learning theories cannot provide an adequate account of the hallmark re-experiencing symptoms.

INFORMATION PROCESSING

More recently, Foa, Zinbarg, & Rothbaum (1992) have also proposed that the symptoms observed in animals subjected to unpredictable and uncontrollable aversive events resemble PTSD. They also argue that the similarity in symptoms between animals and trauma victims may reflect common aetiological factors and that it is the lack of predictability and controllability that leads to the syndrome of learned helplessness.

However, their synthesis of the animal and PTSD literatures also suggests that information-processing constructs are important. The suggestion that information-processing constructs are involved in the aetiology of post-traumatic stress reactions is not a new one. For example, Freud (1919) discussed the nightmares experienced by veterans of the First World War. He argued that emotionally intense events penetrate the ego's defence, flooding it with uncontrollable anxiety. The patient was thought by Freud to remain fixated on the trauma and that this was expressed through dreams of the event.

Furthermore, Janet (1889) suggested that intense emotional reactions cause memories of particular events to be dissociated from consciousness and to be stored as visceral sensations (panic and anxiety) or visual images (nightmares and flashbacks). These intense emotions interfere with the integration of the experience into existing memory schemas. These ideas are remarkably similar to those of today.

Horowitz's Theory

Horowitz's (1975, 1976, 1979, 1982, 1986a, 1986b) information-processing approach is based on the idea that individuals have mental models, or schemata, of the world and of themselves which they use to interpret incoming information. He also proposes that there is an inherent drive to make our mental models coherent with current information (the 'completion principle'). A traumatic event presents information which is incompatible with existing schemas. This incongruity gives rise to a stress response requiring reappraisal and revision of the schema. As traumatic events generally require massive schematic changes, complete integration and cognitive processing take some time to occur. During this time, active memory tends to repeat its representations of the traumatic event causing emotional distress. However, to prevent emotional exhaustion, there are processes of inhibition and facilitation which act as a feedback system modulating the flow of information. The symptoms observed during stress responses, which Horowitz categorises as involving denials and intrusion, occur as a result of opposite actions of a control system

Phases   Common states during each phase of response

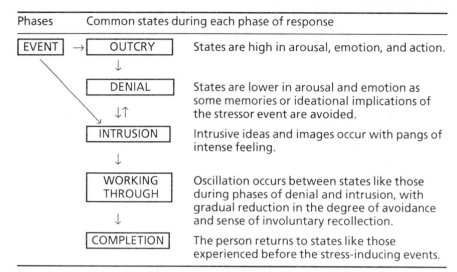

Figure 5.1   Phases of response following trauma (Horowitz, 1979)

that regulates the incoming information to tolerable doses. If inhibitory control is not strong enough, intrusive symptoms such as nightmares and flashbacks emerge. When inhibitory efforts are too strong in relation to active memory, symptoms indicative of the avoidance phase occur. Typically, avoidance and intrusion symptoms fluctuate in a way particular to the individual without causing flooding or exhaustion that would prevent adaptation. The person oscillates between the states of avoidance and intrusion until a relative equilibrium is reached when the person is said to have worked through the experience (see Figure 5.1). The emotional numbing symptoms are thus viewed as a defence mechanism against intrusion.

The information-processing approach of Horowitz draws our attention to the central role that memory plays in the development of post-traumatic stress reactions. Such an approach is compatible with Rachman's concept of emotional processing; both emphasise that post-traumatic stress reactions are signs of incomplete processing, but whereas Horowitz emphasises the need to assimilate and integrate information regarding the event, Rachman emphasises the importance of emotional arousal.

Fear Structures

Applying Lang's (1977, 1985) concept of 'fear structures', Foa and her colleagues (Foa & Kozak, 1986; Foa, Steketee & Rothbaum, 1989; Foa et al., 1992; Foa & Riggs, 1993) have put forward a theory of PTSD which centres around the conditioned formation of a 'fear network' in memory, as a result of traumatisation. This network encompasses: (1) stimulus information about the traumatic event; (2) information about cognitive, behavioural, and physiological reactions to the event; and (3) interoceptive information which links these stimulus and response elements.

This theory leads to the prediction that people characterised by an extensive fear network will show a number of information-processing biases such as an attentional hypervigilance towards trauma-related stimuli (e.g., Foa, Feske, Murdock, Kozac, & McCarthy, 1991; McNally, English, & Lipke, 1993) and consequently an increased probability estimation that traumatic events are likely to happen—it is known that the probability of occurrence accorded a given event is a function of the availability in memory of instances similar to that event (Tversky & Kahneman, 1974).

Activation of the fear network by triggering stimuli (i.e., reminders of the event) causes information to enter consciousness (re-experiencing symptoms). Attempts to suppress such activation leads to the cluster of avoidance symptoms. Successful resolution of the trauma can only occur by integrating the information in the fear network with existing memory structures. Such integration requires, first, the activation of the fear network so that it becomes accessible for modification and, second, availability of information that is incompatible with the fear network so that overall memory structure can be modified.

A number of factors make such integration problematic. Foa and her colleagues argue that the unpredictability and uncontrollability of the event make it difficult to assimilate into existing models in which the world is controllable and predictable. In addition, factors such as the severity of the event disrupt the cognitive processes of attention and memory at the time of the trauma. Foa and her colleagues argue that this disruption leads to the formation of a disjointed and fragmented fear network which is consequently difficult to integrate with existing organised models.

Foa et al.'s theory, whilst useful in explaining fear maintenance and associated cognitive factors, also suffers from the exclusive concentration upon fear. The theory also relies upon a model of stimulus representation which has been found to be inadequate (Teasdale & Barnard, 1993).

Cognitive Action Theory

The cognitive action theory of Chemtob, Roitblat, Hamada, Carlson, and Twentyman (1988) presents a similar perspective to that of Foa and her colleagues but with more detailed analysis of the structure of the fear network which is formulated as a parallel-distributed hierarchical system. Chemtob et al. (1988) argue that, in individuals with PTSD, the fear network is permanently activated causing them to function in 'survival mode' that has proved adaptive during the traumatic event. This permanent activation leads to the symptoms of hyperarousal and re-experiencing.

A possible synthesis?

The cognitive-processing model of PTSD put forward by Creamer, Burgess, and Pattison (1992) is presented as a 'synthesis and reconceptualisation of existing formulations' (p. 453). It combines the central ideas of Horowitz with the network architecture of Foa et al. (1989) and Chemtob et al. (1988).

Creamer et al. (1992) propose that the fear network must be activated for recovery to take place—a mechanism referred to as 'network resolution processing'. This is a concept similar to Horowitz's completion tendency. Creamer et al. (1992) argue for an initial period of intrusion (due to activation of the fear network) which the individual copes with by using a range of defensive and avoidant strategies. Creamer et al. (1992) argue that the extent of initial intrusive symptomatology is an index of the degree of network resolution processing that is occurring. Thus, high levels of initial intrusion are a predictor of successful recovery whereas low levels of intrusion are a predictor of poor outcome and chronic symptoms. Creamer et al. (1992) also argue that intrusion precedes avoidance which is conceptualised as a coping strategy in response to the discomfort that arises from intrusive memories. Although avoidance may reduce immediate distress, excessive reliance on this strategy may be maladaptive because it prevents fear network activation and thus network resolution processing (see Figure 5.2).

Creamer et al's. (1992) model is significant in that it is based on longitudinal data and makes clear predictions about outcome. In a test of the model with 158 office workers following shootings, it was found that intrusive activity at 4 months, as measured using the IES, was predictive of lower distress scores at 8 months, and intrusion at 8 months was predictive of lower distress at 14 months. Avoidance was not found to predict distress.

However, the opposite pattern of results were found by McFarlane (1992a). McFarlane also noted that, although intrusive thinking is diagnostic of disorder, it also represents part of the normal process of trauma appraisal. But, in contrast to Creamer et al., he suggested that greater frequency of intrusive thinking should be predictive of poorer subsequent outcome.

In a test of this prediction, McFarlane (1992a) examined data from 290 firefighters who had completed questionnaires at 4, 11, and 29 months after exposure to bush fires in Australia. A higher frequency of intrusive thinking at 4 months, as assessed using the IES, was predictive of greater distress at 11 months and a higher frequency of intrusive thinking at 11 months was predictive of greater distress at 29 months.

Findings similar to those of McFarlane have been reported in longitudinal studies of survivors of the *Herald of Free Enterprise* disaster (Joseph, Yule, & Williams, 1994) and for survivors of the *Jupiter* cruise ship disaster (Joseph, Yule, & Williams, 1995a).

The reason for these discrepant results is not clear and, to further complicate the picture, other research has failed to show a relationship between early

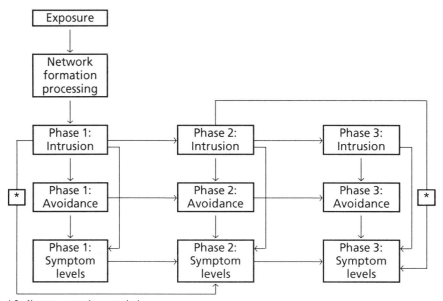

* Indicates a negative association.

Figure 5.2 The longitudinal model of cognitive processing proposed by Creamer et al. (1992). (Copyright © 1992 by the American Psychological Association. Reprinted with permission)

intrusion and avoidance and later symptoms in survivors of a terrorist attack (Shalev, 1992). This might be, as McFarlane (1992b) suggests, because Shalev's data were collected only days following the attack:

> In the initial days after a traumatic event, intrusive memories are a universal phenomena indicative of a normal process of reappraisal of the experience. Various representations of the trauma are developed and an attempt is made to integrate them with existing psychological schemata. It is unclear at which state traumatic memories develop the relatively inflexible quality that represents the failure to resolve the issue of meaning. (McFarlane, 1992b, p. 599)

The importance of the timing of intrusions has also been noted by Brewin and colleagues (Brewin, Dalgleish, & Joseph, 1996) who, in an attempt to provide a conceptual framework for these data suggest that two factors need to be considered: first, the intensity of the event and, second, the timing of the assessment of intrusive and avoidant activity. Like McFarlane, Brewin et al. suggest that the presence of intrusive memories immediately after substantial trauma is a normal reaction that, as Shalev (1992) found, will not predict subsequent adjustment. After some weeks or months, however, continuing intrusive activity, as argued by Rachman (1980), signals a failure to emotionally process the experience and the longer the time elapsed since the trauma, the more likely that intrusive thoughts will predict poor outcome.

One study which would seem to support this possibility was carried out with hospitalised burn patients in which it was found that the severity of intrusive and avoidant thoughts during the first week of hospitalisation did not predict the development of PTSD. This is consistent with the findings of Shalev (1992). But the severity of intrusive thoughts at two months predicted PTSD at six months and the severity of avoidant thoughts at six months predicted PTSD at 12 months (Perry, Difede, Musngi, Frances, & Jacobsberg, 1992). The authors of this study conclude, like McFarlane (1992a), that intrusive and avoidant mental processes immediately after a severe trauma may be normal and should only be defined as pathological if they persist.

With survivors of the *Herald of Free Enterprise* disaster, we found that greater frequency of intrusive thinking and avoidance behaviour at three years, as assessed using the IES, following the event was predictive of greater distress at five years (Joseph, Dalgleish, Thrasher, Yule, Williams, & Hodgkinson, 1996).

But what of the prediction by Creamer et al. that intrusions represent network resolution processing and so should predict less PTSD? It may be that there is a period of time after which intrusions become indicative of a failure to process the experience but before which they are normal reactions, in which emotional processing is ongoing. For some people, this initial period will lead to unsatisfactory emotional processing and chronic distress, but for others this stage will lead to satisfactory emotional processing and recovery. It is the content of the intrusive thinking that will determine whether emotional processing is satisfactory or unsatisfactory.

Similarly, an ambiguity in the role of avoidance has been discussed (Williams, Joseph, & Yule, 1994) and it might be suggested that, early on, avoidance is a normal response and that as the weeks and months pass it becomes increasingly pathological. But before it becomes indicative of unsatisfactory emotional processing some forms of avoidance may be helpful whereas other forms may be harmful. This would require analysis of the specific avoidant cognitions and behaviours used in any given situation.

SOCIAL-COGNITIVE PERSPECTIVES

The work of Janoff-Bulman (1985, 1989, 1992) is of interest in that it focuses on the cognitive schemata that individuals hold, and thus complements the work of Horowitz. Janoff-Bulman suggests that there are common psychological experiences shared by victims who have experienced a wide range of traumatic situations. She proposed that post-traumatic stress following victimisation is largely due to the shattering of basic assumptions that victims hold about themselves and the world.

The number and extent of assumptions that are shattered are dependent upon the individual, but central to Janoff-Bulman's thesis is a common and core belief in personal invulnerability. She argues that although we may recognise that crimes, accidents, and illness occur to a large proportion of the population, it is also possible to believe simultaneously that these misfortunes will not happen to us. There is evidence that people will rate themselves as less likely than others to be victims of diseases, crimes, and accidents (Perloff, 1983), and to underestimate their likelihood of experiencing negative events (Weinstein & Lachendro, 1982). Victimisation shatters this assumption of invulnerability, Janoff-Bulman argues, leaving the person feeling vulnerable to future victimisation.

The sense of vulnerability appears to be tied, Janoff-Bulman believes, to the disruption of three core beliefs: (1) the world as benevolent; (2) the world as meaningful; and (3) the self as worthy (Janoff-Bulman, 1985, 1989, 1992). However, one of the most important underlying assumptions, Janoff-Bulman believes, is that of justice and fairness.

According to the just world hypothesis formulated by Lerner (1975, 1980; Lerner & Miller, 1978), individuals have a need to believe that they live in a world where people get what they deserve and deserve what they get. The belief in a just world enables the individual to confront the physical and social environment as if it were stable and orderly. It is a belief that individuals are reluctant to give up, and evidence that the world is not really just can be extremely distressing.

Janoff-Bulman (1985, 1989, 1992) also writes that people generally operate under the assumption that they are worthy decent people. Victimisation may lead to a questioning of these self-perceptions. This rests, in part, on the notion of the just world. If one deserves what one gets, the experience of victimisation would suggest that one is not a worthy decent person after all. Coping with victimisation involves the person coming to terms with these shattered assumptions and re-establishing a conceptual system that will allow him or her to function effectively.

While bringing out the cognitive contents of the survivor's shattered experience and having considerable face validity, little work has been done as yet to test out these ideas. Janoff-Bulman (1989) has devised a 32-item 'World Assumptions Scale' self-report questionnaire which has been found to have adequate reliability and to distinguish between traumatised and non-traumatised university students. One might question the appropriateness of a questionnaire, however, to assess tacit meaning, which, by definition may not be accessible to consciousness. This level of assessment represents a challenge to cognitive scientists.

TOWARDS AN INTEGRATIVE PSYCHOSOCIAL MODEL

A common theme in the above theories is the integration within memory of trauma-related information with pre-existing schemas. Horowitz suggests that there are phases of intrusion and avoidance as the people gradually dose themselves with information. Although Horowitz's model remains the single most influential perspective in understanding post-traumatic stress reactions there are a number of important criticisms.

Jones and Barlow (1990) note that although Horowitz's model accommodates the signs and symptoms characteristic of PTSD, it is limited in that it fails explicitly to incorporate psychosocial factors that may influence the differential development in the severity and chronicity of symptoms. Indeed, it has been suggested that the most important function of any aetiological model is to explain the absence of symptoms in some individuals (Jones & Barlow, 1990). We will outline those psychosocial factors, based on the work of Rachman (1980) which might operate to impede or promote emotional processing.

Furthermore, little attention is given to the process of appraisal and how the individual's interpretations may mediate between the traumatic event and adjustment. Our approach emphasises the role of appraisal processes as emphasised in the social-cognitive theory of Janoff-Bulman.

Finally, Chemtob et al. (1988) note that Horowitz places an emphasis on a 'drive for completion' for which there is little evidence. An integrative model must therefore outline those psychosocial factors which might operate to impede or promote emotional processing as well as explicate the process of how the individual's interpretations may mediate between the traumatic event and adjustment. Although we will also argue that there is a drive for completion it will be recognised that the emotional processing of traumatic experiences can become blocked so that intrusive and avoidant phenomena are indicative of psychopathology.

However, it is argued that different types of intrusion and avoidance are distinguishable: whereas phenomena indicative of processing or working through seem to be under conscious control, i.e., ruminative thoughts and behavioural avoidance, states viewed as pathological are less under conscious control, i.e., nightmares, and dissociation. Differentiating between types of intrusion and types of avoidance might help to clarify the conflicting data discussed above concerning the predictive role of these phenomena.

Janet (1909) considered dissociation in the context of trauma to result from a state of physiological hyperarousal which results in memory disturbance. The information conveyed by the traumatic event is not available to ordinary conscious representation and so cannot be processed. Instead it persists as a fixed idea that is split off from consciousness and experienced in nightmares. Available empirical data substantiate the view that dissociation at the time of trauma is associated with later post-traumatic symptomatology (Bremner et al., 1992; Holen, 1993; Marmar et al., 1994).

Each of the theories reviewed can tell us about some of the clinical characteristics. We would argue that there are two main assumptions that need to be made before understanding the psychological processes underlying PTSD (see Weiss, 1993b). First, that the symptoms of PTSD have an evolutionary origin, and, second, that both conscious and nonconscious processes are involved.

An Evolutionary Perspective

It has been argued that the cognitive features of chronic PTSD found in combat veterans, such as hyperalertness, excessive startle responses, focused concentration, appear to be derivative of a special 'survival mode' of functioning (Chemtob et al., 1988). Such reactions are likely to be adaptive in a combat situation as they enable the soldier to react quickly to threat, thus increasing the chance of survival. From an evolutionary perspective, post-traumatic reactions might be considered to be a normal and adaptive reaction. A similar evolutionary significance might be attached to the protective function of dissociation when stress exceeds the capacity of coping resources.

A similar argument is presented by Marks and Nesse (1994) who review the evolutionary origins and functions of the capacity for anxiety. However, the persistence of these reactions into civilian life interferes with everyday social functioning and can be highly distressing. Thus, theoretical approaches need, first, to explain the development of post-traumatic reactions as a normal psychological reaction to an extreme stressor; and second, to account for the persistence of these post-traumatic reactions once the stressor is no longer present.

One mechanism which might help to explain the persistence of reactions in the time subsequent to the traumatic event has been described by Brown and Kulik (1977) as flashbulb memory. Brown and Kulik argued that there is a special mechanism which exists for encoding emotion-laden memories. Such a mechanism would have evolutionary survival value. Flashbulb memories might enable the organism to learn quickly about threat in the environment without having to undergo repeated exposure to the stimulus, e.g., if a lion jumps out suddenly and our ancestor was able to escape from the lion, having learnt from that one experience to stay away from lions in future will have survival value. Such a mechanism of encoding emotional-laden information might help to account for the re-experiencing phenomena. Wright and Gaskell (1992) have presented a view of flashbulb memories which is compatible with current thinking on the nature of trauma-related imagery. Flashbulb memories, they argue, develop initially as a result of the person having difficulty storing the event within an existing memory structure.

Conscious and Nonconscious Processes

The acceptance that nonconscious as well as conscious mental processes are involved is important. Research suggests that sensory input is subject to conscious and nonconscious processing (see Brewin, 1988, 1989; Epstein, 1994, for reviews). It has been proposed that dual representations in memory of traumatic experience are the minimum cognitive architecture necessary to understand PTSD (Brewin, Dalgleish, & Joseph, 1996). The first set of representations are the person's conscious experience of trauma, which Brewin (1989) refers to as 'verbally accessible knowledge' because it can in principle be deliberately retrieved from the store of autobiographical experiences. The second set of representations is not verbally accessible but refers to the output of extensive nonconscious processing which may be accessed automatically when the person is in a context whose physical features or meaning are similar to those of the traumatic situation. Later we will argue that this information can be accessed through imagery. Brewin (1989) refers to this second set of representations as 'situationally accessible knowledge'. Briefly, Brewin et al. (1996), in applying this theoretical structure to PTSD, propose that the sensory (i.e., visual, auditory, olfactory, etc.), physiological and motor aspects of traumatic experience are represented in situationally accessible knowledge in the form of analogical codes that enable the original experience to be recreated. The person may only become aware that these representations have been accessed when emotional arousal, motor impulses, flashbacks, or dissociative states are experienced. Verbally accessible knowledge, on the other hand, is viewed as consisting of a series of autobiographical memories that can be deliberately and progressively edited in an attempt to assign meaning to the trauma in terms of verbally accessible constructs (Brewin et al., 1996). A dual representation theory, Brewin et al. believe, provides the minimum cognitive architecture needed to synthesise the various theories reviewed earlier. Teasdale and Barnard (1993) suggest a more complex theory of cognitive representation, the 'interacting cognitive subsystems approach' in which nine different kinds of information and their interrelationships are explicitly recognised. Teasdale and Barnard's emphasis has as yet been upon the explication of depression. The implications for PTSD remain to be explored.

A further set of representations are the person's pre-existing schematic representations about the self and the world which reflect prior experience. These representations would be similar to those discussed by Janoff-Bulman and include beliefs about the self and the world—beliefs that are themselves not easily accessible to verbalisation. Prior life-experiences, particularly those in early childhood between the infant and caregiver, can have an important bearing on later schematic representations which influence how the traumatic event is processed.

Psychosocial Factors in the Post-trauma Environment

There has been much interest in the possible psychosocial factors that contribute to adjustment following exposure to a traumatic event. Green, Wilson, and Lindy (1985c) presented a psychosocial framework for understanding positive and negative outcomes following a traumatic event. Their model starts with exposure to specific aspects of the event, such as violent loss, threat to life, and exposure to grotesque injury. Exposure leads to psychological processing such as that proposed by Horowitz which takes place in the context of two sets of factors: (1) those which the person brings to the situation (e.g., past psychological problems); and (2) those in the recovery environment (e.g., social support). Although not addressing the issue of PTSD specifically, Hobfoll (1989) proposed the Conservation of Resources model. This model focuses on the extent to which individuals are able to maintain social and personal resources. Hobfoll's model proposes that the loss of these resources leads to diminished coping capacity and psychological distress and that it is through replenishing resources that the individuals are able to enhance their coping and reduce their distress.

We suggest that a traumatic event presents an individual with stimulus information which, as perceived *at the time*, gives rise to extreme emotional arousal but interferes with immediate processing. Representations of these *event stimuli* are held in memory, due to their personal salience and to the difficulty they present for easy assimilation with other stored representations. These *event cognitions* take two forms corresponding to the dual representation theory of Brewin et al. (1996): information that is not available to conscious inspection and information which is deliberately retrievable and can be easily edited. Event cognitions provide the basis for the re-experiencing phenomena or intrusive recollections of the trauma which are sometimes full and realistic enough to be experienced as if the event were really happening again (flashbacks). These traumatic cognitions will idiosyncratically reflect the individual's prior experience, personality, basic assumptions, and the specific components of an event that presented the individual with the greatest subjective threat. Intrusive ideation is therefore influenced by *personality* and/or representations of earlier experience (i.e., 'top-down processing').

These images can then form the subject of further cognitive activity called *appraisals* and *reappraisals*. Any stimulus is capable of being perceived in a variety of ways: what is dangerous to an inhabitant of Manhattan may not seem so to someone who has lived on the Ganges and vice versa. Although it is the appraisal that is important in determining subsequent reactions, some stimulus characteristics may render a stimulus to be perceived in the same way by all observers. To this extent we can say that some stimuli are universally judged to be objectively dangerous, unpredictable and uncontrollable: factors which are thought to be important in the aetiology of PTSD (Foa & Kozak, 1986; Foa et al., 1989, 1992).

Appraisal cognitions are distinguished from traumatic cognitions in being thoughts *about* the information depicted and its further meanings, drawing more extensively and consciously upon past representations of experience and/or aspects of personality. (This analysis is similar to Salkovskis (1985) cognitive model for Obsessional-Compulsive Disorder which also features ego-dystonic intrusive cognitions.) These appraisal cognitions might therefore take two forms: (1) automatic thoughts (Beck, 1976; Hollon & Kendall, 1980) associated with automatic schematic activation and with strong emotional states and reappraisals; and (2) conscious thinking through of alternative meanings, influenced by disclosure to others in the social network. These appraisal cognitions might be considered as ruminative behaviour and constitute a further form of intrusive activity. Depending on the content of this intrusive activity, emotional processing might be impeded or promoted. For example, self-blaming ruminative activity which encourages a sense of control and appropriate activity might be expected to promote emotional processing. In contrast, self-blaming ruminative activity which encourages a sense of shame and withdrawal from social support sources might be expected to impede emotional processing.

Current views of how personality and environmental influences are represented in memory encompass various concepts such as associative networks, cognitive styles, schema and other theoretical models (e.g., Teasdale & Barnard, 1993). This part of the model awaits further work. Examples of these representational concepts are noted in Figure 5.3 with a two-way interaction with appraisals (and reappraisals), the specific contents of conscious cognition. In other words, appraisals are influenced by representations and representations are modified by new appraisals (assimilation).

The occurrence of event cognitions and automatic thoughts will be associated with strong *emotional states* (e.g., fear, panic, grief, guilt, and shame) which will themselves become the subjects of cognitive appraisal, influenced by personality. Hence, we suggest that there is a two-way interaction between emotional states and appraisals, each being influenced by the other. As a result of the appraisal process, emotional states are capable of generating further emotional states, e.g., shame about fear, depression about anger, etc.

The occurrence of these event cognitions, appraisals, and emotional states will all engender distress and attempts at *coping* including, most notably, avoidance thoughts and behaviours: avoidance of stimuli (triggers for re-experiencing), thoughts and images (intrusive and automatic), emotions and activities. Some avoidance may take the form of thinking: voluntary, ruminative, worry thoughts directed at problem-solving and the avoidance of strongly emotive imagery and associated with generalised anxiety (Wells & Matthews, 1994). It is suggested that some successful avoidance may be an important aspect of coping but that too much emotional suppression (avoidance) will result in the emotional state of numbness and the dissociation of cognitive and emotional activity. Cognitive suppression will result in the recurrence of intrusive trauma cognitions (Wegner, Shortt, Blake & Page, 1990; Clark, Ball & Pape, 1991). An important component of coping will be the seeking of *social support* from the environment. Input from others can interact via appraisal processes to influence the individual's meaning attributions, emotional states, memory structures and coping in a helpful manner or to induce more distress.

In the 'normal' case, then, following Horowitz, the individual goes through a repetitive cycle of intrusions and appraisals and associated emotional reappraisals and coping resulting in more intrusive cognitions and more appraisals, with feedback into memorial representations until such time that mental models are adjusted to produce new models that are coherent but allow for the new information. On examination the factors distinguished in this analysis bear

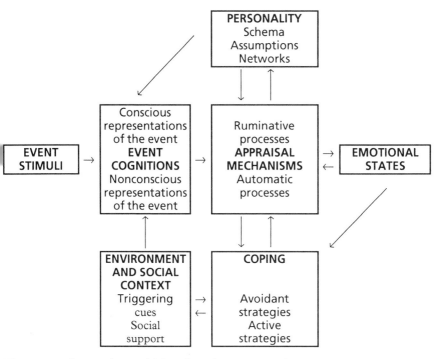

Figure 5.3 Integrative model for adaptation to traumatic stress

close resemblance to Rachman's factors that may impede 'emotional processing', although we are suggesting that the factors that impair emotional processing *at the time* of an event continue into the post-event period, event cognitions acting for event stimuli.

The process of adaptation is extended over time and involves a number of states of mind rather than one static mental state. Some have suggested stages of adaptation characterised by a sequence of emotions (e.g., Kubler-Ross, 1969) whereas others have questioned the necessity of a standard sequence to these states and have emphasised the multifaceted nature of the processes of adaptation. For example, there are likely to be differing needs for support over time (Jacobson, 1986). In this model, adaptation to trauma is seen as a function of both conscious and nonconscious processes.

In this model, which is schematically represented in Figure 5.3, individual variation is attributable to a complex interaction between components that constitute variables which may contribute to outcomes at different points in time. The model offers a way of integrating research findings and points the way to multivariate research which may investigate the patterns of interrelationships.

From a therapeutic perspective, the model delineates phenomenological components of individual experience which may be valuable to analyse and offers points at which therapeutic intervention can be addressed. For example, while emotional states are intense and intolerable, an individual may need help with coping techniques which provide relief, involving avoidance and distraction. When coping is established, individuals who fear 'going crazy' as a result of their intense emotions may need help in reappraising their emotional state before they will risk eliciting the emotion in talking about the incident in detail. Other individuals who have no such emotion cognitions may be able to enter straight into reappraising the event stimuli in a supportive environment where appraisals of culpability and weakness can be examined and reality tested. Seen within this framework, the criteria for PTSD above are observable or introspectable products of emotional processing (an in principle unobservable process) viz.: thoughts of and about the trauma, corresponding highly emotional states, and coping responses including avoidance.

CONCLUSION

In this chapter we have reviewed the main theories that have been put forward to explain post-traumatic reactions. We have outlined an integrative psychosocial model of adaptation which emphasises the role of appraisal factors, personality factors, emotional state factors, and activity factors. In Chapter 6 we shall discuss the evidence for each of the components of this model.

SUMMARY POINTS

1. A number of theoretical paradigms have been applied to the understanding of PTSD. These include 'emotional processing', conditioning theory, learned helplessness, and information processing models.
2. All models have their advantages and limitations to the extent that they explain the phenomena of post-trauma responses.
3. Some attempts to integrate and reconceptualise earlier theories are described, including a new psychosocial model which brings into the picture the importance of the social environment in influencing an individual's adaptation after trauma.
4. Our psychosocial model points to the interactions between a number of key elements, environmental, personal and social in determining an individual's symptomatic 'outcome' and emphasises the importance of appraisal in mediating response to the environment.
5. Important distinctions are drawn between re-experiencing cognitive representations of aspects of the traumatic event itself and ruminations about both the event and emotional reactions. All might be influenced by the individual's personality, coping techniques and social environment.
6. Implications for therapeutic intervention are suggested.

Chapter 6

EVIDENCE FOR AN INTEGRATIVE MODEL OF ADJUSTMENT

INTRODUCTION

Although exposure to a traumatic event is a necessary causal factor in the development of post-traumatic reactions, it is not thought to be sufficient and there has been much interest in the possible factors that may mediate the effects of traumatic events and moderate their impact on mental health. In Chapter 5 we introduced our integrative model of adjustment following traumatic stressors. The main components of this model are stimulus factors, appraisal factors, personality factors, activity factors, and emotional state factors. Stimulus factors were reviewed in Chapter 4. In this chapter we will discuss the experimental literature about the impact of each of these factors.

Key Topics

Appraisal factors
Personality factors
Emotional state factors
Activity factors
Sociocultural factors
Conclusion

APPRAISAL FACTORS

Although appraisal is very much an idiosyncratic process that does not lend itself easily to empirical studies having group designs, it is central to our model of adaptation presented in the previous chapter. We have argued that appraisal processes mediate between the traumatic event and subsequent adjustment. Appraisal processes can constitute one type of intrusive experience; one that is potentially under conscious control although the roots of such activity may be in the form of less consciously accessible 'automatic thoughts' (Beck, 1976). For example, an automatic thought such as 'I should have acted differently' can pop into mind spontaneously, but having done so, that thought is then accessible to conscious inspection and controllable rumination, perhaps in an attempt to resolve questions such as, 'But could I really have done things differently?', 'What would other people have done in that situation?', and so on. Rumination, in itself, will not necessarily lead to better or worse outcome although, as discussed in the previous chapter, it is likely to become pathological after a certain amount of time if it becomes repetitive and stereotyped, indicating that emotional processing has been unsatisfactory and issues of meaning have not yet been resolved. However, early on, depending on the content of the ruminative activity, it might promote or impede processing.

Attributional Perspectives

One aspect of appraisal that helps us to understand some of the processes involved in adaptation is causal attribution. As we have seen, several theorists have noted the importance of the constructs of controllability and predictability in post-traumatic stress reactions. The reason why the constructs of uncontrollability and unpredictability might be important rests on the general theoretical viewpoint that people have a need to predict the future and control events (e.g., Harvey & Weary, 1985; Heider, 1958; Rotter, 1966). The consequence of this is that people who are exposed to unpredictable and uncontrollable events are strongly motivated to explain why the event occurred (Weiner, 1985, 1986; Wong & Weiner, 1981). This has been demonstrated following physical illness (Watts, 1982), cancer (Taylor, 1983), and accidents (Dollinger, 1986) and evidence shows that perceptions of being out of control are predictive of poorer adjustment (e.g., Craig, Hancock, & Dickson, 1994).

As well as the need for perceived predictability and controllability, people also have a need for self-esteem (e.g., Steele, 1988; Tesser & Cambell, 1980). Self-esteem, like perceptions of predictability and controllability, is thought to serve a stress-buffering function (Greenberg et al., 1992, 1993). Causal attribution is the central cognitive mechanism involved in the attempt to establish and maintain self-esteem as well as perceptions of the world as predictable and controllable.

One study which illustrates the need to explain misfortune was carried out by Taylor (1983) who reported that 95% of her sample of women diagnosed as having cancer made some explanation for its occurrence. Women attributed their cancer to stress, the taking of birth-control pills, living near a chemical dump, hereditary factors, or diet. The question is: Do different explanations lead to different ways of coping with the event and different emotional states? Attribution theorists believe that they do (e.g., Antaki & Brewin, 1982; Brewin, 1985, 1988; Janoff-Bulman, 1979; Joseph, Yule, & Williams, 1993d; Shaver & Drown, 1986; Tennen & Affleck, 1990; Turnquist, Harvey & Anderson, 1988; Weiner, 1986) and several theoretical perspectives exist which can help us to make predictions regarding particular types of explanation.

Hopelessness theory

One model that has received much attention is the reformulated model of learned helplessness (Abramson, Seligman, & Teasdale, 1978), since revised as the hopelessness theory of depression (Abramson, Metalsky, & Alloy, 1988, 1989; Alloy, Abramson, Metalsky, & Hartledge, 1988). This theory predicts that, following a negative event, individuals who make causal attributions for the event's occurrence to stable factors (i.e., the cause is perceived as something that persists across time) and global factors (i.e., the cause is perceived as something that affects a wide range of outcomes in one's life) will experience an expectation of hopelessness which may lead to a subtype of depression characterised by hopelessness. Feelings of hopelessness have been observed to underlie a variety of mental health problems (e.g., MacLeod & Tarbuck, 1994) and the hopelessness theory has been applied to understanding a wide variety of illnesses and injuries (e.g., DeVellis, & Blalock, 1992). Although the hopelessness theory does not make explicit predictions regarding PTSD, hopelessness is a common theme expressed by survivors of traumatic events (e.g., Harvey et al., 1995) and the expectation of hopelessness is echoed throughout Janoff-Bulman's (1985, 1992) theory of shattered assumptions. Many of the new beliefs about the world that survivors develop can be considered under the conceptual umbrella of hopelessness expectation. For example, Janoff-Bulman suggests that the cognitive schemata of traumatised populations emphasises the randomness and malevolence of the world, beliefs that reflect stable and global perceptions that bad things will continue to happen. Symptoms are further compounded by lowered self-esteem if the stable and global attributions are also internal (i.e., the cause is perceived as residing within the person). Other variables, such as the lack of social support, are thought to contribute to this expectation of hopelessness.

Although there is evidence for the role of causal attributions with a variety of outcomes (Brewin, 1985; 1988; Sweeney, Anderson, & Bailey, 1986), the hopelessness model remains to be tested in its application to PTSD. However, there is reason to suggest that the hopelessness theory might be an appropriate model for predicting at least some of the clinical characteristics of PTSD. As we have seen in Chapter 2, many of the symptoms of hopelessness depression are diagnostic criteria for PTSD.

It is suggested that a syndrome of post-traumatic hopelessness provides a core construct that can help to resolve some of the discrepancies over the classification of symptoms associated with PTSD by providing a bridge between anxious and depressive phenomena. Although anxiety and depression are considered to be phenomenologically distinct, it has proven difficult to distinguish these constructs empirically (Feldman, 1993).

Although the hopelessness theory may be an appropriate model for predicting at least some aspects of PTSD it does not adequately account for the full range of symptoms associated with the diagnosis of PTSD. To extend attribution theory to account for other PTSD symptomatology, the work of Weiner (1986) is useful. Weiner suggests that there are links between causal attributions and specific emotional states. Weiner draws attention to the way in which specific emotional states appear to depend on causal attributions for events. For example, feelings of rage and anger are generally experienced in the context of negative and externally controllable outcomes.

So, although self-blame has been associated with negative outcomes among victims of threatening events in a variety of studies, there is other evidence that blaming others may also be associated with poorer adjustment in a variety of circumstances (Tennen & Affleck, 1990). One reason for this may be that blaming others leads to the emotional states of rage and anger, states which are frequently reported by survivors of assault and which may lead to the development and maintenance of PTSD (Riggs, Dancu, Gershuny, Greenberg, & Foa, 1992). Other work has shown that anger and hostility in Vietnam veterans was associated with detachment (Silver & Iacono, 1984) and it may be that such emotional states which result out of other-blame may be seen as a form of defence or denial (Tennen & Affleck, 1990).

However, it may be important to differentiate between causal attributions for the events occurrence and causal attributions for what takes place during the event. Guilt and shame are common reactions. In survivors of the *Herald of Free Enterprise* disaster it was found that between one-third and two-thirds said that they felt guilty about things they did or failed to do during the capsize (Joseph, Hodgkinson, Yule, & Williams, 1993b). Feelings of guilt are generally experienced in the context of negative and internally controllable outcomes. Shame, on the other hand, tends to be experienced when an attribution is made to an internal stable cause (Weiner, 1986).

Two studies based on Weiner's (1986) work have investigated the causal attributions made by survivors about events that occurred during a disaster and their relationship to symptomatology. In the first, Joseph, Brewin, Yule, and Williams (1991) investigated the relationship between causal attributions and psychiatric symptoms in civilian survivors of a shipping disaster in which 193 people died: the *Herald of Free Enterprise* disaster. For purposes of legal assessment, 20 survivors provided a detailed account of their experiences during the disaster. From these, causal attributions were extracted and rated along external—internal and uncontrollable—controllable dimensions. Although ratings were generally uncontrollable there was much variation on the externality—internality dimension. For example, some of the survivors provided accounts of their attempts to climb up a rope to safety: 'I had several attempts to climb the rope but was unable to do so. There were no knots in it and it was very slippy.' This was rated as external and uncontrollable, whereas the statement 'I was unable to climb the rope because my legs had gone numb' was rated as internal and uncontrollable. Ratings were based on the attributional coding system developed by Stratton and his colleagues (Stratton et al., 1986). In this study it was found that more internal and controllable attributions were related to intrusive thoughts, depression, and anxiety at 8 and 19 months following the disaster. These findings are consistent with Weiner's (1986) cognitive theory of emotions which suggests that internal and controllable causal attributions for negative outcomes are related to feelings of guilt which in turn, it was suggested, may exacerbate symptoms. This finding is also consistent with the prediction of Foa, Steketee, and Rothbaum (1989) that symptoms of PTSD would be exacerbated by the perception of unexercised control.

A second study by Joseph, Brewin, Yule, and Williams (1993a) replicated the above study with 16 adolescents who survived the *Jupiter* cruise ship disaster. In this study, however, attributions were overwhelmingly uncontrollable so only the externality—internality dimension was rated. For example, the statement 'It was not easy swimming because I had my jeans and sweater on' was rated as external whereas the statement 'I found it very hard to swim out of the suction as I am not a strong swimmer' was rated as internal. The results confirmed that for adolescents causal attribution is an important aspect of disaster response. More internal attributions for disaster-related events were associated with greater depression and intrusive thoughts one year later. However, whereas it was hypothesised that the results with the *Herald* survivors reflected the operation of guilt, the virtually complete absence of personally controllable attributions in the *Jupiter* survivors suggested that it might be shame in this case that provides the link with symptoms.

Although both of these studies suggest an intriguing link between causal attributions and post-traumatic stress, the samples were small and highly selected. Also, no evidence was found to support a causal relationship between attributions and symptoms, although it should be noted that symptoms were probably too stable to permit the demonstration of causal effects. However, even if causal attributions are not responsible for the onset of symptoms they may be responsible for their maintenance. Attributions may be important in the way survivors cope subsequent to disaster, which in turn may exacerbate symptoms.

In addition, survivors may make causal attributions for their emotional state (Solomon, Benbenishty, & Mikulincer, 1988a; Mikulincer, Solomon, & Benbenishty, 1988). Mikulincer et al. investigated how battle events contribute to the formation of PTSD. It was shown that the experience of particular battle events, notably officers' errors during battle, and problems in unit functioning, were associated with fewer long-term disturbances. One possible explanation for this, they suggested, is that soldiers who experience such events can attribute their combat stress reaction (CSR) to external factors beyond their control. In contrast, those who do not experience such events cannot fall back on situational attributions and, therefore, tend to attribute their CSR to personal weakness. The attribution of CSR to personality deficits would have negative consequences for self-image and long-term mental health. A similar explanation was offered by Solomon et al. (1988a) for their finding that soldiers who experienced physical deprivations such as hunger, or who suffered the consequences of error, such as coming under fire by their own forces, exhibited less severe psychological symptoms than those who did not have such experiences. Both physical deprivations and errors, Solomon et al. (1988a) argue, are external causes that may serve to prevent soldiers attributing their own inappropriate behaviour to internal and controllable factors. Events can therefore be appraised in a variety of ways and these studies indicate how idiosyncratic people's reactions can be. Other data also suggest that self-blame is associated with higher levels of depressive symptomatology in survivors of rape (Frazier, 1990; Frazier & Schauben, 1994; Hill & Zautra, 1989; Meyer & Taylor, 1986).

Causal attributions, therefore, constitute one aspect of stimulus appraisal that may help to account for some variations in PTSD symptoms as well as specific emotional states such as rage, anger, guilt, and shame. However, it would seem to be necessary to differentiate between causal attributions for the occurrence of an event, behaviours during the event, and subsequent emotional reactions. This distinction might help to resolve some of the conflicting findings in the literature regarding the role of perceptions of control. Furthermore, we would suggest that the resolution of causal attribution may be one aspect of internal experience that actually constitutes a form of intrusive thinking. This would correspond to the ruminative activity discussed previously, some forms of ruminative activity might lead to better outcome whereas other forms might lead to worse outcome. This might explain why, as we have seen in the previous chapter, findings regarding the role of intrusive thinking in determining later outcome are mixed. But ruminative behaviour must be distinguished from those intrusions which are symptomatic of disorder, the most symptomatic intrusions would correspond to what Lifton (1967) described as the death imprint. This consisted of intrusive images of the impact, the sight of bodies dismembered or crushed, the sounds of screaming, and the smell of burning flesh occurring in the waking state or in nightmare.

PERSONALITY FACTORS

A recent survey with a national probability sample in America has suggested that the prevalence of psychiatric problems is greater than previously thought. Fifty per cent of respondents reported at least one lifetime disorder and approximately 30% reported at least one disorder in the previous 12 months. Furthermore, this morbidity is highly concentrated in roughly one-sixth of the population who have a history of three or more co-morbid disorders (Kessler et al., 1994). The question that many researchers have asked is whether people with previous psychological problems are more at risk of developing post-traumatic stress reactions than those who do not have previous psychological problems.

The evidence which has accumulated is generally consistent in showing that prior behavioural and psychological problems are associated with greater distress. This conclusion has been drawn from studies of the effects of personal injury and physical attack (Breslau, Davis, Andreski, & Peterson, 1991; Helzer, Robins, & McEvoy, 1987; Hough et al., 1990), rape (Atkeson, Calhoun, Resick, & Ellis, 1982; Burgess & Holmstrom, 1978; Frank & Anderson, 1987; Frank, Turner, Stewart, Jacob, & West, 1981; Ruch, Chandler, & Harter, 1980), mass shooting (North, Smith, & Spitznagel, 1994) disaster (Lopez-Ibor, Soria, Canas, & Rodrigues-Gamazo, 1985; Markowitz & Gutterman, 1986; McFarlane, 1988a, 1988b, 1989; Bromet, Schulberg, & Dunn, 1982b) and previous psychiatric history is recognised as a vulnerability factor for PTSD (APA, 1994).

But interestingly, it has been suggested that the effects of prior psychological problems interact with the intensity of event exposure. For example, Foy, Resnick, Sipprelle, and Carroll (1987) reported that a family history of psychiatric disorders was associated with the development of PTSD in Vietnam veterans but that the effect was greatest for those with the least exposure to combat. This is an interesting suggestion which might help to explain why some other research has not found prior history factors to be associated with distress (Solkoff, Gray, & Keill, 1986; Speed, Engdahl, Schwartz, & Eberly, 1989; Kilpatrick, Veronen, & Best, 1985; Madakasira & O'Brien, 1987). It may be that survivors of these event experienced a traumatic event so intense that the effect of prior psychological problems was minimum. In addition, there are other factors which may need to be taken into account when trying to understand the role of prior psychological problems. For example, in the study by North et al. (1994) of survivors of a mass shooting, it was found that a past history of psychiatric disorder predicted the development of PTSD for women but not for men. Clearly, the role of prior-psychological problems in the development of post-traumatic stress reactions is not straightforward.

Personality is shaped by our life-experiences and some researchers have suggested that particular experiences in the past may lead to a person being vulnerable to the development of psychiatric problems. In particular, childhood experiences are thought to be crucial to later personality development and work has shown that people who are depressed are more likely to have had childhoods characterised by adverse experiences (Brewin, Andrews, & Gotlib, 1993). It might be expected that people with adverse events in their childhood are also prone to the development of post-traumatic stress reactions.

Childhood experiences are thought to be important in the development of our beliefs about ourselves and the world around us and from a cognitive perspective it might be that these belief systems in turn cause the person to be vulnerable to disorder. One set of beliefs that seem relevent to understanding post-traumatic stress are those to do with control.

Attributional style

As we have seen, causal attributions are thought to be important in how a person reacts to an event. Causal attributions themselves reflect not only the situational information available regarding the event but also the person's attributional style (Abramson et al., 1988; Alloy & Tabachnik, 1984; Alloy et al., 1988), a relatively stable personality characteristic (Burns & Seligman, 1989) which refers to people's characteristic way of explaining events.

The hopelessness theory predicts that individuals who characteristically explain negative events in terms of internal, stable, and global causes and explain positive events in terms of external, unstable, and specific causes are vulnerable to the development of depression characterised by feelings of hopelessness accompanied by low self-esteem (Abramson et al., 1988; Alloy et al., 1988). Research which has tested this prediction with a retrospective behavioural high-risk paradigm has presented evidence consistent with the hopelessness theory (Alloy, Lipman, & Abramson, 1992) and there is some correlational evidence that this vulnerable attributional style is also associated with PTSD in Vietnam veterans (McCormick, Taber, & Kruedelbach, 1989) and in women with histories of child sexual abuse and who are suffering from low self-esteem and poorer adjustment (Gold, 1986; Wolfe, Gentile, & Wolfe, 1989).

Another study by Mikulincer and Solomon (1988) investigated whether attributional style was associated with emotional distress in Israeli combat veterans at two and three years following the Lebanon War. They found that intensity of PTSD symptomatology, general psychiatric symptomatology, and problems in social functioning were associated with the attribution of good events to more external and uncontrollable causes and the attribution of bad events to more external, stable, and uncontrollable causes. But in contrast to other research which suggests that internality for negative events is associated with poorer outcome, Mikulincer and Solomon (1988) suggest that their finding that externality for negative outcomes is associated with poorer outcome is explained by the denial of personal responsibility by PTSD veterans. It might be that avoidance manifests itself in this particular attributional pattern. Alternatively, it may be that these data reflect the attribution of blame and feelings of anger towards other people.

Locus of Control

A related concept to attributional style is that of locus of control. It has generally been believed that perceptions of control are adaptive in stressful situations (Benassi, Sweeney, & Dufour, 1988). For example, Taylor (1983) reported that in cancer patients the belief that one could control one's own cancer was associated with positive adjustment and there is growing evidence that perceptions of control are also associated with lower distress in combat veterans (Frye & Stockton, 1982; Orr et al., 1990; Solomon, Mikulincer, & Benbenishty, 1989b). However, although it is likely that attributional style and locus of control are vulnerability factors for disorder following traumatic events, there is as yet no evidence to confirm this suggestion. Obtaining pre-morbid personality measures is a particular problem with trauma research. However, the availability of attributional coding techniques which can be used with written material such as letters (Stratton et al., 1986; Schulman, Castellan, & Seligman, 1989) makes this an intriguing possibility for future research.

If attributional style and locus of control do constitute vulnerability factors, it is likely that the intensity of exposure will moderate the association between locus of control and distress. Solomon et al. (1989b) found an association between locus of control and distress in soldiers who had been exposed to low battle intensity but not in soldiers who had been exposed to high battle intensity. The explanation for this, they suggest, was due to the greater informational value of greater battle intensity in helping the soldier to explain his behaviour to himself. High-intensity battle, they argue, leads the soldier to explain his combat stress reaction entirely by the stressful events whereas low-intensity battle leads to explanations affected by locus of control.

Locus of control refers to the person's perceptions of control and it might be predicted that perceptions of control are most adaptive in situations where control can actually be exercised. Locus of control should, however, be distinguished from self-efficacy, the person's conviction of whether or not he or she is able to exercise control (see Litt, 1988).

Attitudes and Beliefs

Beck and Emery (1985), although they do not discuss PTSD as such, suggest that there may be another mechanism whereby an individual's personality may result in extreme and negative conclusions following traumatisation. They suggest that vulnerable individuals have dysfunctional assumptions which predispose them to the development of depression and anxiety. These asumptions are rules for living acquired during childhood but which can be too rigid, extreme, and absolute in form. For example, the need for control is sometimes represented in absolute black and white terms so that any deviation from absolute control tends to be conceived in terms of absolute lack of control. This could be a mechanism by which a primitive belief could come to be shattered by the operation of automatic, schematic processing rather than discrepant information impacting on a basic belief.

Drawing upon Beck's concept of dysfunctional assumptions, as well as the work of Rachman (1980), Williams (1989) has hypothesised that negative attitudes towards emotional expression (e.g., 'I think you should always keep your feelings under control', 'I think you should not burden other people with your problems', 'I think getting emotional is a sign of weakness', 'I think other people don't understand your feelings') would act to block the processing of emotionally charged information and constitute one vulnerability factor for the development or maintenance of post-traumatic stress reactions.

Tests of this prediction have been carried out with survivors of the *Herald of Free Enterprise* disaster showing that those who held the most negative attitudes towards emotional expression had the highest distress scores (Williams, Hodgkinson, Joseph, & Yule, 1995) and that more negative attitudes towards emotional expression at three years were associated with greater distress at five years (Joseph, Dalgleish, Williams, et al., 1997).

EMOTIONAL STATE FACTORS

The role of emotional state at the time of the event has received some attention and DSM-IV (APA, 1994) has, as we have seen in Chapter 2, introduced the category of Acute Stress Disorder. To qualify for a diagnosis, the person must exhibit dissociative symptoms, persistent re-experiencing, marked avoidance of reminders, anxiety and increased arousal. Acute Stress Disorder is most likely to develop under conditions of extreme stress and it is thought that individuals with this disorder are at increased risk for the development of PTSD although at present the relationship between Acute Stress Disorder and PTSD is not understood and we have to rely on data which have been collected on other acute syndromes such as Combat Stress Reaction (CSR) (see Oei, Lim, & Hennessy, 1990). CSRs may be brief, lasting only a few hours to a few weeks. Israeli soldiers who suffered from CSR in the 1982 Lebanon War were more likely to go on to develop PTSD than those soldiers who had not suffered from CSR but had experienced an equal level of combat exposure. In the first year after the war, the PTSD prevalence rate was 62% for the CSR group compared to 14% in the non-CSR group. At three years, the prevalence rates were 43% and 10% respectively (Solomon, 1993). Although these data provide some evidence in support of the causal link between acute reactions and PTSD, the specific features of acute reactions that are most likely to predict PTSD remain unclear. A prominent feature of Acute Stress Disorder is dissociation and it has been suggested that this may provide the link between acute and chronic reactions. There is some evidence for the role of dissociation with survivors of a North Sea oil rig disaster (Holen, 1993) and Vietnam veterans (Marmar et al., 1994).

In addition, personality variables and pre-existing mental disorders may influence the development of Acute Stress Disorder. However, not all those who develop Acute Stress Disorder go on to develop PTSD and so the relationship between these two states must be moderated by other factors.

Theorists who propose a stage model of processing have drawn attention to the multiple emotional states experienced following trauma. Although some theories have emphasised fear (e.g., Foa et al., 1989) with thoughts of recurrence of the trauma and helplessness in the face of it, PTSD is not synonymous with fear and anxiety. It would appear that the full range of negative emotions are felt, not only fear and anxiety but grief, guilt, and shame as well as rage and anger. Indeed, processing gives rise to not only one state but a series of states as the event comes to be examined from different perspectives.

As already noted, Weiner (1986) points out how specific emotional states appear to depend upon causal attributions for events. It has been suggested that the relationship between internal and controllable attributions and symptoms in a sample of survivors of a ferry disaster was mediated by the emotional state of guilt (Joseph et al., 1991); whereas it was suggested that the internal and uncontrollable attributions of a group of adolescent survivors could reflect the emotional state of shame (Joseph et al., 1993a). However, further research is clearly needed to substantiate these data. In particular, it is not known whether particular emotional states are exclusively related to attributions for specific types of events, for example, events which involve another person. In addition, although causal attributions and attributional style have been found to be associated with post-traumatic symptoms, there is at present no evidence supporting a causal path between these variables. In addition to longitudinal research, it is also suggested that future research should attempt to address the association between causal attributions for real events and attributional style for hypothetical events in order to explore a vulnerability model for the development of post-traumatic stress reactions.

As already discussed, emotional states themselves may be subject to appraisal. Emotional states that are perceived of as inappropriate may be associated with behavioural inhibition, concealment and denial (or avoidance). The emotional states can be appraised as frightening, depressing, etc. and lead to secondary emotional reactions. Foa et al. (1989) emphasise the importance of these secondary reactions because of their association with avoidant coping strategies. As Horowitz (1976) pointed out, an individual may feel threatened by the emotional state itself and use avoidance as self-protection. Such reactions to powerful emotional states may then both block processing and render the individual beyond the scope of social support.

Foa, Zinbarg, and Rothbaum (1992) present evidence that rape victims diagnosed with PTSD two months post-rape were unlikely to recover spontaneously. This and other evidence with survivors of a variety of events suggests that after 3–4 months, PTSD, if present and without treatment, is likely to remain stable over time and that symptoms early on are able to predict later chronicity of symptomatology (McFarlane, 1988a, 1988b; Perry, Difede, Musngi, Frances, & Jacobsberg, 1992; Solomon, Weisenberg, et al., 1987c).

ACTIVITY FACTORS

The role of causal attributions may be to influence the coping strategies employed following adversity which, in turn, may exacerbate PTSD symptoms. There is good evidence for this relationship in normal populations. Brewin, MacCarthy, and Furnham (1989), for example, investigated whether causal attributions concerning negative outcomes were related to seeking social support. It was found that individuals who blamed their own inadequacies for a specific negative event were more likely to have withdrawn socially and were less likely to have used coping strategies involving family and friends. Previously we discussed the role of appraisal in determining specific emotional states such as guilt or shame. Recent work on the role of guilt and shame and psychopathology suggests that they may have a differential relationship to post-traumatic response. Tangney, Wagner, and Gramzow (1992) note that, although both shame and guilt involve negative affect, each has a distinct focus which is related to unique symptom clusters.

> In guilt, the object of concern is some specific action (or failure to act). There is remorse or regret over the 'bad thing that was done' and a sense of tension that often serves as a motivation for reparative action. The tension, remorse, and regret engendered by guilt can be quite uncomfortable, particularly when reparation is blocked for one reason or another... In shame, the object of concern is the entire self. The 'bad thing' is experienced as a reflection of a 'bad self', and the entire self is painfully scrutinized and negatively evaluated. With this painful scrutiny of the self is a corresponding sense of shrinking, of being small, and of being worthless and powerless. Shame also involves a sense of exposure. (Tangney, Wagner, & Gramzow, 1992, p. 469)

One important phenomenological difference between guilt and shame, then, is that shame motivates us to hide whereas guilt motivates us to take reparative action. This has implications for the choice of coping behaviour. It might be expected that shame leads to the use of avoidant coping whereas guilt leads us to use approach coping. However, where reparative action cannot be taken, the person may be obliged to relive the events over in his or her mind. Strong feelings of guilt may then be associated with intrusive thinking whereas shame may be associated with avoidant behaviour. Interestingly, there are similarities here to the distinction drawn by Lifton (1967) between 'animating guilt' and 'static guilt'. Animating guilt is a spur to self-examination whereas static guilt keeps the victim bound to the experience and unable to move on. A variety of strategies may be used to cope with traumatic events. For example, Green, Grace, and Gleser (1985a), in their study of survivors of the Beverly Hills Supper Club fire, assessed coping using an open-ended question to which responses were grouped into one of three categories. These were denial (e.g., using drugs or turning to work to avoid thinking about the situation), philosophical/intellectual (e.g., turning to religion), and interpersonal (e.g., talking to others). North et al. (1994), in their study of survivors of a mass shooting, found that the most widespread method of coping was seeking support from family and friends (88%).

Coping refers to the person's cognitive and behavioural efforts to manage (reduce, tolerate, master) the demands (both internal and external) of a stressful transaction (Lazarus & Folkman, 1984). Much evidence has accumulated showing that coping mediates between stressful events and psychological distress (Billings & Moos, 1981, 1984; Carver et al., 1989; Endler & Parker, 1990; Folkman & Lazarus, 1985, 1988; Folkman, Lazarus, Dunkel-Schetter, De-Longis, & Gruen, 1986a; Pearlin & Schooler, 1978). A basic distinction often employed is between problem-focused and emotion-focused coping (Folkman & Lazarus, 1985). The former refers to acts taken to remove or mitigate the source of stress, the latter to attempts to reduce the psychological distress. Findings regarding the use of emotion-focused and problem-focused strategies seem, at first, somewhat inconsistent and confusing. Greater emotion-focused coping has been found to be associated with less distress following the Three Mile Island leak (Baum, Fleming, & Singer, 1983a), and more distress in Israeli combat veterans (Solomon, Mikulincer, & Flum 1988c), American combat veterans (Nezu & Carnevale, 1987), civilians following the SCUD missile attacks on Israel during the Gulf War (Zeidner & Ben-Zur, 1994), and women with HIV infection (Commerford, Gular, Orr, Reznikoff, & O'Dowd, 1994).

In addition, the role of coping may be modest following events associated with great loss (Freedy, Darlene, Jarrell, & Masters, 1992). There are as yet no clear answers to the question of which strategies, or combination of strategies, are most beneficial. The Conservation of Resources stress model (Hobfoll, 1989) suggests that whichever particular strategy, or combination of strategies, leads to the most efficient acquisition of resource losses will be the most adaptive for psychological health. If event-related resource loss allows for the person to take control, then problem-focused coping should be adaptive. However, if the event-related loss does not allow the person to take control, then emotion-focused strategies should be adaptive (Carver et al., 1989; Folkman & Lazarus, 1988; Hobfoll, 1989). Thus, it would seem that the effects of coping can only be understood in relation to the nature of the event and its appraisal.

Avoidance

Various forms of avoidant coping have been found to be associated with less distress in uncontrollable situations such as the political violence in Northern Ireland (Cairns & Wilson, 1984, 1989), the length of survival following the diagnosis of cancer (Greer, Morris, & Pettingale, 1979). In addition, Whittington and Wykes (1991) found that psychiatric nurses who reported using denial also reported fewer problems in the year following a violent assault. There are some suggestions from empirical studies, then, that using coping strategies that involve avoidance strategies may be helpful. In contrast, McFarlane (1988a/b) found that in a sample of volunteer firefighters exposed to Australian bush fires, a reported tendency to avoid thinking about negative experiences was associated with more symptoms. Also, Green, Grace, and Gleser (1985a), in their study of the Beverly Hills Supper Club fire, found that those using avoidant strategies exhibited higher levels of pathology and it is generally believed that coping which involves exposure (without escape) to feared stimuli can help to ameliorate anxiety (Beck & Emery, 1985; Clark, 1986; Marks, 1981). As a type of coping with perceived threats, avoidance is believed to play a role in the spiralling cycle that characterises anxiety disorders (Beck & Emery, 1985) and to be associated with a range of health problems (Suls & Fletcher, 1985). As we have seen, however, Horowitz (1976, 1979) sheds a different light upon the role of avoidance. According to Horowitz's theory, as a part of normal adaptation, an individual will go through phases of re-experiencing and avoiding thinking about the trauma. Thus the role of avoidance in coping with stress seems ambiguous: first, avoidance impedes emotional processing and maintains anxiety; but second, avoidance may be necessary to protect a traumatised individual from being overwhelmed by emotion and plays a part in normal processing of the event.

Avoidance is not a simple concept and can implicate different coping responses: behavioural avoidance (i.e., staying away from reminders); cognitive avoidance (i.e., not thinking about the event); and affective avoidance (i.e., blocking an affective response). It is possible that different types of avoidance are associated with different outcomes. Specifically, if emotion is required in processing, it might be that affective avoidance would have the most generalised inhibitory effect and would be associated with the greatest signs of blocked emotional processing and functional impairment. The studies which have shown avoidant strategies to be adaptive have generally used measures of either cognitive or behavioural avoidance rather than affective avoidance. It is suggested that affective avoidance may be predictive of emotional disorder.

Inhibition

The inhibition-disease framework developed by Pennebaker and his colleagues (Pennebaker, 1985; Pennebaker & Beall, 1986; Pennebaker & Chew, 1985; Pennebaker & O'Heeron, 1984; Pennebaker, Hughes, & O'Heeron, 1987; Pennebaker, Kiecolt-Glaser, & Glaser, 1988) suggests that the act of restraining ongoing thoughts or behaviour requires physiological work resulting in increased psychosomatic symptoms. One explanation for this effect is that, by disclosure, individuals change the way in which trauma-relevant material is represented in memory. Pennebaker and his colleagues (Pennebaker, 1993; Hughes, Uhlmann, & Pennebaker, 1994) present evidence that what is important is the construction of a coherent story together with the expression of negative emotions.

Similarly, Foa et al. (1989) argue that recovery from victimisation requires that, first, the fear memory be activated, and, second, that new information incompatible with what is already in the fear structure be introduced.

Evidence suggests that a tendency towards thought suppression is associated with obsessive thinking and emotional reactivity. It has been suggested that intention to suppress a thought produces two mental processes: a conscious effortful operating process that searches for distractors, and an unconscious, relatively effortless monitoring process that searches for the unwanted thought (Wegner & Zanakos, 1994). It may be then that avoidant strategies can actually increase the cognitive accessibility of information.

SOCIOCULTURAL FACTORS

Social Support

A considerable body of evidence has been accumulated documenting the stress-buffering effects of social support (Brown & Harris, 1978; Cohen & Wills, 1985; Dalgard, Bjork, & Tambs, 1995; Roy & Steptoe, 1994) and much research has now been carried out showing greater social support to be associated with better outcome following toxic exposure (Bromet, Parkinson, Schulberg, Dunn, & Gondek, 1982a), rape (Burgess & Holmstrom, 1974a, 1974b, 1978; Kilpatrick et al., 1985), combat (Fontana & Rosenheck, 1994c; Foy, Sipprelle, rueger, & Carroll, 1984; Foy et al., 1987; Frye & Stockton, 1982; Keane, Scott, Chavoya, Lamparski, & Fairbank, 1985a; Roberts, Penk, Robinowitz, & Patterson, 1982; Solkoff et al., 1986; Solomon, Mikulincer, & Avitzur, 1988b; Stretch, Vail, & Maloney, 1985) as well as a range of civilian disasters (Cook & Bickman, 1990). However, social support has been variously defined in these studies.

Definitions of social support emphasise behaviour relevant to coping needs. Schaefer, Coyne, and Lazarus (1981) distinguished between the emotional, tangible and informational support functions of support. Emotional support includes intimacy and attachment, reassurance and being able to confide in and rely on another: factors which contribute to the feeling that one is loved, or cared about, and that one belongs. Tangible support involves direct aid, and includes loans, gifts of money, and the provision of services. Informational support includes giving advice and providing feedback.

The demands evoked by any event may unfold over time and Jacobson (1986) has emphasised the need to consider social support in its temporal dimension. To the extent that stressful situations are sequential, different kinds of support will be called for at different times. Weiss (1976) outlined a model in which the types of support are related to the sequencing of stressful events. First, there is 'crisis', which is defined as a situation of sudden onset and limited duration, severely threatening to one's well-being, and marked by emotional arousal. In a crisis the most useful form of help is emotional support which provides a person with reassurance that others are able and willing to help in the struggle to regain equilibrium. Second, there is 'transition', which is defined as a period of personal and relational change involving a shift in the person's 'assumptive world'. In transitions, the primary type of help is cognitive support that helps the individual to come to terms with the meaning of the changes experienced. Third, there are 'deficit states', which are situations in which the individual's life is characterised by excessive demands. Here material aid and direct action are needed to remedy an imbalance between needs and tangible resources.

A study by Cook and Bickman (1990) investigated the relationship of perceived availability of social support to self-reported psychological symptomatology at various points in time over a period of six months following a flood. Their results indicated that respondents experienced severe distress immediately following the disaster, that this distress decreased sharply at six weeks after the flood, and decreased more gradually in the following months. Perceived availability of social support was not related to distress immediately following the disaster nor five months later. Social support and symptomatology were, however, significantly correlated during the intermediate time. Cook and Bickman (1990) suggest that their data have important methodological considerations for the conduct of research following traumatic events:

> Not only did the effects of the distress decay but also the relationship between an important social variable such as social support and symptomatology changes over time. These results can possibly explain some of the inconsistent findings in this field. Differing results may be obtained depending on the time since the occurrence of the stressor. (Cook & Bickman, 1990, p. 555)

Buffering hypothesis

A major debate in the conceptualization of social support has been whether to consider it as acting as an antecedent to stressful life-events that serves to protect individuals from negative health outcomes, versus viewing it as playing a buffering role in situations of high stress (Cohen & Wills, 1985; Gore, 1981; House & Kahn, 1985; Thoits, 1982). Cohen and Wills (1985) reviewed the existing literature in detail in an attempt to consider the process by which support has a beneficial effect on well-being. Their review concludes that there is evidence consistent with both models. Evidence for a main effect model was found when the support measure assessed the person's degree of integration in a social network. Evidence for a buffering model is found when the support measure assesses interpersonal resources that are responsive to the needs elicited by a stressful situation.

Raphael (1986) notes that survivors often have a compelling need to talk about their experiences, and thus empathic listening is a principal component of the necessary emotional support following crisis. One study which has examined the buffering role of support offers impressive evidence that it is related to a reduced risk of depression following a crisis. In a longitudinal study of working-class women, it was found that retrospective reports of crisis support received from a husband, lover, or very close friend following a severe event or major difficulty were strongly associated with a reduced risk of depression. Crisis support was said to have been received if, following a provoking agent, there had been a high level of confiding with a high level of active emotional support, as long as it was not accompanied at some point by a negative response from the person confided in (Andrews & Brown, 1988; Brown, Andrews, Harris, Adler, & Bridge, 1986).

Studies which have investigated the role of crisis support with survivors of the *Jupiter* cruise ship disaster (Joseph, Andrews, Williams, & Yule, 1992a; Joseph, Yule, Williams, & Andrews, 1993e) and the *Herald of Free Enterprise* sinking (Dalgleish, Joseph, Thrasher, Tranah, & Yule, 1996) have also found that higher self-reported ratings of crisis support received from family and friends are predictive of lower levels of distress.

With civilian burns patients, Perry, Difede, Musngi, Frances, and Jacobsberg (1992) found less emotional support to be predictive of PTSD up to 12 months later. Thus, there is growing evidence for the role of social support as a protective factor against emotional distress following exposure to a traumatic event. It has been suggested that one way in which social support works is by enhancing perceptions of control over the environment. For example, social support acts as a vehicle for the transmission of information for problem solving.

Solomon et al. (1988b) examined the relationship between coping, locus of control, social support, and combat-related PTSD. Their sample consisted of 262 Israeli soldiers who suffered a combat stress reaction episode during the 1982 Lebanon War. In contrast to much previous work that has set out to examine the impact of personal and social resources on the development of PTSD among CSR casualties, Solomon et al. (1988b) employed a longitudinal design, focusing on two points in time: two years and three years following combat. They examined, first, the relation between personal resources and social resources and PTSD at each point in time; and, second, the relation between changes in the course of PTSD and changes in both personal and social resources. The intensity of PTSD declined between the two points of time, reflecting a process of recovery. In addition, locus of control became more internal, there was less emotion-focused coping, and more perceived social support. As hypothesised, associations were found at each point in time between PTSD intensity and personal and social resources. Both in the second and third years after the war, more intense PTSD was associated with external locus of control, emotion-focused coping style, and insufficient social support. With regard to locus of control, although correlated at both times with PTSD, the removal of the contributions of coping strategies and social support to PTSD variance cancelled out the significance of locus of control. It is suggested that this is consistent with the idea that internal locus of control is associated with the use of more task-relevant problem-focused coping strategies, and less task-irrelevant emotionally-focused strategies (Anderson, 1977). The findings are thus thought to point to coping strategies as mediating between locus of control and PTSD. However, this study is limited by several methodological problems in common with much of the disaster literature. First, the subjects have PTSD prior to the start of the study, the findings cannot provide definitive evidence as to the direction of causality between resources and PTSD, and once established one would expect a mutually reinforcing relation between resources and PTSD. Second, the conceptualisation of emotion-focused coping as including avoidant strategies can actually be viewed as an expression of PTSD symptomatology rather than as a contributing factor. Third, assessments of personal and social resources are retrospective, and thus may be influenced by the current psychological state. Although people with an internal locus of control may be more able to get support in a time of crisis, other research has suggested that the buffering effect of social support might only apply to those people with an external locus of control (Dalgard et al., 1995).

However, over-reliance on the social network can create dependency and there is some research which suggests that marriage may actually exacerbate the negative psychological consequences of disaster for women (Gleser et al., 1981; Solomon, Smith, Robins, & Fischbach, 1987a). It may be that married women are relied on for support by others, creating additional stress. Other life-events will often occur in the period after disaster, some perhaps triggered by it (Janney, Masuda, & Holmes, 1977) and which might serve to exacerbate symptoms. It is known from numerous studies that stressful life-events are implicated in the onset and maintenance of psychiatric problems (Brown & Harris, 1978; Lloyd, 1980; Breslau & Davis, 1986). McFarlane (1988a, 1988b), in his study of survivors of the Australian bush fire, found that individuals with PTSD had more adverse life-events before and after the trauma. Karlehagen et al. (1993) report that railway drivers who suffered from negative psychological outcomes following railway accidents were more likely to have had previous similar accidents. In their work on Dutch hijackings, van der Ploeg and Kleijn (1988) note that hostages who had to cope with other major life-events besides having been held hostage reported a greater number of negative after-affects. Following extreme catastrophe, post-disaster life-events are inextricably bound up with the traumatic event itself. Goenjian et al. (1994), in their study of the survivors of the Armenia earthquake, note that the persistence of symptoms one and a half years later may also have been related to the unremitting multiple post-disaster adversities such as the relocation of families, loss of possessions, lack of housing and crowded living conditions, unemployment, and so on. Also, they note that the undisposed of debris and destroyed buildings served as constant reminders of the event.

Social Context

Responses to trauma are also linked to sociocultural events. Summerfield (1993), for example, draws attention to the Vietnam War following which the

US veterans were disowned by their society and contrasts this to the Falklands War in which British veterans returned to popular acclaim. The social context helps to determine the meaning of particular experiences and subsequent emotional reactions. The relationship between emotional reactions and social context is illustrated in an interesting study carried out by Bartone and Wright (1990) who investigated group recovery following a military air disaster which showed a response pattern of adaptation that included both intrusion and avoidance. A chartered US Army jetliner crashed in 1985 killing all who were on board. This was the second of three flights carrying soldiers home from the Sinai for Christmas. Bartone and Wright collected monthly data using unstructured interviews over a period of six months following the crash on 140 individuals from the battalion. Their data indicated four relatively distinct phases, each lasting 4–6 weeks: (1) Numb Dedication; (2) Anger–Betrayal; (3) Stoic Resolve; and (4) Integration. This first phase in weeks 1 to 6 was characterised by denial, generalised affective detachment, and numbness.

> The work atmosphere was sombre but business-like. Soldiers working at the battalion staff offices at this time described a 'feeling of unreality, like this isn't really happening,' 'like I'm on automatic pilot,' and feeling as if 'I'm here, but I'm not really here.' Many described feeling 'numb' or 'cold,' with 'no real feelings at all.' (Bartone & Wright, 1990, p. 528).

Bartone and Wright (1990) note that although this phase was dominant, various intrusive reminders sometimes triggered periods of uncontrollable crying and dreams were common. Other symptoms observed included those of startle response and survivor guilt. Near the six-week point, Bartone and Wright describe how this first phase of Numb Dedication shifted to one dominated by Anger–Betrayal. What is interesting about Bartone and Wright's work is that they attempt to integrate these stages with a sociopsychological context. They note that the transition into this phase was marked by the publication of a report indicating poor airline safety practices as contributing to the cause of the crash and also the explosion of the space shuttle *Challenger* in 1986.

> Unit survivors resented what they perceived as greater public concern for seven astronaut lives than for 248 soldier lives. This was attributed to a presumed public attitude that 'a soldier's blood is cheap,' that soldiers represent the lower strata of society and are therefore more expendable than others ... anger was frequently expressed toward the charter airline for alleged safety violations ... and toward the upper-echelons of Army command for not assuring the safety of military charter flights. This was coupled with a sharp sense of betrayal; many felt the trust they placed in the army to care for their safety and welfare had been profoundly violated. (Bartone & Wright, 1990, p. 531)

However, Bartone and Wright also note that during this phase there was a high degree of support within the group and that many members tried to direct their anger into constructive channels, for example, using it to care for the bereaved families. Also, there was no notable decline in symptoms like insomnia, dreams, guilt, or startle reactions and many reported an increased use of alcohol or tranquillisers to relieve tension. At around the tenth week, following the burial of the last dead soldier, there was another marked turning point characterised by a sense of relief.

> Expressions of sadness and anger were replaced by an attitude of 'stoic resolve' to continue on with work and life. Many individuals reported having made a conscious decision to focus attention on the present and future, with the aim of bringing the battalion back to a strong and healthy state. The crash itself became a taboo topic. All emphasis was on training and readiness. When some reference to the crash became necessary, as was the case at memorial services, indirect or euphemistic terms were used (e.g., 'the plane that was lost'; 'our Sinai heroes'; 'our soldiers who didn't make it home'). (Bartone & Wright, 1990, p. 532)

This phase, although still marked by reported symptoms of sleep disturbance and increased alcohol use, was characterised as one of avoidance. Also, during this period a major training exercise was conducted which gave the replacement troops the opportunity to integrate within the unit. The end of the training exercise in week 20 marked the final recovery phase which was characterised by Bartone and Wright as one of integration. As already noted, new replacement troops had by now become incorporated within the unit, and most of the veteran unit members were now looking forward to the future, having accepted the loss. Integration, Bartone and Wright note, was evident in the memorial displays and plaques which have been erected around the post and which they suggest

> . . . may serve the paradoxical function of permitting survivors to turn their conscious attention away from the disturbing event, without contributing to a sense of guilt. Survivors consistently walked past such displays without observing them directly, and yet they also reported strong beliefs that it was right and honorable to preserve the memory of the Gander victims through such memorials. (Bartone & Wright, 1990, p. 534)

Bartone and Wright help to put the phenomenology of PTSD within a social context. They suggest that intrusion and avoidance may manifest in different forms at particular times with different functions, depending on the changing social context. Bartone and Wright's work suggests an initial avoidance phase characterised as numb dedication. This was dominated by a detached almost unconscious avoidance, punctuated by a high frequency of intrusive reminders at both the individual and group level. This was followed by an intrusion phase characterised as anger-betrayal followed by an avoidance phase characterised as stoic resolve and finally integration. Interestingly, Bartone and Wright note that those who maintained avoidance throughout fared less well than those who followed this pattern. These 'total-deniers', as they are referred to, never discussed their feelings and avoided memorial services and other reminders. Their model of group recovery shares important features with Horowitz's description of individual responses to trauma and demonstrates the role social events might play in helping survivors to process events.

CONCLUSION

This chapter has provided an overview of empirical work in the area of psychosocial approaches to post-traumatic reactions. It would seem that personality factors (including previous mental history) are associated with an increased likelihood of developing PTSD, although it does not seem that these factors are necessary for the development of the disorder. What does seem likely, however, is that personality factors help to shape the specific cognitions of and about the traumatic event. Cognitions in turn help to determine the nature and intensity of emotional states, such as guilt, shame, fear, or rage. Emotional states in turn influence the choice of coping strategy and the level of social support received. It would seem to us to be useful in helping to explain the individual differences in the severity and chronicity of reactions of survivors to take into account the role of stimulus, appraisal, personality, state, and activity factors. Although we have tried to integrate the results of previous research and, where possible, specify the interactions of the various components of our model, there are inconsistencies in the literature and there remains a lack of data in several areas. The model may offer a useful heuristic for guiding future research and clinical practice.

SUMMARY POINTS

1. Evidence has been reviewed implicating a role for causal attributions in mediating emotional distress. More internal and controllable attributions for events during a shipping disaster were related to measures of intrusive thoughts, depression and anxiety. External attributions for emotional responses during battle may, in reverse, be associated with less emotional distress.

2. Evidence also has been reviewed for a relationship between history of psychological problems and distress after trauma. It seems that such an effect is strongest when the intensity of the trauma is lower. Such an effect may be related to attributional style although there are some inconsistencies in the literature that remain to be explained.

3. Some little evidence has also been described relating dysfunctional beliefs about emotional expression to emotional distress.

4. There are some suggestions that severe emotional distress at the time of

the trauma may be predictive of later PTSD. Different emotional states such as shame and rage may be related to causal attributions.

5. Some inconsistencies exist in the empirical literature relating to coping and distress. It is suggested that choice of coping can only be evaluated in relation to aspects of the traumatic event such that in some instances emotion-focused coping may be more helpful and in others where action is possible, coping related to problem resolution may relieve distress.

7. Some studies show a protective function for coping by avoidance. Others show a positive relation between avoidance and distress. It is suggested that 'avoidance' is a complex construct which needs further examination. Some types of avoidance may be more blocking of processing than others.

8. Some evidence has been reviewed which indicates a protective function of crisis support following trauma. The effects of social support may be mediated by enhancement of self-esteem and appraisals of control. Needs for social support may vary as a function of time.

Chapter 7

INTERVENTION AND TREATMENT

INTRODUCTION

While any particular mental health service may go for years without having to respond to the psychosocial sequelae of a major event, when they do occur, services are all too often ill-prepared and overwhelmed. Given the well-documented increase in morbidity following traumatic events, mental health services need to plan their crisis intervention and longer-term treatment to meet the needs of survivors well in advance. In the absence of such planning, problems arising from failures in communication and coordination and from competition between rival services have been seen. In Chapter 6 we discussed the role of psychosocial factors in the aetiology and maintenance of post-traumatic stress reactions. Although the processes through which these factors may be related to adjustment are not entirely clear at present, the available evidence does suggest that one aim of intervention should be to provide social support where it is lacking. It is often the role of the social services and volunteers to provide emotional or practical support in the form of outreach programmes, whereas mental health professionals may be employed for crisis intervention and longer-term therapy. These services require coordination. In the present chapter we will outline the various outreach programmes that have been employed as well as the various forms of therapeutic intervention that are commonly used.

Key Topics

Outreach to survivors
Key areas in psychosocial care
Crisis intervention
Treatment strategies
Direct exposure therapies
Cognitive-behavioural therapies
Encouraging activity and social support
Planning for the future
Conclusion

OUTREACH TO SURVIVORS

The death and destruction following major natural disasters calls for massive relief. For example, during the 1988 Armenian earthquake on 7 December 1988, four major cities and 350 villages were destroyed. Estimates indicate that up to 100,000 people were killed and 530,000 people left homeless. Many of these people were refugees who had fled the pogroms perpetrated against Armenians in Azerbaijan and had settled in the earthquake zone (Goenjian et al., 1994). The task of the Armenian Relief Society of the Western United States was to organise and implement a mental health relief programme following the earthquake to treat survivors and to provide training to local mental health workers and teachers (Goenjian et al. 1994). In extreme circumstances, organisations such as the Red Cross move in to give help, offering food, clothing, and shelter. Surrounding communities will be called upon to complement this assistance. Outreach may be required on a massive scale bringing together local agencies as well as international bodies and relief from other countries. Such relief must initially be directed towards life-saving and providing basic human needs for food, water, and shelter.

Much of current thinking about planning for the provision of psychological relief has been shaped from the work carried out in the Netherlands in the 1970s. In the 1970s there were a large number of political hijackings in the Netherlands. Civilians were taken hostage and used in negotiation with the authorities. Several people were killed. In response to the suffering of many of the victims, a strategy for outreach treatment was introduced as early as 1975. Van der Ploeg and Kleijn (1988) outline the outreach programme for hijackings. A group of health care providers, consisting of workers at a local level and at a regional and national level, are brought together immediately subsequent to the hijack. Each victim and their family are visited at home within one week of the hostage's release. They are invited to talk about the events and their immediate reactions in a friendly, permissive atmosphere. They are informed about coping strategies, about 'normal' reactions, and about individuals, organisations, and addresses capable of offering help and after care. After a few weeks, a second call is made in most cases. In addition, the family's general practitioner is asked to offer help and to visit the victim. It is essential, however, that outreach is not forced upon the victims. The Netherlands provided the basic model of intervention. However, much experience has since accumulated (see Adshead, Canterbury, & Rose, 1994).

The *Herald* Assistance Unit

In the UK, the *Herald of Free Enterprise* disaster provided much instructive experience. Following the disaster, the Herald Assistance Unit was set up by Kent Social Services. This service provided, over a 15-month period, a 24-hour telephone help line, a newsletter, proactive outreach visits to the passenger survivors and bereaved, and longer term counselling and group work for the crew survivors and bereaved in Dover. Further therapeutic services were also provided by the local mental health services in Dover. The Departments of Psychology and Psychiatry at the Institute of Psychiatry in London were extensively involved in the assessment of survivors and bereaved for the purposes of compensation and became involved in the treatment of some survivors (Yule & Williams, 1990).

Those affected themselves set up the Herald Families Association as both a pressure group and a support network, and across the UK many volunteers and helping professionals became involved with individual families. Some 30 children under the age of 16 years were on board the *Herald of Free Enterprise*. A few months later, most of the children and their families were also referred to the Psychology Department at the Institute of Psychiatry for assessment for legal purposes and for whatever help could be offered.

It is obviously important that survivors and bereaved are put in touch with outreach programmes and self-help groups. It is inevitable, however, that not all survivors will turn to professional services for help. Blake et al. (1990b) found that one-third of the combat veterans in their study reporting PTSD symptoms did not seek psychiatric help. Some populations, then, may be characterised by hiding the levels of distress although other factors may operate such as the availability of community or religious services and the perceived helpfulness of mental health professionals. In particular, work with women following sexual assault has demonstrated that the majority of survivors do not seek services from mental health professionals, rape crisis centres, or victim assistance programmes (Burnam et al., 1988; Kilpatrick, Saunders, Veronen, Best, & Von, 1987; Kimerling & Calhoun, 1994). Other populations, however, may be more willing to seek help. For example, North, Smith, and Spitznagel (1994) reported that 71% of survivors diagnosed with PTSD following a mass shooting had sought help from a doctor or counsellor, although this still leaves a substantial minority who had not sought help. Although services will not be needed by all survivors, it is important that a support team should make an initial proactive contact in which they assess risk factors and potential needs, and refer on to other services for more specialised therapies where appropriate.

Proactive Contact

Since one of the main features of PTSD is avoidance of trauma-related information, many of the severely affected may not present themselves to the services for help. In most cases, survivors will be people unaccustomed to seeking help for psychological problems, and may believe that they should be able to cope without outside help. For this reason it is recommended that an initial contact is made to all those who have been affected in order to offer the opportunity to talk through their experiences with a member of the support team. This initial contact provides an occasion for a debriefing in which the counsellor provides normalising information about how people react to disaster and gives a further point of contact if later help is required.

Following the Australian bush fires, mental health workers developed a leaflet describing common reactions to major personal crises and indicating when and where to seek further help. The leaflet was adapted and distributed after the Bradford fire, the capsize of the *Herald of Free Enterprise*, the Kings Cross fire, and other recent major disasters (Hodgkinson & Stewart, 1991). This leaflet, now entitled 'Coping with a Personal Crisis', is distributed by the British Red Cross. In the 30-month follow-up of survivors of the *Herald of Free Enterprise* disaster (Yule, Hodgkinson, Joseph, Parkes, & Williams, 1990a) we found that, to the majority, the response team's visit and leaflet were helpful. However, we also found that a small minority recalled that they had been upset by these contacts and judged them to be harmful rather than helpful. What sort of help should be provided?

KEY AREAS IN PSYCHOSOCIAL CARE

Much has been written on psychosocial care. The following discussion will highlight what have been recognised as key areas: the prevention of long-term disorder; the identification of vulnerable individuals; and the provision of specialised services for individuals with more severe and chronic problems (Williams, Joseph, & Yule, 1993). It must be stressed, however, that although there is a considerable amount of expertise developing and many theoretical notions about how to achieve these aims, the concrete evidence about the effectiveness of services, particularly for civilian disasters, is still very sparse. In our model of psychosocial adaptation we have emphasised the temporal sequence of reactions and the recognition that the phenomenology of post-traumatic stress reactions alters over time. This has guided our thinking about what psychological provision should be provided.

Immediate Impact Phase

The immediate necessity for the rescue of survivors may obscure the practical needs of individuals who may have lost all their possessions and lost contact with companions and be ignorant of the exact nature of what happened, including loss of lives. Thus, in this phase, assigned volunteer helpers could be useful in providing information, solving practical problems, and in making contact between those separated in the disaster. Brom and Kleber (1989), in describing a programme of preventative work, point out that the importance of practical help in the early stages is often underestimated. Individuals who are in shock may need quiet to rest and protection from the most intrusive agents of the media. When ready, survivors may benefit from talking through their experiences either individually or in groups and giving expression to the strong feelings that these generate. There is some evidence that talking through at a relatively early stage can protect individuals from a more severe reaction later, although such an intervention needs to be held off until the immediate phase of shock has passed (Hodgkinson & Stewart, 1991).

To minimise the agonising uncertainty that relatives and friends may experience as to the fate of their loved ones who are caught up in the disaster, adequate telephone lines for information and support need to be established and be well publicised. The needs of relatives and friends at this time emphasise the central importance of accurate, up-to-date information being available as the details of what happened and to whom become clearer over time. Staff answering information and help lines should be trained to expect to deal with high levels of anxiety and anger in stressed callers.

Space should be assigned, with relevant services, for relatives who wish to visit the site of the disaster. Helpers assigned to individual families can give support, information, and help to solve the practical problems the family may have. In the case of death, a family member will be required by the police to provide identification. Distressed and worried relatives may be further distressed when asked to give the name of the missing person's dentist so that dental records may be compared. Assigned workers should be available to explain procedures such as this, conveying information about the condition of bodies or the likelihood and time of recovery.

Viewing Human Remains

Bereaved individuals may wish to view the body. It has been suggested that this can be helpful in the process of accepting the reality of a sudden, unexpected death, and in finding out how the person died, even if the body is disfigured or if deterioration has occurred (Cathcart, 1988; Hodgkinson & Stewart, 1991). Singh and Raphael (1981) report that following the Granville train disaster, 36 of 44 bereaved had not seen the body, and of these 22 regretted not viewing. Those who had viewed had lower scores on the GHQ at 15-18 months. However, it may be that in some cases where the body is not recovered for some time and begins to decompose, viewing is harmful rather than helpful.

In a study of those bereaved following the *Herald of Free Enterprise* (Hodgkinson, Joseph, Yule, & Williams, 1993), 22 reported that the body was recovered on the night of the disaster, 13 reported that the body was recovered in the following weeks, and 43 reported that the body was recovered when the ship was righted one month later. Each individual was asked if he or she had viewed the body. Of the 22 respondents answering questions concerning bodies recovered on the first night, 10 viewed and 12 did not: only 1 person who viewed said that they regretted it whereas 5 people who did not view regretted this choice. Of the 13 respondents answering questions concerning bodies recovered in the weeks following the disaster, 5 viewed and 8 did not: 3 people

Table 7.1 Viewing human remains following disaster

	Viewed		Did not view	
	Mean	SD	Mean	SD
Body recovered *on the night:*				
IES intrusion	19.90	8.35	28.67	6.85*
IES avoidance	16.50	10.35	26.59	9.10*
GHQ-28	10.10	7.31	12.83	8.65
Body recovered in *the weeks following disaster:*				
IES intrusion	28.00	4.69	21.50	10.21
IES avoidance	15.40	14.26	17.50	11.55
GHQ-28	19.80	5.63	8.38	7.44*
Body recovered when *the ship was righted:*				
IES intrusion	15.00	11.31	23.81	8.27*
IES avoidance	12.00	11.36	20.62	10.40*
GHQ-28	8.60	5.13	12.14	8.71

* Indicates a significant difference between mean scores. Adapted from Hodgkinson, Joseph, Yule, & Williams (1993).

who viewed regretted doing so whereas only 1 person who did not view regretted this choice. Of the 43 respondents answering questions concerning bodies recovered when the ship was righted, 5 viewed and 37 did not: none of those who viewed regretted doing so whereas 19 people who did not view regretted this choice.

These data were part of the survey carried out 30 months after the disaster at which time survivors also completed the GHQ-28 and the IES (see Chapter 3). Those who viewed relatives' bodies where recovery was made on the first night or on the righting of the ship, reported lower scores on intrusive and avoidant symptoms than those who did not view (see Table 7.1). No differences were found between these groups on the GHQ-28. Although these results would seem to support the benefits of viewing, it may be that those who requested to view had less severe symptoms in the first place or differed in some other uncontrolled way.

In contrast, where body recovery was many weeks following disaster, there were no significant differences on the IES between those who viewed their relatives' bodies and those who chose not to, but those who had viewed had significantly higher GHQ-28 scores. Although these results may be due to the small numbers in this sample and factors specific to these families, it may be that the results are due to the state of the bodies themselves having been washed up on the shore.

Hodgkinson et al. (1993) conclude that although no one should be encouraged to view, what must be ensured is that those who wish to do so are not prevented. Even if the person does not wish to view, it will often be the case that recovered bodies are photographed as part of the procedure for the coroner's report and assigned helpers should explain to relatives that they have the right of access to all documents and should, therefore, have access to photographs at a later stage if they so wish.

On this point, relatives are often unclear of the purposes of an inquest and will probably be unfamiliar with the procedures of a coroner's court. The hearing may actually take place several months after the disaster, and this is often the first time the relatives have an opportunity of finding out exactly how their loved one died. At present it is probably true to say that following most of the recent mass civilian disasters in the UK, the needs of relatives have not been well considered, often provoking further distress in the families.

We have so far placed much emphasis on effective communication systems being set up to benefit survivors and their families. This requires further discussion. By their nature, disasters are often unexpected and the immediate impact phase is one of chaos. The specific details necessary in setting up an effective information network cannot always be planned in advance; however, much can be planned and should be. To avoid endlessly overlapping questioning by staff from different agencies and the loss of vital information, standard forms should be drawn up beforehand which can then be adapted, if necessary, to collect information. Accordingly, thought needs to be given to the storage of the information in an accessible and central system. Arguments on the access to this database and considerations on how best to protect survivors' confidentiality should also be discussed and sorted out at the planning stage. Likewise, thought should be given to the ways of accessing the database for later research and evaluation.

CRISIS INTERVENTION

Crisis intervention has received much attention by clinicians in recent years. It is thought that early intervention facilitates emotional processing, although data are sparse on this. It has been noted that post-traumatic stress responses, once they have become chronic, can be extremely difficult to treat (Watson, 1987). Several writers have commented on this and recommended early crisis intervention. Stein (1977), for example, outlines a model of crisis intervention counselling which includes on-the-scene support with follow-up within two days. Similarly, Mitchell (1983) states that interventions within the first 72 hours are effective in reducing the long-term effects of events in emergency workers and Solomon (1986) recommends confidential debriefing within three days and preferably within 24 hours. The function of early crisis intervention is to support and facilitate emotional release in a safe supportive environment (Raphael, 1986) and has been used extensively with victims of rape (Burgess & Holmstrom, 1974a) and armed robbery (Manton & Talbot, 1991).

Manton and Talbot (1991) outline a system they developed to assist victims of armed hold-ups. First, they describe the process of making initial observations. Following the hold-up, the counsellor aims to arrive at the scene within an hour, during which a sense of the atmosphere is obtained.

> There may be people who appear to be working normally, small groups chatting or comforting each other, individuals who are isolated and in shock, and there may be one or more who is visibly and audibly overwrought. Sometimes there is a complete eerie silence and stillness and at other times there is high-pitched out-of-control laughter or someone crying quietly. You can smell the fear. (Manton & Talbot, 1991, p. 511)

Those identified as being highly overwrought are attended to first and contact established with those locked into their own internal processes. The aim is to see all staff members before they leave for home and provide an initial debriefing.

Debriefing

Manton and Talbot (1991) see the purpose of debriefing as one of providing comfort, defusing the frightening situation, allowing expression of anxieties, and normalising reactions. They describe their approach as 'empathic listening, with awareness that people may experience many different emotions, all of which are valid . . .'. The debriefing session, they believe, '. . . is almost certainly the most important preventative measure and an opportunity for rapport building which will be essential later on' (Manton & Talbot, 1991, p. 512).

> With each individual we start by observing their behaviour—observing whether they want to talk to us or not and keeping that in mind while talking to them. Then asking 'How are you?' and if that brings no response we might say 'Would you be willing to tell me what happened?' which can lead to fairly basic level empathy and deepening if necessary or as appropriate. If they are not willing to talk we can then start to give them information. For example, 'I have been to a lot of hold-ups and talked to a lot of people. It seems that reactions vary, sometimes people feel this and sometimes people feel that and some people find it very hard to talk. Later though you may want to.' Sometimes victims do not fully realise what has hit them until they get home and then there may be no one to talk to. The focus of the discussion is to make it clear to them that we are there to listen. We want to hear how it feels for them. Part of the debriefing session is reassurance, caring for the person, making the event smaller and cutting it down to size without minimising their reaction: accepting, supporting and understanding, and permission giving. (Manton & Talbot, 1991, p. 512).

At this stage, Manton and Talbot (1991) note there may be feelings of guilt over letting others down which can become projected as anger directed at the organisation. However, they argue that although at this stage it is useful to empathise with these feelings it may not be appropriate to help the victim to change the projection. 'Victims need to be able to express and vent their feelings. It is a normal response, albeit inappropriately placed' (Manton & Talbot, 1991; p. 512).

Manton and Talbot (1991) note that following armed hold-ups there are issues about returning to work and taking medication that victims need to be aware of. Issues of information giving will be central to the debriefing of survivors of all traumatic events. However, they raise the issue of how this information is presented and argue that it should be done permissively and not as advice. The intervention continues the next day and is seen as a continuation of the previous day. Everyone is seen individually if required or perhaps in small groups, depending on various factors such as the size and cohesiveness of the existing group. Here, Manton and Talbot (1991) note that there are a variety of reactions which may be observed, some of which are coloured by the individuals' previous history or their current life situation. They argue that follow-up is essential in order to identify those at risk of further problems.

Hayman and Scaturo (1993) outline a protocol for debriefing military personnel, although there are clear applications of their protocol to other populations as well. The first general guideline from their procedure is that debriefing should begin as soon as possible so as to help defuse the intensity of reactions and prevent negative coping behaviours from becoming habitual. This last point is particularly important as it is crucial for survivors to be able to make effective use of their social support networks. Second, it is recommended that standardised screening instruments are employed so as to facilitate referral for treatment. Third, they maintain that, throughout the debriefing process, it is essential to reinforce the expectation of returning to pre-combat levels of psychosocial functioning. Fourth, they recommend the use of group sessions for married couples, which might include exploration of the impact of separation and relationship skills enhancement. They also emphasise that the debriefing should proceed at a speed comfortable for the participants. The protocol involves 12 sessions, beginning with a clarification of the purposes of debriefing and the nature of emotional reactions through to the exploration of the personal impact of combat and homecoming, through to learning about managing moods and resolving current life stressors, and finally, facilitating the impact of the group termination (Hayman and Scaturo, 1993).

However, despite the widespread use of debriefing there remains relatively little evidence for its efficacy. One study examined 137 consecutive admissions to a burns unit. Patients completed a battery of standardised self-report measures on admission and were randomly allocated to either a psychological debriefing group or a control group which received no intervention. Three months later most of the 137 were interviewed in their homes where they again completed several self-report measures. It was found that debriefing did not prevent psychological sequelae but it was perceived to be useful by most of those who received it. Furthermore, those who received debriefing were more likely to continue with the research, a finding which the authors suggest points to the important role of debriefing in helping to engage patients in a more comprehensive treatment package (Bisson, Jenkins, & Bannister, in press). Debriefing involves some kind of exposure to the trauma-related stimuli. According to Fairbank and Nicholson (1987) and van der Kolk, Boyd, Krystal, and Greenberg (1984b), exposure to stimuli related to the trauma is an essential part of treatment. But unlike other treatment intervention strategies which may form part of longer-term support services, i.e., systematic desensitisation and implosive therapy, and which are also based on the principle of exposure, debriefing is concerned with prevention rather than the amelioration of symptoms.

Long-term Support Services

Building on the experiences of services after the Bradford football stadium fire, Kent Social Services quickly set up a longer term response and support team for survivors and relatives from the *Herald of Free Enterprise* disaster. It has now been recommended (Department of Health, 1990) that such a support service should be set up and financed for at least two years following a disaster. As discussed earlier, there is evidence that many survivors remain highly symptomatic even after this time. Indeed, distressed people may still present to services for the first time years after the disaster. Although services will not be needed by all survivors, it is important that a support team should make an initial proactive contact in which they assess risk factors and potential needs, and refer on to other services for more specialised therapies where appropriate.

TREATMENT STRATEGIES

For the mental health professional involved in diagnosis, it becomes necessary to enquire about a range of the clients' emotions and behaviours in order to make a complete assessment. Often the length of time required to capture the full picture is not available, or the client may be reluctant to undergo such a lengthy procedure involving many personal questions. It is necessary, therefore, for mental health professionals to be aware of the range of possible difficulties and the various measurement instruments available. Once the clinician has clearly identified what the focus of treatment is to be, he or she will be in a better position to select the most efficacious method of treatment.

Since the inclusion of PTSD in the diagnostic literature, there have been numerous descriptive summaries of various treatment approaches to PTSD. However, there remains relatively little empirical information concerning the effectiveness of psychological interventions. In addition, much of the work has been with Vietnam veterans and findings may not always generalise to survivors of civilian trauma. However, the work reviewed in Chapter 6 offers evidence that although exposure to a traumatic event is the necessary aetiological factor in the development of PTSD, other psychosocial variables are involved in the development of post-traumatic stress reactions.

Emotional processing in survivors of traumatic events is thought to be a normal adaptation process although processing can be excessively prolonged or even blocked. This process is determined by identifiable factors. Although, it is acknowledged that the role of other variables may be small, particularly following extremely traumatic events, what is important is the fact that they are modifiable. Thus, there is scope for the treatment of distressed individuals. Our model suggests a conceptual framework for planning therapeutic interventions with survivors with post-traumatic stress reactions.

The model contains different components of the adaptation process where it may be possible to intervene:

- promoting re-exposure to the event and to stimuli associated with the event for reappraisal;
- promoting reappraisal of the traumatic experience and its meanings and in promoting reappraisal of the emotional states to which appraisals give rise;
- promoting the direct reduction of emotional arousal;
- promoting helpful coping strategies to deal with emotional arousal; and
- promoting the reviewing of previously held cognitive styles and rules for living, some of which may be maintaining symptoms through blocking re-exposure, others of which may determine primary traumatic appraisal.

The choice of strategy can be determined by the therapist's formulation of the role played by each factor in an individual case. In some cases, stimulus factors may predominate and the individual's needs may best be met by the use of direct exposure techniques (DETs) (Richards & Rose, 1991) which help the survivor to confront the traumatic event. However, given our formulation of stress reactions in terms of blocked processing, the task for the clinician may be the identification of the block to permit natural processes (completion tendency) to continue rather than the indiscriminate treatment of each and every client within an exposure framework.

The importance of such flexibility within an overall conceptualisation echoes the conclusions of McFarlane (1994) who points to the impact of allegiance to therapeutic models in the evaluation of their efficacy and the degree of partiality which is prominent in psychotherapy. Space precludes an exhaustive discussion of treatment options. Our choice is determined by methods that have most empirical support.

DIRECT EXPOSURE THERAPIES

DET techniques have received the most attention by researchers and can be grouped according to the medium of exposure (imaginal vs in vivo), the length of exposure (short vs long), and the amount of arousal induced by the exposure (low vs high) (Rothbaum & Foa, 1992).

Systematic Desensitisation

When the length of exposure is short and the amount of arousal is low it is termed systematic desensitisation. Both forms of systematic desensitisation were based on the conditioning of incompatible relaxation responses with traumatic stimuli (although this explanation of treatment effects has since been challenged). The client is taught a formal relaxation technique and later employs this technique while a graduated series of increasingly anxiety-provoking imaginal or in vivo cues are presented. By remaining relaxed as successive cues are presented, the client learns to associate the cues with feelings of relaxation rather than anxiety (Lyons & Keane, 1989). Systematic desensitisation has been used with combat veterans with some success (e.g., Bowen & Lambert, 1986). Lyons and Keane (1989), however, note that in certain cases desensitisation may not be feasible:

> Memories of combat may be so potent that they override both the therapist's attempts to present very gradual exposure and the patient's capacity to remain relaxed. For such cases, implosive therapy may be the treatment of choice. (Lyons & Keane, 1989, p. 138).

Implosive Therapy

In contrast to systematic desensitisation, which is based on classical conditioning theory, implosive therapy is based on an operant extinction model (Stampfl & Levis, 1967). Implosive therapy involves prolonged exposure to a stimulus during which time high levels of arousal are induced. In practice, clinicians often employ a graded prolonged exposure procedure in which cues are presented in increasing order of threat. The client is exposed to trauma-related cues until there is a reduction in anxiety associated with the cues (Lyons & Keane, 1989). Implosive therapy has been used with some success with adults (e.g., Black & Keane, 1982; Fairbank, Gross, & Keane, 1983a; Fairbank & Keane, 1982; Keane & Kaloupek, 1982), and with children (Saigh, 1987). For example, in the Keane and Kaloupek (1982) study, a 36-year-old Vietnam veteran was treated for the anxiety-related symptoms of PTSD. Therapy consisted of 19 sessions over a 22-day inpatient hospitalisation. The purpose of their study was to test the efficacy of treating a combat-related disorder by imaginally presenting the aversive events surrounding the patient's trauma.

The patient frequently experienced nightmares and flashbacks of three events from Vietnam. For example, one recurrent scene was the death of a buddy in an ambush attack. Measures included daily anxiety ratings, hours of sleep, frequency of nightmares and flashbacks. Following a three-day baseline period, treatment consisted of the presentation of a scene preceded by 10 minutes of relaxation. There was a reduction in anxiety as well as an overall improvement which was maintained over a 12-month period. Keane and Kaloupek (1982) concluded that, for some patients at least, imaginal flooding was an effective treatment.

Gersons (1989) gives case illustrations of treatment with two police officers who had been involved in a shooting incident. Treatment consisted of, first, recalling to mind every detail of the traumatic event. Gersons notes that the use of newspaper articles and photographs are helpful at this stage. Relaxation and closing one's eyes is beneficial in inducing a trance-like state in which experiences can be vividly recalled. The stimulation of re-experiencing the event helps release hidden emotions which, Gersons notes, is often a totally new experience for 'very walled-off' officers. Five to ten sessions, Gersons reports, can be enough to work through all the affects associated with the event, and the PTSD symptoms steadily disappear, although follow-up therapy may be necessary in certain cases. Other uncontrolled single case studies for a variety of types of traumatic event are reported by Richards and Rose (1991) who emphasise the importance of self-exposure in homework assignments, incorporating the use of tape-recorded imaginal exposure sessions and in-vivo exposure exercises to promote extinction. Richards, Lovell, and Marks (1994) have also studied the relative merits of imaginal and in-vivo exposure, finding that in-vivo exposure to trauma-related stimuli was of advantage only for the amelioration of phobic anxiety, in some cases. The authors report improvement in focal PTSD symptoms, measures of general psychiatric well-being and in work and social adjustment. However, self-reported depression before treatment was low in this group. Treatment gains reported were highly significant (65–80% reduction) and were maintained over one year's follow-up.

Implosive therapy has also been used in the treatment of an adult victim of sexual abuse (Rychtarik, Silverman, & Van Landingham, 1984).

A cautionary note is sounded by Pitman et al. (1991). These authors report six illustrative case vignettes where unforeseen complications have arisen during prolonged exposure. They suggest that concurrent problems such as depression and alcohol abuse may lead to emotional problems such as panic and guilt which do not extinguish with exposure, pointing to the importance of other therapeutic methods being needed. It is sometimes unclear to what extent therapists are using a more complex therapeutic regime from their descriptions. Thompson, Charlton, Kerry, Lee, and Turner (1995), for example, describe their open trial under the rubric of 'deconditioning' although explicitly employing cognitive as well as behavioural exposure methods.

The use of these exposure techniques is illustrated in the case of David,

CASE HISTORY 10

(An adult case involving exposure therapy)

David is a 29-year-old lecturer in design and technology who also runs a successful computer graphics consultancy. He had a good relationship with his long-standing partner and they enjoyed a very comfortable lifestyle until this was shattered in a boating accident. They were celebrating with friends on a river boat when, late at night, the boat was sunk in collision with a barge. David and his partner were among those who survived.

At first, he felt lucky to be alive, but then he was haunted with guilt that he had not done enough to help his partner, nor managed to save any of his friends who had drowned. He found it very difficult to sleep and was constantly fending off intrusive images of what had happened to him when he was under the water. On one occasion, he was travelling home on a night bus. As the bus crossed a bridge over a river, he saw lights reflecting off the surface of the water and immediately he had a terrifying flashback in which he believed that he was back on the boat as it went under. It took him many hours to calm down and get back in touch with reality.

He found great difficulty concentrating at work and his consultancy business foundered. He began smoking and drinking a great deal, to the point that he was making himself ill. He went to a counsellor for a couple of sessions but did not engage. He was referred for treatment over a year after the accident.

After taking a full and careful history, including a detailed account of his experiences during the accident, David was offered exposure therapy along the lines described by Richards and Rose (1991). It was explained to him that by avoiding dealing with his emotional reactions, the memories remained and interfered with his recovery. While confronting the memories in detail would probably be painful, he should experience a lowering of tension and anxiety and a greater ability to control his reactions. It was emphasised that the treatment would not rid him of the memories as they were now an important part of him. Rather, he would be able to control his reactions to them.

In the first session, he was seated comfortably and the tape recorder was switched on. He was then asked to describe in detail, in the first person present tense, as if it was happening currently, precisely what happened in the accident. He was asked to say what he was seeing, hearing, feeling, tasting, smelling, and so on, as well as what he was thinking and the emotional reactions he was having. What then happened was remarkable. David began in a steady voice describing how they had gone on board the boat and settled to have a drink in the bar as the boat pulled out into the river. They were laughing, joking, and relaxing when suddenly they felt a great bump and heard the noise of the two vessels tearing against each other. Immediately, everything went dark as the lights went out and all he could see was the reflections of lights from the shore on the water pouring in through the smashed windows. As he described all this, so his demeanour changed. His descriptions were graphic, but so was his body language. As he recalled pulling himself through a smashed window, he writhed in his chair; as he recalled hitting the bottom of the river and then surfacing to see people carried away on the current, he began to shiver with cold and almost shake off the water. He rated his anxiety as near maximum while recounting this.

At the end of more than an hour, he was given the recording of the session to take home and asked to listen to it daily. He managed to do so about four times in the week before the second session. Then, he was able to expose himself in imagination to the whole episode, but reporting a much lower level of anxiety. The therapist watched his reactions intently and any time that it appeared that David was blocking on a part of the experience or was otherwise skipping over it, he would ask David to go back to that section and conjure up the image in greater detail. In this way, all the worst memories were confronted and after eight sessions David's levels of distress were lowered to within normal, acceptable levels.

someone who survived a very unpleasant boating disaster. It illustrates how lengthy exposure sessions can initially induce strong, unpleasant emotions which then habituate with repeated exposure (Case History 10).

Children

Although the adult literature is increasingly full of examples of the successful application of behaviour therapy to reduce intrusive thoughts, startle reaction, and phobic and avoidance behaviour, there is little information available on children. One study is, however, reported by Saigh (1986) of the in-vitro flooding treatment of PTSD exhibited by a $6\frac{1}{2}$-year-old Lebanese boy who had been traumatised by a bomb blast. Two years after the event, he suffered nightmares, intrusive thoughts and avoided areas associated with the bombing. Four scenes were successfully worked on in therapy and rapid improvement was obtained in 10 sessions, and improvement was maintained over six months. Saigh (1986) notes that earlier attempts to treat other children with systematic desensitisation failed, and in this case, each session began with 15 minutes of relaxation followed by 24 minutes of flooding. This extended exposure to the fear-inducing stimuli fits in well with Rachman's (1980) views on factors that accelerate successful emotional processing.

It is trickier using exposure therapy with children and adolescents because of the need to ensure that one has informed consent for any treatment and especially for ones which are, in part, unpleasant initially. The rationale is described more fully elsewhere (Saigh, Yule, & Inamdar, 1996). As with interventions with adults, there are a number of successful case studies with children being published but, as yet, no systematic, randomised controlled trials. Work with groups of children has been described and there is some evidence that group approaches to debriefing children after accidents and disasters can be successful.

COGNITIVE-BEHAVIOURAL THERAPIES

The difficulties some clients have in dealing with exposure has led to the suggestion that anxiety management techniques (AMT) (Fairbank & Nicholson, 1987) might be used to help the survivors improve their management of high anxiety and other symptoms. Lyons and Keane (1989) conclude that implosive therapy must be embedded in a strong and supportive therapeutic relationship, and that it appears to be most effective when used in conjunction with skill-building techniques aimed at developing coping skills. Kilpatrick and Veronen (1983) have described a 4–6-hour treatment package for survivors of rape. The package includes behavioural procedures with elements of rape crisis counselling which attempt to promote realistic beliefs and adaptive coping skills.

Meichenbaum (1993) presents detailed instructions for carrying out Stress Innoculation Training (SIT), a therapy consisting of 8–14 sessions in individual and group formats. The therapy protocol has three phases: (1) an educational stage in which the client is introduced to the nature of dysfunctional emotions and their origins; (2) a skills acquisition stage in which coping strategies are introduced in relation to the tripartite model of emotions (physiological, behavioural, and cognitive-emotional); (3) a stage in which the client is helped to apply the training via imagery rehearsal, role-playing, and graded in-vivo exposure.

Cognitive Therapy

Cognitive-behavioural theorists propose that emotional disorders, including anxiety and depression, stem from dysfunctional interpretations of environmental events. Therapy aimed at challenging these interpretations should therefore lead to a change in emotional state. There is a considerable body of outcome research which suggests that cognitive therapy (CT) is effective in comparisons with control therapies for depression (see Hollon, Shelton, & Davis, 1993, for a review) and anxiety disorders (see Chambless & Gillis, 1993, for a review). The high level of success recently reported for the treatment of panic disorder by Clark (1986, 1991) should have clear implications for the treatment of PTSD in view of the overlap in symptomatology. Although there has been little application of CT to PTSD to date, the theoretical approach of CT with its emphasis upon psychoeducation and the acquisition of skills lends itself well to a condition which, as we have seen, may have manifold components with global impact upon the individual's functioning. CT's emphasis is upon the challenging of appraisals and the identification of dysfunctional attitudes that may block processing. (See Treatment 1.)

The identification of psychological vulnerability factors has much implication for therapeutic intervention. For example, causal attributions for trauma-related experience may be connected to emotional states and, as we have outlined earlier in Chapter 6, may be one of the possible mechanisms that may operate to impede or promote emotional processing. If this is true, then there are implications for therapeutic intervention based on attributional style therapy (Layden, 1982). The direction of attributional change will, however, depend on individual circumstances insofar as realistic causal attributions may involve a shift in the direction of greater or less personal controllability (Fösterling, 1985). (See Treatment 2.)

An important methodological issue in the cognitive-behavioural therapies (CBTs) is the degree to which it is necessary to intervene in modifying cognitions to achieve therapeutic ends. Exposure practitioners would assert that cognitions change spontaneously as Horowitz's theory of a 'completion tendency' would perhaps also propose. An interesting variant of CBT called 'Imagery Rescripting' has been described by Smucker, Dancu, Foa, and

TREATMENT 1

(See Case History 1, p. 2)

Pauline had spent some sessions with a CPN prior to referral in which she had talked about the trauma and reported feeling less distressed now when talking about it. This was evidenced by the first interview and Pauline's relatively low avoidance score on the IES, although the score for intrusive experiences was still high. It was therefore decided to start treatment within a cognitive model and to direct intervention at cognitions and symptoms that seemed to reflect event appraisals. Pauline was introduced to the cognitive model on the first sessions and the link was made between her expectation of future catastrophe and her situational anxiety, her depression and pessimism about the future. Pauline began making written records of her 'automatic thoughts' associated with negative emotions, day to day. We became aware of worries that she would have a panic attack in social situations and, when travelling, with thoughts such as 'what will people think?' and 'I'm out of control'. These self-observations led to cognitive intervention addressing panic. At one stage Pauline and her therapist ran together up three flights of stairs to create autonomic arousal. They then sat quietly together and noticed Pauline's relative difficulty in dealing with this physical activation leading to her relative slowness at calming down. An exposure hierarchy was drawn up, including physical activity such as running, medical situations and social situations especially giving a presentation at work, the latter being a problem prior to the trauma. Pauline was also trained in slowed breathing to cope with panic and to use this skill in anxiety-provoking situations. An exploration of Pauline's anger with other people and her alienation from them led to a full examination of her veiws about friendship and the discovery of black and white thinking in this area (viz., if you do not support me all the time you have let me down). A lengthy and important examination of 'What's going to happen next?' led to a changed view of the predominance of adverse events, taking her life as a whole although the fear remained at a lower level of intensity. Discussion of ending sessions after about six months led to a recurrence of worries about future adversity and inability to cope alone. At termination, Pauline was revealing frequent and horrifying images of hospital-isation, being helpless, unable to communicate, staff ignoring her, and of her being unable to cope, screaming and resisting. Some attempts to use both exposure and restructuring of imagery were made but these were relatively unsuccessful. Pauline was not prepared to overcome avoidance of medical situations at present and therapy was terminated. Pauline was considerably less depressed and anxious at termination. There remained some problems, especially with fears of hospitalisation, which maintained her fear of repetition but it was hoped that Pauline had the tools to deal with these if and when she wanted to.

Niederee (1995) which aims to achieve change in deep schemas for PTSD adult survivors of sexual abuse. The procedure combines some initial pro-longed exposure with the addition of a modification procedure in which the abusive imagery is altered to introduce mastery and complete the memory with a more positive ending. Throughout the imagery rescripting, dysfunctional schemas underlying abuse cognitions are identified and challenged, the thera-pist going in and out of the image to work on cognitions or go back to the image. Smucker is clear to point out, however, that modifications to the script follow the client's own wishes and are not directed by the therapist who plays a facilitative role, asking questions to prompt the new imagery. The 10 sessions,

TREATMENT 2

Roy is a 35-year-old single man, currently unemployed and cohabiting with a partner. Roy had suffered a depressive reaction when a successful career in business had ended in bankcruptcy in the economic recession. Both Roy and his twin sister had suffered severe psychological difficulties at this time and, associated with severe symptoms, he began to remember incidences of repeated sexual, physical, and emotional abuse in childhood. These memories which were intrusive and highly disturbing were corroborated by two out of his three siblings.

Roy came into therapy wanting to address these traumatic experiences in the past which he felt were holding him back from full recovery and affecting his confidence and his relationships. After some initial sessions in which he was introduced to the cognitive model and the role of avoidance in maintaining beliefs and symptoms and problems, one perceived major block was discovered, namely his attitude to expressed emotion. Roy thought emotions were bad and tended to present himself to others, including his therapist, in a cheerful, confident manner while feeling depressed and anxious inside. He failed to confide in others who had commented that they did not really know him. This 'avoidance' had the result of maintaining his fear that he was unlovable and that others would reject him if they got to know him intimately. In order to deal with these fears, therefore, therapy proceeded to embark on an exploration of his childhood experiences as perceived and remembered as a way of unlocking the emotions and allowing processing to occur. Roy was able progressively to give way to feelings in sessions and to explore the associated cognitions. Prominantly emerged a need for explanation: Why did the abuse happen? The answers that he gave to this question were that his father did not love him and that he was unlovable and that his father was a monster. Since he also loved his father he was unable to hold on to the external attribution. He was enraged by his father's continuing denial of his behaviour which he linked in his mind to being loved and being unlovable: if his father loved him he would admit to his offences. An important discussion of the functions of denial led to a lessening of his hopeless need for validation and to a more complex understanding of human motivation and therefore to the implications he can read into the behaviour about himself.

---

each lasting 90 minutes, also involve the practice of self-comforting or 'nurturing' imagery. Initial outcome results in comparison with SIT are yielding comparable effects (Smucker et al., 1995).

Comparative Outcome Studies

Studies comparing the effects of different therapies are few in the literature. Brom, Kleber, and Defares (1989) compared the effects of brief psychodynamic therapy, hypnotherapy and desensitisation and a waiting-for-therapy-control condition in a group of 112 adults, mainly female and suffering from traumatic bereavements. All treatments were effective in comparison with waiting. At three months' follow-up, psychotherapy had more impact upon avoidant symptoms, desensitisation upon intrusion.

Boudewyns and Hyer (1990) compared implosive therapy and counselling for Vietnam veterans. Both treatments were equally effective at the end of treatment but implosive therapy produced a stronger effect upon overall adjustment at three months' follow-up. Foa, Rothbaum, Riggs, and Murdock (1991) compared implosive therapy, SIT, counselling and waiting-for-therapy in rape survivors. They found that at the end of therapy, SIT was superior in reducing symptoms but at three months' follow-up, the implosion group was superior to both SIT and counselling on all measures. Much more work needs to be done on establishing the relative merits of different interventions for different types of trauma, different combinations of problem, and for different durations after the event.

Eye-movement Desensitisation and Reprocessing Therapy

Shapiro (1995) describes the serendipitous discovery and development of eye-movement desensitisation and reprocessing therapy (EMDR), which is widely practised as a rapid treatment for the symptoms of PTSD (see Box 7.1). Shapiro herself had been troubled by intrusive thoughts until one day, out jogging, she noticed they began to diminish. She linked this to rapid movements of her eyes. She then tried to conjure up the disturbing thoughts and found that they were not so disturbing. She asked colleagues to try pairing eye movements with thinking disturbing thoughts and they too found that the strength of the images waned. She then tried out this technique carefully with clients who had PTSD. The early case studies she reported showed people with distressing intrusive thoughts and images getting symptomatic relief in as little as a single one-hour session. Later, she found that other, non-specific, factors in therapy had to be given greater emphasis and so EMDR was born.

In the session, clients are asked to conjure up their distressing scene and then to follow the therapist's finger with their eyes. The therapist moves the finger across the field of vision at a rapid rate and after 20 or more passes, asks the clients to rest. The clients ask for feedback about what has happened to the image and at various points the clients are asked to rate subjective distress on a 10-point scale. Clients often report that the image changes, more detail may be recalled and then the image fades while, simultaneously, the distress goes down. The therapist, unlike in more orthodox cognitive and exposure therapies, does not interrogate the clients for details or try to make new connections between the changing images and other aspects of the traumatic event.

There have been many case examples and clinical studies published that claim extraordinarily good results, but there is a lack of larger scale studies involving double blind randomised controls and long-term follow-up (see Smith and Yule, in press, for a review). But this is a familiar story in psychotherapy research. More worrying is that there is no clear model of why this inherently implausible therapy should work at all. Is it that the eye-movement procedure permits the subjects to expose themselves in imagination and that it is exposure and habituation that are the processes whereby the treatment is effective? Or is it that the eye movements do somehow have a facilitating or inhibiting effect within the central nervous system? At present, the jury is out.

Box 7.1   Eye Movement Desensitisation and Reprocessing Therapy (EMDR)

Recently, Eye Movement Desensitisation and Reprocessing Therapy (EMDR) has been introduced as a treatment for intrusive traumatic memories (Shapiro, 1989a, 1989b) and some support for its clinical effectiveness has begun to accumulate (Marquis, 1991; Puk, 1991; Wolpe & Abrams, 1991; Vaughan, Wiese, Gold, & Tarrier, 1994) although other studies have not found it to be effective (Jensen, 1994) and the mechanisms underlying this treatment remain unclear (Dyck, 1993).

The EMDR procedure involves the client creating in his or her mind a visual image of the traumatic event and then isolating a word or phrase which represents a belief about the visual image. For example, 'I am helpless', or 'I have no control' (Shapiro, 1989b, p.204). The client then repeats these phrases while bilateral saccadic eye movements are induced by following the clinician's fingers which are moved rapidly across the visual field. Subsequently, negative belief statements are replaced by alternative positive belief statements such as 'I have control', 'I am worthy' (Shapiro, 1989b, p. 204) while the clinician again induces bilateral saccadic eye movements.

What is emerging is that the eye movements themselves may not be a necessary component of the procedure. Renfrey and Spates (1994) found that eye movement versus fixating a blinking light were equally effective in reducing PTSD.

Clearly, any procedure that seems to reduce suffering quickly and inexpensively even in a minority of cases is worthy of further investigation. If one could identify suitable candidates for EMDR then this would potentially save a great deal of suffering and also save on the scarce resource of experienced therapists.

There are other rapid treatment techniques which make extravagant claims for their efficacy in treating PTSD. Sometimes, they are merely variants on exposure therapy that emphasise one particular facet of the treatment. Other rapid treatments have little or no theoretical rationale and cannot be recommended until proper outcome studies have been undertaken. People with PTSD are often vulnerable to promises of rapid cures and the therapeutic community owes them a duty of care that incorporates a healthy scepticism towards brief, miraculous interventions. (See Treatment 3.)

Group Therapy

Many workers in the field of disaster research are agreed that group debriefing sessions are desirable, and that they reduce later morbidity (Stallard & Law, 1993; Yule & Udwin, 1991). If this is true, the explanation may be that de-briefing sessions expose individuals to information of how others react to the same stimuli. Yule and Williams (1990) note that the child survivors of the *Herald of Free Enterprise* disaster who attended group meetings were clear that merely being together was helpful. However, Yule and Williams (1990) also note that

TREATMENT 3

(Geoff: treated by EMDR)

Geoff, aged 10, was referred for treatment three years after he had been badly frightened in an accident in which the car he was seated in was hit from the side by another car, causing quite a bit of damage but no injury to the occupants. Geoff though he was going to be badly hurt, if not killed. Shortly afterwards, Geoff started to have nightmares and kept waking in the night. There were times when he was scared to sleep. He kept seeing pictures of the other car that hit them. He also developed a very strong fear of death.

When seen, he still had worries about travelling by car. He still saw recurring pictures of what happened and these were upsetting. His nightmares occurred at least once per week. He has occasionally had flashbacks when it felt as if it was all happening all over again. He did not like watching programmes on television that involve car crashes. He felt shaky and scared. He often had to sleep in his parents' bed. He had become much more aware of dangers when he was in a car or walking on a pavement. He tried to stay in the middle of the seat when in the car.

He said that he did not feel miserable or depressed, but was anxious. He worried about death. He got upset by sudden loud noises. Geoff completed some questionnaires and scored as follows:

Scale	July	September
Impact of Events	32	2
Birleson Depression	14	6
Child Anxiety	21	1

There were no concerns about his development prior to the accident. It was followed immediately by the appearance of many symptoms of stress reactions and anxiety. As a direct consequence of the accident, Geoff developed a positive psychiatric disorder, namely a Post-Traumatic Stress Disorder of moderate severity but which ran a chronic course and he still met criteria for the diagnosis three-and-a-half years later.

Geoff agreed to try EMDR. In the first session, after the first set of eye movements while he was visualising the accident, he was experiencing a high level of distress but he also began to recall considerable detail of what had happened three years previously. He could describe the type of clothing worn by workmen who were working at the other side of the place they were parked. He could describe details of what his mother and brother did and said at the time of the accident—details that appeared to have been inaccessible to him when he first described the accident to the therapist. With successive exposures and eye movements, he recalled more detail and his subjective distress subsided. Gains made in the clinic generalised to the home.

Following only two sessions of 'Eye-Movement Desensitisation and Reprocessing', there was a remarkable drop in the level of reported symptoms, as can be seen in the table of scores. His mother confirmed that he was greatly improved and he no longer met criteria for a diagnosis of PTSD.

...In the children's group, they were allowed to express their sadness and fears and so learn that others shared similar reactions. They were encouraged to think of strategies for coping and out of the discussions emerged some practical ways of dealing with their problems. In the adults group, parents were also relieved to learn that some of the uncharacteristic behaviours shown by their own children were also exhibited by others. They were able to discuss how to react to problems presented by their children and, lastly but not least, they were able to face their own reactions to the disaster and share these. (Yule & Williams, 1990, p. 292)

Thus, a situation that provides consensual information seems to be welcomed by survivors. From a more cognitive point of view it may be that group experiences enable people to undergo a shift in their attributional patterns. However, it is also possible that debriefing may, depending on individual circumstances, foster an attributional pattern that would serve to increase a person's emotional distress. The concern must be to help the survivor resolve issues of meaning in a way that is not only satisfactory but is also realistic as to the situation.

Resick and Schnicke (1992) report a controlled evaluation of a variant of CT called Cognitive Processing Therapy carried out in a group format with survivors of rape. The therapy consisted of 12 sessions, each lasting 90 minutes. Following some educational and 'exposure' sessions in which clients wrote and experienced the emotions of the trauma, subsequent sessions dealt with cognitive aspects: self-blame and then issues of safety, trust, power, esteem, and intimacy. Written materials addressing these themes were used. In a comparison with a waiting list group, individuals who experienced the group therapy showed significantly reduced PTSD and other symptoms, and improved social adjustment post-therapy.

Children

Therapeutic intervention for child victims of disaster has often been aimed at alleviating the immediate distress of traumatic experiences with counselling techniques. Some workers have found that adjustment may be facilitated through a more guided cognitive and emotional re-experiencing, restructuring and re-enacting of the disaster under controlled circumstances (Galante & Foa, 1986; Pynoos & Eth, 1986). Going over what happened in this way is likely to result in the child changing his or her causal attributions for particular events. Therefore, attribution style therapy may also be beneficial for children suffering from post-traumatic reactions. A similar argument is presented by Stallard and Law (1993) who carried out a group debriefing with school pupils who had been involved in a minibus accident. They found debriefing was effective in reducing intrusive thoughts.

Changing beliefs

The evidence would suggest that some beliefs are more adaptive than others; for example, those that help to maintain a sense of control and protect self-esteem. However, the clinician is faced with the question of whether it is appropriate to encourage such beliefs when they are unrealistic (Calhoun &

Tedeschi, 1991). While discussing the role of attribution therapy, it is important to note the role of the therapist. Milgram (1986) makes the interesting point that the framework within which therapy takes place is in itself important. He suggests that efficacious treatment of PTSD requires the patient to take responsibility for the progress of his or her own therapy. It is probably true to say that most therapists actively discourage self-blame. However, in her discussion of reactions to rape, Janoff-Bulman (1979) distinguishes between characterological self-blame (attributions to aspects of the self that cannot be changed), versus behavioural self-blame (attributions to aspects of the self that can be changed). She suggests that behavioural self-blame is related to better recovery because it is associated with a sense of future control and, therefore, therapeutic intervention that discourages all self-blame could actually be harmful. However, evidence would suggest that people do not always seem to make the distinction between characterological and behavioural self-blame (Frazier & Schauben, 1994).

ENCOURAGING ACTIVITY AND SOCIAL SUPPORT

Survivors who are overwhelmed with traumatic recollections may benefit from planning activities and structuring their day. Activity planning can serve various functions: to learn control and mastery of distress which may have useful impact upon self-esteem and depression and provide an alternative to drug-use; to address practical problems that may have been overlooked because of the emotional experience (also impacting upon depression and self-esteem and preventing further cascade of disaster); to establish a 'normal' pattern of exposure and avoidance which is managable; to aid integration with family or other social network; to engender hope that life can go on.

Traumatic events often interfere with the normal functioning of social support networks through the death of others, or through disruptions caused by responses to the event (Solomon, 1986). For example, McFarlane (1987) showed that families who had been exposed to the Australian bush fires were characterised by increased levels of irritability and fighting.

Others have, however, commented that communality can increase in the aftermath of disaster (Wright, Ursano, Bartone, & Ingraham, 1990). There is evidence that social support is related to later post-traumatic symptoms. In cases where a low level of social support is identified, intervention aimed at increasing support may be possible. As has been argued earlier, attribution therapy may be feasible in helping survivors deal with specific emotional states such as guilt or shame that may block processing. Such emotional states, it is believed, may also lead to social withdrawal and hence making little use of coping strategies that rely on family and friends. Thus, the alleviation of these feelings may lead to increased support seeking. There is good evidence that higher levels of support received are predictive of later adjustment.

TREATMENT 4

(See Case History 4, p. 22)

Sarah's problems in relating with others was a problem that frequently recurred in therapy. Either she reported feeling very irritable and angry and then guilty about feeling that way or else she was afraid of meeting people and dealing with other people's questions about her problems which added to her general avoidance. Initially we tried getting Sarah to accept her feelings, as components of her reaction to the trauma that anyone would experience, to reduce the guilt. How bad was it to be irritable and snappy, given the full range of bad behaviours a person might engage in? Was her boyfriend unable to deal with it and understand how she felt, given her totally unwanted and unbidden state of dependence? We tackled what might happen if she met someone in the street, role-played how she could deflect intrusive enquiries if she wanted to and looked at her feelings of shame that she still had emotional problems, three years after the accident. Examining her angry feelings further we found that Sarah was angry with her sister for not helping her more and angry that she had to help others with *their* feelings of distress about her problems. They did not understand: they infantilised her and gave her advice or they failed to appreciate the emotional impact of her disabilities and did not see how vulnerable and helpless she felt and how hard she was trying to combat her problems. This exploration led us into thinking more about how she presented herself to others, as the chirpy survivor and did not give them a chance to understand the darker side of her feelings. This led us back into issues of control and lost independence which she characterised in a black and white way, thereby obscuring her awareness of her gradual regrowth of independence.

The support received from others is also a function of the support providers' perception of the victims' need for help. It has been suggested that the self-presentational coping stance taken by victims can play an important role in the support providers' reaction (Silver, Wortman, & Crofton, 1990). Silver et al. (1990) argue that victims who are able to portray 'balanced coping'—conveying that although they are distressed, they are attempting to cope through their own efforts—are most likely to receive support from others. Problems in perceiving and receiving support are demonstrated by our client, Sarah, who was badly physically damaged in a car accident and who was forced to depend upon others over a long period. (See Treatment 4.)

On this basis, it may be feasible for therapists to focus on the self-presentational stance employed by survivors. Part of the self-presentational stance taken by survivors is their expression of causal attributions for the event's occurrence. For example, women who blame themselves for rape have been shown to be perceived as less well-adjusted and as more responsible for the rape (Thornton et al., 1988). Because of their interpersonal nature, group therapies can provide opportunities for social support, social reintegration, and learning more adaptive social behaviours and can be particularly useful for treating patients with PTSD (Allen & Bloom, 1994). Family members who were not involved are often also highly distressed by the event (van der Ploeg & Kleijn, 1988) and may be in need of some form of professional intervention. With regard to research into the efficacy of treatment programmes, Perconte (1988) notes that the wide range of problems associated with PTSD (for example, alcohol and drug abuse, marital and family conflicts) may interfere with any treatment programme that focuses exclusively upon alleviating symptoms and problems associated with re-experiencing the trauma. Perconte notes that:

> Successful treatment of PTSD must follow a number of stages corresponding to the variety of problems experienced, and also directed toward overcoming secondary problems which may interfere with long-term rehabilitation. (Perconte, 1988, p. 133)

Perconte (1988) lists some of the problems found in the course of treatment with veterans. This includes incomplete treatment for addiction. Substance abuse can also be a problem with civilian survivors and deserves special attention. Many survivors will use drugs as a way of coping and the therapist may find it valuable to discuss drug-related beliefs (e.g., 'I can't handle stress without a drink') with a view to introducing cognitive therapy for substance abuse as part of the treatment package (Liese, 1994).

Other problems noted by Perconte (1988) include subsequent life-events resulting in an increase of symptomatology; failure to address phobic behaviour; failure to maintain communication with family and friends; and failure to establish new activities to replace intrusive thoughts and behaviour patterns.

In addition to social support, communities can offer important group experiences that can help survivors to process their memories. Johnson, Feldman, Lubin, and Southwick (1995) report on the therapeutic use of ritual and ceremony in the treatment of Vietnam veterans. The authors have developed four ceremonies that form part of an intensive group inpatient programme which focus on the relations within the veteran's family. They comment that these ceremonies are effective in accessing and containing intense emotions and are rated as extremely helpful by a very high proportion of veterans, family, and staff members.

What is clear, then, from this selective review is that successful treatment must depend on attention to a wide range of factors as well as the core PTSD symptomatology. Furthermore, although data from controlled trials of pharmacotherapy are limited, the available evidence suggests that antidepressants can be helpful for core PTSD symptoms (see Sutherland & Davidson, 1994, for a review of psychopharmacological treatment in PTSD).

PLANNING FOR THE FUTURE

To facilitate an effective and efficient response to an unpredicted traumatic event, working relationships should be established well before any incident between the relevant organisations, which include the emergency services and police, social services, health authorities, education authorities, voluntary agencies, and religious bodies. In the UK, the Report of the Disasters Working Party (Department of Health, 1990) recommended that Local Authority Departments of Social Services should take the lead role in coordinating a response. As far as responding to disasters that affect children, the school system is the obvious means through which to reach and help large numbers. Schools have been urged to develop contingency plans to prepare for both large and small disasters (Yule & Gold, 1993). Some agencies have argued for a central disaster fund to which local authorities could make an application, perhaps along the lines of the US Federal arrangements after a major disaster area is declared centrally.

In addition to the existing plans for rescue, under the responsibility of the police, protocols need to be established with the police for the provision of psychosocial care in the immediate aftermath. Training in the planning phase should include use of communication systems by administrators and for all individuals, across disciplines, in the psychological effects of trauma. It is important to also recognise that all workers involved in the aftercare of survivors should be prepared for the effects of massive stress on themselves. Some have argued for a national disaster squad of expert professionals who could be held in readiness to respond immediately and to consult and supervise a response to a disaster in any particular locality.

The role of such a national squad needs very careful consideration. It would be impossible as well as undesirable for a small specialised team to take responsibility for treating all those affected by a disaster. Far better, local services should be facilitated in responding to local disasters. They would need advice on particular aspects, but they will already have many relevant skills in dealing with anxiety, depression, and bereavement. The function of a specialist unit should not be inadvertently to deskill local staff. Rather, they should have an important role in disseminating information in training, and in mounting high-quality research. In Norway, armed forces mental health professionals are used to attend disasters in times of peace, thereby using resources efficiently in tasks that may be relevant in times of conflict. It may well be worth other countries considering the virtues of this model of service delivery.

The development of effective services for survivors, as we have seen, involves a diversity of professionals. It is crucial, therefore, for researchers to communicate their knowledge of the effects of trauma, and the factors involved in more severe and chronic disturbance, to these interested agencies. Gersons (1989), in his study of police officers involved in a shooting incident, reported that none of the general practitioners visited by the officers recognised or reported a post-traumatic stress reaction. Furthermore, Westermeyer (1989) discusses some of the problems faced by professionals working with patients from other cultures. He notes that often there is a failure to recognise organic factors, such as head injuries, among torture victims, concentration camp internees, and refugees. Westermyer argues that there is a need for professionals with expertise in neuropsychology and neuropsychiatry to be on hand when dealing with such groups.

Support Staff and Vicarious Traumatisation

In the planning stages attention should be drawn to the importance of selecting staff who are able and willing to cope with the nature of the work. There will be volunteer staff involved who should be given clear information about the work being highly stressful. This is true also for volunteers who are trained professionals. Specialised training should be given where possible, for example, in dealing with distressed relatives, being exposed to bodies, or being trained to break difficult and distressing news.

Although mental health professionals have generally spent a considerable amount of time in training it must be remembered that they are not immune to the powerful emotions aroused through exposure to their clients' traumatic memories. Workers may develop many of the symptoms of the survivors themselves and resort to strategies like increasing cigarette and alcohol consumption to cope. McCann and Pearlman (1990) refer to the psychological impact of working with trauma victims as vicarious traumatisation. This may involve symptoms analogous to that of the survivors, a disruption of the therapists' own basic assumptions of trust, safety, invulnerability, independence, self-worth, and so on. McCann and Pearlman (1990) note that helpful coping strategies for the therapists include: striving for balance between their personal and professional lives; and balancing traumatised with non-traumatised treatment work. It is important that helpers are themselves embedded within their own wider support network.

Certain professional groups may develop a 'macho' image and deny any emotional impact of confronting death and disfigurement. It has been recommended that staff involved in disaster work attend a stress debriefing group (Hartsough & Myers, 1985) either immediately following the work or within 24–48 hours. Mitchell (1983) described a structured group usually run by a mental health professional experienced in emergency work, in which, as well as sharing factual experiences, workers are encouraged to express the feelings that they experienced during and after the rescue work with a view to normalising their appraisal of their reactions and preparing them for further symptoms and the availability of further help should the need arise. As has been recommended for the survivors themselves, it is suggested that re-experiencing events in this way can help in emotionally processing the event. However, the effects of such critical incident stress debriefing remains to be fully evaluated.

Also, as McFarlane's (1987) study demonstrated, the experience of disaster and PTSD symptoms are associated with impaired family functioning. There is the recommendation, therefore, that attention be paid to the possible impact on the functioning of the helper's family.

CONCLUSION

This chapter has described strategies for intervention and treatment, focusing upon those methods that have received the most empirical evaluation in the literature. Intervention for trauma is a broad area encompassing planning for emergency services, the provision of information in the immediate aftermath, crisis and outreach approaches, individual and group therapies for the most severely affected.

We are aware of a great increase in professional knowledge and in public awareness over the 10 years since we became involved in this field. Much as this is to be welcomed, there is still a great deal that needs to be researched, particularly in the area of treatment intervention, as we as yet know little about the effectiveness or relative effectiveness of different treatment approaches, nor yet about the indications for treating any individual by any particular method. Although we would like to see people being offered help when suffering post-trauma disorders, we strongly hope that treatments will continue to be researched and funding found for this work, so that these important questions can be addressed and our ability to help others in the future can be improved.

SUMMARY POINTS

1. Recent experiences in dealing with the aftermath of disasters has led to the recommendation that outreach services be set up to locate survivors who may not come forward for help.
2. In the immediate impact phase, the following issues have been discussed as critical: the setting up of good information systems for the relaying of up-to-date news on what has happened to survivors and affected relatives; practical help for survivors and relatives; deciding upon the viewing of human remains.
3. Immediate intervention in the form of crisis counselling and debriefing is popular and carries our wish to prevent the development of later severe and prolonged problems but at present is not well supported by empirical evidence.
4. Various longer term treatment methods are in use and we can relate these to our psychosocial model, indicating at which points they are operating.
5. Direct exposure therapies seem to operate through representing event stimuli for reappraisal and habituation of high arousal that may impede reappraisal.
6. Cognitive-behavioural therapies aim to promote reappraisal more directly and also to teach coping techniques to manage high arousal.
7. Cognitive therapy specifically embraces the reviewing of pre-existing

beliefs and coping strategies which may be dysfunctional in relation to coping with trauma.

8. Eye-movement desensitisation and reprocessing therapy is one of several new approaches that lack any clear rationale but which seem to promise rapid and relatively painless effects for some patients. Controlled trials are called for in the further evaluation of this method.

9. Group therapies seem especially effective in normalising post-trauma reactions and providing a supportive environment for reprocessing trauma experiences.

10. Community support action can provide vital practical and emotional support for survivors. Communities can also supply important communal experiences which some find useful in processing trauma, such as memorial services and official inquiries.

11. Throughout we have emphasised the importance of prior planning to facilitate the coordination of different services. Planning includes the selection and training of personnel and the provision of services for these key people who may also suffer trauma in the context of their work or vicarious traumatisation as a result of working with survivors.

CHAPTER 8

CONCLUSIONS

In the past two decades there has been an explosion of research into the psychological effects of traumatic events. But on reading the preceding chapters it is clear that much remains to be investigated. The present chapter will discuss some of the issues that strike us as promising foci for future work. In particular, although the diagnostic category of PTSD provided the impetus for research, the architecture of post-traumatic stress reactions remains unclear.

Key Topics

Architecture of symptomatology
Implications and directions
Conclusion

ARCHITECTURE OF SYMPTOMATOLOGY

As already noted in Chapter 2, the criteria for PTSD have largely reflected Horowitz's (1975, 1976, 1979) formulation of stress responses as consisting of alternating phases of intrusions and attempts to ward off intrusive thinking. These are the hallmark characteristics of PTSD. But despite the influence of the two-factor model (Gersons, 1989), the grouping of symptoms within the diagnostic criteria remains controversial and only partially reflects Horowitz's operational criteria.

To illustrate, sleep disturbances, hypervigilance, exaggerated startle response (which Horowitz considered as intrusions), memory loss, and difficulties in concentration (which Horowitz considered as denials) have been placed in section D of the DSM criteria for PTSD (APA, 1980, 1987, 1994). Section D has been described as a miscellaneous section and it has been argued that the section D symptoms should be divided between the two dimensions of repetition phenomena and defensive phenomena and that these two symptom groupings should consist of two patterns: (a) a re-experiencing symptom pattern, divided into (1) intrusion symptoms and (2) hyperarousal symptoms; and (b) a denial symptom pattern, divided into (1) numbing and (2) cognitive difficulties (Laufer, Brett, & Gallops, 1985).

Factor Analytic Studies

Although the symptom groupings proposed by Laufer et al. (1985) provide an appealing structure, the question of whether there is an underlying and identifiable symptom structure to post-traumatic reactions or whether they are simply arbitrary groupings of symptoms can only be resolved by psychometric studies. Surprisingly few studies have, however, investigated the grouping of symptoms within a broader perspective on the phenomenology of post-traumatic stress reactions.

Silver and Iacono (1984) carried out a factor analysis of 33 symptoms associated with PTSD which were self-rated by over 400 Vietnam veterans selected from Outreach Centers in the USA. A four-factor solution was obtained which identified a first factor characterised as depression and dysthymic disorder; a second factor characterised as survival guilt; a third factor characterised as re-experiencing the trauma; and a fourth factor identified as numbed responsiveness and detachment including feelings of anger and hostility (see Table 8.1). Although these data provide support for the separate groupings of intrusive and avoidant symptoms, they do not provide evidence that a two-factor structure provides the most parsimonious architecture for conceptualising reactions. Furthermore, their data show that depressive symptoms account for most of the variance in reactions. Silver and Iacono (1984) suggest that their data may more accurately represent the PTSD symptom structure for war veterans than they do for PTSD as defined by the APA, which may be more accurately described as a generic classification.

This is an important point. Although the classification of PTSD has provided a common language for researchers and fuelled interest into the study of the psychological effects of traumatic events, there remains debate over whether or not there is a generic PTSD. It may be that the structure of post-traumatic stress reactions is dependent on the type of event. It has been suggested that the term PTSD should be qualified as in rape-related PTSD, combat-related PTSD, and so on.

Furthermore, the evidence does not strongly support the grouping of symptoms as listed in DSM, i.e., intrusion, avoidance, and hyperarousal. Factor analytic data using the DSM-III criteria with 131 Vietnam veterans have been reported (Watson, Kucala, Juba, Manifold, & Anderson, 1991b). All respondents were male patients at a veteran medical center who had been administered a DSM-III interview schedule (PTSD-I: Watson, Juba, Manifold, Kucala, & Anderson, 1991a) and had qualified for a DSM-III based diagnosis of PTSD. Five factors were generated (see Table 8.2). Factor 1 was labelled as 'intrusive thoughts and their effects'. Factor 2 was labelled as 'increased arousal'. Factor 3 was labelled as 'impoverished relationships'. Factor 4 consisted of 'guilt' items and 'nightmares'. Factor 5 was labelled as 'memory and concentration' problems. Although these data provide some support for the DSM groupings (e.g., factor 2 resembles the DSM-IV arousal section and

Table 8.1 Symptoms loading on each factor

Factor 1: Depression
Trouble concentrating
Low interest in job or other activities
Feeling worthless or unsure about the self
Difficulty keeping a job
Depression
Suicidal feelings or attempts
Problems with memory

Factor 2: Survival guilt and grief
Guilt about what I did in Vietnam
Guilt for surviving Vietnam
Grief or sorrow

Factor 3: Reexperiencing the trauma
Nightmares
Violent dreams or fantasies
Flashbacks to Vietnam
Reacting when surprised, using military training

Factor 4: Detachment and anger
Feeling angry or irritable
Losing temper easily
Difficulty in relations with others
Mistrust of others or government
Jumpiness or hyperalertness
Feeling emotionally distant from family and others
Anxiety
Difficulty feeling emotions
Painful moods and emotions
Feeling separated from others, from country or society
Fear of loss of control
Depression
Having arguments with others

Adapted from Silver and Iacono (1984).

factor 3 resembles the DSM-IV avoidance/numbing section) the evidence does not support the three-factor structure inherent in DSM. Such studies only tell us about the structure of the DSM symptom menu. This point is illustrated by the inclusion of guilt in those studies conducted using DSM-III criteria. Not surprisingly, studies using DSM-III-R criteria in which guilt was omitted do not yield a guilt factor.

Factor analytic data of DSM-III-R criteria have shown four factors: numbing of general responsiveness; intrusion; avoidance; and sleeping problems (Hovens et al., 1994a). A similar four-factor structure has been reported in a variety of other studies of survivors of shipping disasters using the IES (Joseph, Williams, Yule, & Walker, 1992b: Joseph, Yule, Williams, & Hodgkinson, 1993g; Yule, Ten Bruggencate, & Joseph, 1994) and victims of armed robbery (Hodgkinson & Joseph, 1995). However, these data, although informative, do

Table 8.2 Five factors of Watson et al. (1991b)

Factor 1: Intrusive thoughts and their effects
Intrusive memories
Trauma-like stimuli worsen symptoms
Diminished interests
Nightmares
Avoiding trauma-like stimuli
Flashbacks
Detachment

Factor 2: Increased arousal
Hyperalertness
Exaggerated startle response
Sleep difficulties
Nightmares

Factor 3: Impoverished relationships
Numbed to intimacy
Constricted affect
Detachment
Decreased sexual pleasure
Avoiding trauma-like stimuli

Factor 4: Guilt and nightmares
Guilt over behaviours
Guilt over survival
Nightmares

Factor 5: Memory and concentration
Memory problems
Concentration difficulties

Adapted from Watson et al. (1991b).

not tell us about the structure of post-traumatic reactions very broadly defined. In order to obtain a clear idea of the symptom structure of post-traumatic reactions, it would be necessary to have a comprehensive menu of all symptoms associated with trauma, and not just those provided in the diagnostic classification systems.

It might therefore be argued that rather than qualify the term PTSD, the term PTSD should be dropped altogether and retained only as an umbrella term for an area of study in which investigators discuss the specific types of symptoms that are present.

The evidence would suggest that even the groupings of intrusive and avoidant symptoms need to be clarified further as there appear to be two distinct forms of intrusive thinking (the first characterised as deliberate ruminative activity and the second characterised best by 'flashbulb' nightmares and flashbacks) and two distinct forms of avoidance (the first characterised as conscious coping efforts and the second characterised as emotional numbing and detachment).

The empirical distinction between these forms of intrusion and avoidance is important theoretically as it has been suggested that different cognitive mechanisms underlie each of these phenomena. Deliberate ruminative activity and conscious coping efforts are best understood within those theoretical frameworks such as the social-cognition perspective of Janoff-Bulman which reflect the operation of conscious processes, whereas nonconscious processes may underlie the occurrence of nightmares, flashbacks, and symptoms of emotional numbing. In our theoretical model we distinguish between trauma cognitions, which refer to intrusive imagery which has its roots in nonconscious processes and ruminative behaviour which can best be understood in terms of appraisal processes which are largely conscious—although influenced by cognitive schemata which, in themselves, may reflect underlying beliefs about the self and the world which are largely nonconscious.

Anyone may develop post-traumatic stress reactions insofar as such reactions reflect normal cognitive processes with their roots in evolutionary history and which reflect the processes of working through. Post-traumatic stress reactions are not here conceptualised as disorder, although it is recognised that the process of working through can become blocked. Recent thinking on the nature of mental disorder conceptualises one defining quality of 'disorder' as 'dysfunction' where dysfunction is a scientific term referring to the failure of a mental mechanism to perform a natural function for which it was 'designed' by evolution (Wakefield, 1992). Applying this definition to PTSD, we would suggest that PTSD does not represent the dysfunction of a mental mechanism but rather the function of normal cognitive processes of adaptation, most often the case where the completion tendency remains persistently in conflict with defensive mechanisms that impede processing. However, when the process of working through becomes blocked it is not completely clear whether this might in some cases represent a failure of a mental mechanism, e.g., where cognitive deficits result in an impairment in the process of assimilation. We would not want to rule this out.

IMPLICATIONS AND DIRECTIONS

The goal of research is to provide better methods for treatment and much research has compared survivors with and without PTSD on various psychosocial factors in an attempt to identify potentially modifiable targets for intervention. However, because different cognitive mechanisms may be involved in different reactions, we would suggest that specific symptom clusters and their relationship to psychosocial factors be investigated. Certainly, there is growing evidence for a differential relationship between the intrusive and avoidant symptom categories and other variables. For example, evidence suggests that antidepressant medication may be effective in reducing symptoms of intrusion but not symptoms of avoidance (Sutherland & Davidson, 1994). It is of importance that therapeutic goals are stated precisely.

A problem arises when global rather than specific measures of dysfunction are used. It may be that psychosocial variables do not mediate between the traumatic event and either intrusion or avoidance, but rather exert their effect on overlapping depressive or anxious symptomatology. In order to clarify these issues, research needs to examine specific relationships between personal and social factors and post-traumatic symptoms.

As well as emphasising a symptom-based approach to research, we would also emphasise the temporal variation in the nature of post-traumatic reactions and how this might affect research findings. Horowitz (1975, 1976, 1979) suggests that intrusion and avoidance are phasic states which oscillate in ways particular to each person eventually reaching a period of stability when a period of completion is said to have been reached. This has implications for research seeking to demonstrate links between post-traumatic stress and other personal or social factors. Specific personal or social factors may be predictive of particular outcomes only at certain times in the period of adjustment.

Timing is, of course, the main problem confronting trauma researchers. There is the difficulty in obtaining pre-event measures. Also, if respondents have PTSD prior to the start of any study the findings cannot provide definitive evidence as to the direction of causality between PTSD and other variables. Clearly, future studies should attempt to obtain measures before the development of severe and chronic PTSD. In particular, there is also a need to understand the relationship between Acute Stress Reaction and PTSD.

It is often said that further research is needed. But this is especially true in trauma studies as they so often have to rely on naturalistic methods of investigation and where relatively little is known about the generalisabilty of results from one situation to another. For example, the *Herald of Free Enterprise* disaster involved a substantial loss of life and in this respect is a very different event from the *Jupiter* cruise ship capsize in which relatively few lives were lost. But both these events share a number of other common characteristics. Both were uncontrollable and unpredictable sudden disasters at sea which invoked in many the fear of drowning. In turn, both of these events are very different from a flood which results in substantial property loss. Even within a single event, the intensity of exposure, both objectively and subjectively defined, may range from minimal to extreme depending on individual differences in experience and perception. We have attempted to draw together the various approaches to understanding individual differences in adjustment into a coherent and testable framework.

There is accumulating evidence that the suspicion about biased reporting in litigants is exaggerated (Green, Grace, Lindy, Titchener, & Lindy, 1983; Cohen, 1987). But although the issue of compensation litigation may introduce a biasing complication in rare cases, it is nevertheless a social reality that some survivors of disaster have a case for compensation when negligence can be proved and hence the ordeal to 'prove' that they have been adversely affected is a part of the consequences of being a survivor. Furthermore, it may be that disasters resulting from human negligence represent a special case and may result in problems of a particular kind. For these reasons, we would argue that litigants from such disasters are important to study further. It may be that involvement in litigation has a biasing effect on self-reports. It has been suggested that psychological reactions might be produced or maintained by a compensation claim, often referred to as 'compensation neurosis' (Weighill, 1983). However, it is a difficult question to investigate whether this is true as often the only survivors available for study are involved in litigation.

Although there are many unavoidable difficulties in the study of people's reactions following exposure to traumatic events, it should also be emphasised that the study of trauma-affected populations provides a unique opportunity to assess the relationship between adversity and illness that is not possible with traditional life-event methodology. As McFarlane (1985) noted: the occurrence of a natural disaster and its impact are obviously not caused by any illness and are therefore independent events; problems of recall are minimised; documenting the effects of a single event is much simpler than trying to unravel the combined effects of a number of highly personal experiences; all subjects experience the same event on the same day at the same time. However, as we have seen, the definition of trauma is problematic and the boundaries of PTSD indistinct. It may be that findings from trauma research will have implications for understanding reactions to stress over a wider range of severity.

CONCLUSION

It would seem that although post-traumatic stress reactions arise as a direct result of exposure to the experience of a traumatic event, the chronicity and severity of reactions are also a function of other psychosocial factors. In particular, the person's appraisal of his or her experiences, the support received from others, and the life-events experienced subsequent to disaster may all exacerbate symptoms. For this reason, we have adopted an integrative model of adaptation to traumatic stressors which emphasises that post-traumatic stress reactions are indicative that the experience has in some way not yet been assimilated. It is important that mental health professionals should have a thorough knowledge of the main research findings and are familiar with those signs of incomplete emotional processing which may indicate risk of later disorder. It should then be possible for victims at high risk to be identified in the early stages and given help to work through and assimilate their experiences.

REFERENCES

Abrahams, M. J., Price, J., Whitlock, F. A., & Williams, G. (1976). The Brisbane floods, January 1974: Their impact on health. *Medical Journal of Australia*, 2, 936–939.
Abramson, L. Y., Metalsky, G. I., & Alloy, L. B. (1988). The hopelessness theory of depression: Does the research test the theory? In L. Y. Abramson (Ed.), *Social cognition and clinical psychology: A synthesis*. New York: Guilford.
Abramson, L. Y., Metalsky, G. I., & Alloy, L. B. (1989). Hopelessness depression: A theory based subtype of depression. *Psychological Review*, 96, 358–372.
Abramson, L. Y., Seligman, M. E., & Teasdale, J. D. (1978). Learned helplessness in humans; critique and reformulation. *Journal of Abnormal Psychology*, 87, 49–74.
Achenbach, T. M., & Edelbrock, C. (1983). *Manual for the child behaviour checklist and revised child behaviour profile*. Burlington, VT: University of Vermont.
Adler, A. (1943). Neuropsychiatric complications in victims of Boston's Coconut Grove disaster. *Journal of the American Medical Association*, 123, 1098–1101.
Adshead, G., Canterbury, R., & Rose, S. (1994). Current provision and recommendations for the management of psychosocial morbidity following disaster in England. *Criminal Behaviour and Mental Health*, 4, 181–208.
Affleck, G., Tennen, H., Croog, S., & Levine, S. (1987). Causal attribution, perceived benefits, and morbidity after a heart attack: An 8-year study. *Journal of Consulting and Clinical Psychology*, 55, 29–35.
Allen, S. N. (1994). Psychological assessment of post-traumatic stress disorder. *Psychiatric Clinics of North America*, 17, 327–349.
Allen, S. N., & Bloom, S. L. (1994). Group and family treatment of post-traumatic stress disorder. *Psychiatric Clinics of North America*, 17, 425–437.
Alloy, L. B., Abramson, L. Y., Metalsky, G. I., & Hartledge, S. (1988). The hopelessness theory of depression: attributional aspects. *British Journal of Clinical Psychology*, 27, 5–21.
Alloy, L. B., Kelly, K. A., Mineka, S., & Clements, C. M. (1990). Comorbidity in anxiety and depressive disorders: A helplessness–hopelessness perspective. In J. D. Maser & C. R. Cloninger (Eds), *Comorbidity in anxiety and mood disorders* (pp. 499–543). Washington, DC: American Psychiatric Press.
Alloy, L. B., Lipman, A. J., & Abramson, L. Y. (1992). Attributional style as a vulnerability factor for depression: Validation by past history of mood disorders. *Cognitive Therapy and Research*, 16, 391–407.
Alloy, L. B., & Tabachnik, N. (1984). The assessment of covariation by humans and animals: the joint influence of prior expectations and current situational information. *Psychological Review*, 91, 112–149.
Anderson, C. R. (1977). Locus of control, coping behaviours, and performance in a stress setting: A longitudinal study. *Journal of Applied Psychology*, 62, 446–451.
Antaki, C., & Brewin, C. R. (Eds). (1982). *Attributions and psychological change: Applications of attributional theories to clinical and educational practice*. London: Academic Press.
Andrews, B., & Brown, G. W. (1988). Social support, onset of depression and personality. *Social Psychiatry and Psychiatric Epidemiology*, 23, 99–108.
APA (1952). *Diagnostic and statistical manual of mental disorders* (1st edition). Washing-

ton, DC: American Psychiatric Association.

APA (1968). *Diagnostic and statistical manual of mental disorders* (2nd edition). Washington, DC: American Psychiatric Association.

APA (1980). *Diagnostic and statistical manual of mental disorders* (3rd edition). Washington, DC: American Psychiatric Association.

APA (1987). *Diagnostic and statistical manual of mental disorders* (3rd edition, revised). Washington, DC: American Psychiatric Association.

APA (1994). *Diagnostic and statistical manual of mental disorders* (4th edition). Washington, DC: American Psychiatric Association.

Arroyo, W., & Eth, S. (1985). Children traumatized by Central American warfare. In S. Eth & R. S. Pynoos (Eds), *Post-traumatic stress disorder in children*. Washington, DC: American Psychiatric Press.

Astor-Dubin, L., & Hammen, C. (1984). Cognitive versus behavioural coping responses of men and women: A brief report. *Cognitive Therapy and Research*, **8**, 85–90.

Atkeson, B. M., Calhoun, K. S., Resick, P. A., & Ellis, E. M. (1982). Victims of rape: Repeated assessment of depressive symptoms. *Journal of Consulting and Clinical Psychology*, **50**, 96–102.

Baider, L., Peretz, T., & Kaplan De-Nour, A. (1992). Effect of the Holocaust on coping with cancer. *Social Science and Medicine*, **34**, 11–15.

Ballard, C. G., Stanley, A. K., & Brockington, I. F. (1995). Post-traumatic stress disorder (PTSD) after childbirth. *British Journal of Psychiatry*, **166**, 525–528.

Bard, M., & Sangrey, D. (1980). Things fall apart. Victims in Crisis. Evaluation Change (Special issue), 28–35.

Bartone, P. T., & Wright, K. M. (1990). Grief and group recovery following a military air disaster. *Journal of Traumatic Stress*, **3**, 523–540.

Basoglu, M., & Paker, M. (1995). Severity of trauma as predictor of long-term psychological status in survivors of torture. *Journal of Anxiety Disorders*, **9**, 339–350.

Baum, A. (1987). Toxins, technology, and natural disasters. In G. R. VandenBos and B. K. Bryant (Eds), *Cataclysms, crises, and catastrophes: Psychology in action*. American Psychological Association.

Baum, A. (1990). Stress, intrusive imagery, and chronic distress. *Health Psychology*, **9**, 653–675.

Baum, A., & Fleming, I. (1993). Implications of psychological research on stress and technological accidents. *American Psychologist*, **48**, 665–672.

Baum, A., Fleming, R., & Singer, J. E. (1983a). Coping with victimization by technological disaster. *Journal of Social Issues*, **39**, 117–138.

Baum, A., Gatchel, R. J., & Schaeffer, M. A. (1983b). Emotional, behavioral, and physiological effects of chronic stress at Three Mile Island. *Journal of Consulting and Clinical Psychology*, **51**, 565–572.

Baum, A., O'Keefe, M. K., & Davidson, L. M. (1990). Acute stressors and chronic response: The case of traumatic stress. *Journal of Applied Social Psychology*, **20**, 1643–1654.

Beck, A. T. (1967). *Depression: Clinical, experimental, and theoretical aspects*. New York: Hoeber.

Beck, A. T. (1976). *Cognitive therapy and the emotional disorder*. New York: International University Press.

Beck, A. T., & Emery, G. (1985). *Anxiety disorders and phobias. A cognitive perspective*. New York: Basic Books.

Beck, A. T., Rush, A. J., Shaw, B. F., & Emery, G. (1979). *Cognitive therapy of depression*. New York: Guilford.

Becker, J. V., Skinner, L. J., Abel, G. G., Howell, J., & Bruce, K. (1982). The effects of sexual assault on rape and attempted rape victims. *Victimology*, 7, 106–113.

Becker, J. V., Skinner, L. J., Abel, G. G., & Treacy, E. C. (1982). Incidence and types of sexual dysfunctions in rape and incest victims. *Journal of Sex and Marital Therapy*, **8**, 65–74.

Bernstein, E. M., & Putnam, F. W. (1986). Development, reliability, and validity of a dissociation scale. *Journal of Nervous and Mental Disease*, **174**, 727–735.

Berren, M. R., Beigel, A., & Barker, G. (1982). A typology for the classification of disasters: Implications for intervention. *Community Mental Health Journal*, **18**, 120–134.

Beitchman, J. H., Zucker, K. J., Hood, J. E., DaCosta, G. A., & Cassavia, E. (1992). A review of the long-term effects of childhood sexual abuse. *Child Abuse and Neglect*, **16**, 101–118.

Belkin, D. S., Greene, A. F., Rodrigue, J. R., & Boggs, S. R. (1994). Psychopathology and history of sexual abuse. *Journal of Interpersonal Violence*, **9**, 535–547.

Bell, B. D. (1978). Disaster impact and response: overcoming the thousand natural shocks. *The Gerontologist*, **18**, 531–540.

Benassi, V. A., Sweeney, P. D., & Dufour, C. L. (1988). Is there a relation between locus of control orientation and depression? *Journal of Abnormal Psychology*, **97**, 357–367.

Bennet, G. (1970). Bristol floods 1968: Controlled survey of effects on health of local community disaster. *British Medical Journal*, **3**, 454–458.

Bentall, R. P. (1992). Reconstructing psychopathology. *The Psychologist*, **15**, 61–65.

Billings, A. G., & Moos, R. H. (1981). The role of coping responses and social resources in attenuating the stress of life events. *Journal of Behavioural Medicine*, **4**, 139–157.

Birleson, P. (1981). The validity of depressive disorder in childhood and the development of a self rating scale: A research report. *Journal of Child Psychology and Psychiatry*, **22**, 73–88.

Bisson, J. I., Jenkins, P. L., & Bannister, C. (in press). A randomised controlled trial of psychological debriefing for victims of acute burn trauma.

Black, J. L., & Keane, T. M. (1982). Implosive therapy in the treatment of combat related fears in a world war II veteran. *Behaviour Therapy and Experimental Psychiatry*, **13**, 163–165.

Blake, D. D., Albano, A. M., & Keane, T. M. (1992). Twenty years of trauma: Psychological Abstracts 1970 through 1989. *Journal of Traumatic Stress*, **5**, 477–484.

Blake, D. D., Keane, T. M., Wine, P. R., Mora, C., Taylor, K. L., & Lyons, J. A. (1990b). Prevalence of PTSD symptoms in combat veterans seeking medical treatment. *Journal of Traumatic Stress*, **3**, 15–29.

Blake, D. D., Weathers, F. W., Nagy, L. M., et al. (1990a). A clinician rating scale for assessing current and lifetime PTSD: The CAPS-I. *Behaviour Therapy*, **13**, 187–188.

Blanchard, E. B., Hickling, E. J., Taylor, A. E., Loos, W. R., & Geradi, R. J. (1994). Psychological morbidity associated with motor vehicle accidents. *Behaviour Research and Therapy*, **32**, 283–290.

Blanchard, E. B., Kolb, L. B., Gerardi, R. J., Ryan, P., & Pallmeyer, T. P. (1986). Cardiac response to relevant stimuli as an adjunctive tool for diagnosing posttraumatic stress disorder in Vietnam veterans. *Behaviour Therapy*, **17**, 592–606.

Blanchard, E. B., Kolb, L. B., Pallmeyer, T. P., & Gerardi, R. J. (1982). A psychophysiological study of post-traumatic stress disorder in Vietnam veterans. *Psychiatric Quarterly*, **54**, 220–229.

Blank, A. S. (1993). The longitudinal course of posttraumatic stress disorder. In J. R. T. Davidson & E. B. Foa (Eds), *Posttraumatic stress disorder: DSM-IV and beyond*. Washington, DC: American Psychiatric Press.

Bourque, L. B., Aneshensel, C. S., & Goltz, J. D. (1991). Injury and psychological distress following the Whittier Narrows and Loma Prieta earthquakes (abstract). In proceedings of the UCLA International Conference on the Impact of Natural Disasters, Agenda for Future Action. Los Angeles: University of California.

Bowen, G. R., & Lambert, J. A. (1986). Systematic desensitization therapy with post-traumatic stress disorder cases. In C. R. Figley (Ed.), *Trauma and its wake*, Vol. II (pp. 264–279), New York: Brunner/Mazel.

Boudewyns, P. A., & Hyer, L. (1990). Physiological response to combat memories and preliminary treatment outcome in Vietnam veteran PTSD patients treated with direct therapeutic exposure. *Behavior Therapy*, 21, 63–87.

Boyle, M. (1990). *Schizophrenia: A scientific delusion?* London: Routledge.

Bradley, G. W. (1978). Self-serving biases in the attribution process: A re-examination of the fact or fiction question. *Journal of Personality and Social Psychology*, 36, 56–71.

Bravo, M., Rubio-Stipec, M., Canino, G. J., Woodbury, M. A., & Ribera, J. C. (1990). The psychological sequelae of disaster stress prospectively and retrospectively evaluated. *American Journal of Community Psychology*, 18, 661–680.

Bremner, J. D., Southwick, S., Brett, E., Fontana, A., Rosenheck, R., & Charney, D. S. (1992). Dissociation and postraumatic stress disorder in Vietnam combat veterans. *American Journal of Psychiatry*, 149, 328–332.

Breslau, N., & Davis, G. C. (1986). Chronic stress and major depression. *Archives of General Psychiatry*, 43, 309–314.

Breslau, N., & Davis, G. C. (1987). Post-traumatic stress disorder: the etiological specificity of wartime stressors. *American Journal of Psychiatry*, 144, 578–583.

Breslau, N., Davis, G. C., Andreski, P., & Peterson, E. (1991). Traumatic events and posttraumatic stress disorder in an urban population of young adults. *Archives of General Psychiatry*, 48, 216–222.

Brewin, C. R. (1985). Depression and causal attributions: What is their relation? *Psychological Bulletin*, 98, 297–309.

Brewin, C. R. (1988). *Cognitive foundations of clinical psychology*. Hove and London: Lawrence Erlbaum.

Brewin, C. R. (1989). Cognitive change processes in psychotherapy. *Psychological Review*, 96, 379–394.

Brewin, C. R., Andrews, B., & Gotlib, I. H. (1993). Psychopathology and early experience: a reappraisal of retrospective reports. *Psychological Bulletin*, 113, 82–98.

Brewin, C. R., Dalgleish, T., & Joseph, S. (1996). A dual representation theory of posttraumatic stress disorder. *Psychological Review*, 103, 670–686.

Brewin, C. R., MacCarthy, B., & Furnham, A. (1989). Social support in the face of adversity: The role of cognitive appraisal. *Journal of Research in Personality*, 23, 354–372.

Brewin, C. R., & Shapiro, D. A. (1984). Beyond locus of control: Attributions of responsibility for positive and negative outcomes. *British Journal of Psychology*, 75, 43–49.

Briere, J., & Runtz, M. (1989). The Trauma Symptom Checklist (TSC-33): Early data on a new scale. *Journal of Interpersonal Violence*, 4, 151–63.

Brom, D., Kleber, R. J., & Defares, P. B. (1986). *Traumatische ervaringen en psychotherapie* (Traumatic experiences and psychotherapy). Lisse: Swets & Zeitlinger.

Brom, D., & Kleber, R. J. (1989). Prevention of post-traumatic stress disorders. *Journal of Traumatic Stress*, 2, 335–351.

Brom, D., Kleber, R. J., & Defares, P. B. (1989). Brief psychotherapy for posttraumatic stress disorders. *Journal of Consulting and Clinical Psychology*, 57, 607–612.

Brom, D., Kleber, R. J., & Hofman, M. C. (1993). Victims of traffic accidents: Incidence and prevention of post-traumatic stress disorder. *Journal of Clinical Psychology*, 49, 131–140.

Bromet, E. J., Hough, L., & Connell, M. (1984). Mental health of children near the

Three Mile Island reactor. *Journal of Preventive Psychiatry*, 2, 275–301.

Bromet, E. J., Parkinson, D. K., Schulberg, H. C., Dunn, L. O., & Gondek, P. C. (1982a). Mental health of residents near the Three Mile Island reactor: A comparative study of selected groups. *Journal of Preventive Psychiatry*, 1, 225–274.

Bromet, E. J., Schulberg, H. C., & Dunn, L. O. (1982b). Reactions of psychiatric patients to the Three Mile Island nuclear accident. *Archives of General Psychiatry*, 39, 725–730.

Brown, G. W., Andrews, B., Harris, T., Adler, Z., & Bridge, L. (1986). Social support, self-esteem and depression. *Psychological Medicine*, 16, 813–831.

Brown, G. W. & Harris, T. (1978). *Social origins of depression*. London: Tavistock.

Brown, R., & Kulik, J. (1977). Flashbulb memories. *Cognition*, 5, 73–99.

Browne, A., & Finkelhor, D. (1986). The impact of child sexual abuse: A review of the research. *Psychological Bulletin*, 99, 66–77.

Brugha, T., Bebbington, P., Tennant, C., & Hurry, J. (1985). The list of threatening experiences: a subset of 12 life-event categories with considerable long-term contextual threat. *Psychological Medicine*, 15, 189–194.

Bulman, R. J., & Wortman, C. B. (1977). Attributions of blame and coping in the 'real world': Severe accident victims react to their lot. *Journal of Personality and Social Psychology*, 35, 351–363.

Burgess, A. W., Hartman, C. R., McCausland, M. P., & Powers, P. (1984). Response patterns in children and adolescents exploited through sex rings and pornography. *American Journal of Psychiatry*, 141, 656–662.

Burgess, A. W., & Holmstrom, L. L. (1974a). *Rape: Victims of crisis*. Bowie, MD: R. J. Brady Company.

Burgess, A. W., & Holmstrom, L. L. (1974b). Rape trauma syndrome. *American Journal of Psychiatry*, 131, 981–986.

Burgess, A. W., & Holmstrom, L. L. (1978). Recovery from rape and prior life stress. *Research in Nursing and Health*, 1, 165–174.

Burke, H. R., & Mayer, S. M. (1985). The MMPI and the post-traumatic stress syndrome in Vietnam-era veterans. *Journal of Clinical Psychology*, 41, 152–156.

Burnam, M. A., Stein, J. A., Golding, J. M., Siegal, J. M., Sorenson, S. B., Forsythe, A. B., & Telles, C. A. (1988). Sexual assault and mental disorders in a community population. *Journal of Consulting and Clinical Psychology*, 56, 843–850.

Burns, M. O., & Seligman, M. E. P. (1989). Explanatory style across the lifespan: Evidence for stability over 52 years. *Journal of Personality and Social Psychology*, 56, 471–477.

Burnstein, E. M., & Putnam, F. W. (1986). Development, reliability, and validity of a dissociative scale. *Journal of Nervous and Mental Disease*, 174, 727–735.

Butcher, J. N. (1990). *MMPI-2 in psychological treatment*. New York: Oxford UP.

Cairns, E., & Wilson, R. (1984). The impact of political violence on mild psychiatric morbidity in Northern Ireland. *British Journal of Psychiatry*, 145, 631–635.

Cairns, E., & Wilson, R. (1985). Psychiatric aspects of violence in Northern Ireland. *Stress Medicine*, 1, 193–201.

Cairns, E., & Wilson, R. (1989). Mental health aspects of political violence in Northern Ireland. *International Journal of Mental Health*, 18, 38–56.

Calhoun, J. S., Atkeson, B. M., & Resick, P. A. (1982). A longitudinal examination of fear reactions in victims of rape. *Journal of Counselling Psychology*, 29, 655–661.

Calhoun, L. G., & Tedeschi, R. G. (1991). Perceiving benefits in traumatic events: Some issues for practising psychologists. *The Journal of Training and Practice in Professional Psychology*, 5, 45–52.

Card, J. (1987). Epidemiology of PTSD in a national cohort of Vietnam veterans. *Journal of Consulting Psychology*, 43, 6–16.

Carlier, I. V. E., & Gersons, B. P. R. (1995). Partial posttraumatic stress disorder (PTSD): The issue of psychological scars and the occurrence of PTSD symptoms. *The Journal of Nervous and Mental Disease*, **183**, 107–109.

Carr, V. J. (1991). Quake Impact Study: Interim Report. Callaghan, NSW, Australia, University of Newcastle Faculty of Medicine, Discipline of Psychiatry, September.

Carver, C. S., Scheier, M. F., & Weintraub, J.K. (1989). Assessing coping strategies: A theoretically based approach. *Journal of Personality and Social Psychology*, **56**, 267–283.

Cathcart, F. (1988). Seeing the body after death. *British Medical Journal*, **297**, 997–998.

Chambless, D. L., & Gillis, M. M. (1993). Cognitive therapy of anxiety disorders. *Journal of Consulting and Clinical Psychology*, **61**, 248–260.

Chemtob, C., Roitblat, H. L., Hamada, R. S., Carlson, J. G., & Twentyman, C. T. (1988). A cognitive action theory of post-traumatic stress disorder. *Journal of Anxiety Disorders*, **2**, 253–275.

Clark, D. M. (1986). A cognitive approach to panic. *Behaviour Research and Therapy*, **24**, 461–470.

Clark, D. M. (1991). Cognitive therapy for panic disorder. Paper presented at the NIH Consensus Development Conference on the treatment of panic disorder, 23–25 September, Bethesda, MD.

Clark, D. M., Ball, S., & Pape, D. (1991). An experimental investigation of thought suppression. *Behaviour Research and Therapy*, **29**, 253–257.

Clark, L. A., & Watson, D. (1991). Tripartite model of anxiety and depression: Psychometric evidence and taxonomic implications. *Journal of Abnormal Psychology*, **100**, 316–336.

Clayer, J. R., Bookless-Pratz, C., & Harris, R. L. (1985). Some health consequences of a natural disaster. *Medical Journal of Australia*, **143**, 182–184.

Cluss, P. A., Boughton, J., Frank, L. E., Stewart, B. D., & West, D. (1983). The rape victims: psychological correlates of participation in the legal process. *Criminal Justice and Behaviour*, **10**, 342–357.

Cohen, R. I. (1987). Post-traumatic stress disorder: Does it clear up when the litigation is settled? *British Journal of Hospital Medicine*, **27**, 485.

Cohen, S., & McKay, G. (1984). Social support, stress and the buffering hypothesis: A theoretical analysis. In A. Baum, J. E. Singer, & S. E. Taylor (Eds), *Handbook of psychology and health*, Vol. 4 (pp. 253–267). Hillsdale, NJ: Erlbaum.

Cohen, S., & Wills, T. A. (1985). Stress, social support, and the buffering hypothesis. *Psychological Bulletin*, **2**, 310–357.

Colligan, R. C., & Offord, K. P. (1992). The MMPI: A contemporary normative study of adolescents. Norwood, NJ: Ablex Publishing Corporation.

Collins, R. L., Taylor, S. E., & Skokan, L. A. (1990). A better world or a shattered vision? Changes in life perspective following victimization. *Social Cognition*, **8**, 263–285.

Commerford, M. C., Gular, E., Orr, D. A., Reznikoff, M., & O'Dowd, M. A. (1994). Coping and psychological distress in women with HIV/AIDS. *Journal of Community Psychology*, **22**, 224–230.

Cook, J. D., & Bickman, L. (1990). Social support and psychological symptomatology following a natural disaster. *Journal of Traumatic Stress*, **3**, 541–557.

Coyne, J. C. (1978). Depression and responses of others. *Journal of Abnormal Psychology*, **85**, 186–193.

Craig, A. R., Hancock, K. M., & Dickson, H. G. (1994). Spinal cord injury: A search for determinants of depression two years after the event. *British Journal of Clinical Psychology*, **33**, 221–230.

Creamer, M., Burgess, P., & Pattison, P. (1990). Cognitive processing in post-trauma reactions: Some preliminary findings. *Psychological Medicine*, 20, 597–604.

Creamer, M., Burgess, P., & Pattison, P. (1992). Reaction to trauma: A cognitive processing model. *Journal of Abnormal Psychology*, 101, 452–459.

Cronkite, R. C., & Moos, R. H. (1984). The role of predisposing and moderating factors in the stress–illness relationship. *Journal of Health and Social Behaviour*, 25, 372–393.

Crummier, T. L., & Green, B. L. (1991). Posttraumatic stress disorder as an early response to sexual assault. *Journal of Interpersonal Violence*, 6, 160–173.

Curran, P., Bell, P., Loughrey, G., Roddy, R., & Rocke, L. (1988, August). Psychological consequences of the Enniskillen bombing. Paper presented at the First European Conference on Traumatic Stress Studies, Lincoln, UK.

Dakof, G. A., & Taylor, S. E. (1990). Victim's perceptions of social support: What is helpful from whom. *Journal of Personality and Social Psychology*, 58, 80–89.

Dalgard, O. S., Bjork, S., & Tambs, K. (1995). Social support, negative life-events and mental health. *British Journal of Psychiatry*, 166, 29–34.

Dalgleish, T., Joseph, S., Thrasher, S., Tranah, T., & Yule, W. (1996). Crisis support following the *Herald of Free Enterprise* disaster: A longitudinal perspective. *Journal of Traumatic Stress*, 9, 833–846.

Daly, R. J. (1983). Samuel Pepys and post traumatic disorder. *British Journal of Psychiatry*, 143, 64–68.

Davidson, J. R. T., & Foa, E. B. (1991). Diagnostic issues in posttraumatic stress disorder: Considerations for DSM-IV. *Journal of Abnormal Psychology*, 100, 346–355.

Davidson, J. R. T., Kudler, H. S., Saunders, W. B., & Smith, R. D. (1990). Symptoms and comorbidity patterns in World War II and Vietnam veterans with posttraumatic stress disorder. *Comprehensive Psychiatry*, 31, 162–170.

Davidson, L., Fleming. I., & Baum, A. (1986). Post-traumatic stress as a function of chronic stress and toxic exposure. In C. Figley (Ed.), *Trauma and its wake* (pp. 57–77). New York: Brunner/Mazel.

Davidson, L. M., Weiss, L., O'Keffe, M., & Baum, A. (1991). Acute stressors and chronic stress at Three Mile Island. *Journal of Traumatic Stress*, 4, 481–493.

Davis, R. C., & Friedman, L. N. (1985). The emotional aftermath of crime and violence. In C. R. Figley (Ed.), *Trauma and its wake: The study and treatment of Post-Traumatic Stress Disorder*. New York: Brunner/Mazel.

De La Fuente, R. (1990). The mental health consequences of the 1985 earthquakes in Mexico. *International Journal of Mental Health*, 19, 21–29.

Delbo, C. (1995). *Auschwitz and After*. New Haven and London: Yale University Press.

Denny, N., Robinowitz, R., & Penk, W. (1987). Conducting applied research on Vietnam combat-related post-traumatic stress disorder. *Journal of Clinical Psychology*, 43, 56–66.

Department of Health (1990). *Disasters: Planning for a caring response. Draft report of the working party on the psychosocial aspects of disasters*. London: Department of Health.

Derogatis, L. R. (1977). *The SCL-9-R: Administration, scoring, and procedures manual* 1. Baltimore: Clinical Psychometrics Research.

Derogatis, L. R. (1983). *SCL-90-R: Administration, scoring and procedures manual—II* (2nd edn.). Baltimore, MD: Clinical Psychometric Research.

DeVellis, B. M., & Blalock, S. J. (1992). Illness attributions and hopelessness depression: The role of hopelessness expectancy. *Journal of Abnormal Psychology*, 101, 257–264.

Di Nardo, P. A., & Barlow, D. H. (1988). *Anxiety Disorders Interview Schedule-Revised (ADIS-R)*. Albany, NY: Phobia and Anxiety Disorders Clinic.

Dollinger, S. J. (1986). The need for meaning following disaster: Attributions and emotional upset. *Personality and Social Psychology Bulletin*, 12, 300–310.

Dollinger, S. J., O'Donnell, J. P., & Staley, A. A. (1984). Lightening-strike disaster: Effects on children's fears and worries. *Journal of Consulting and Clinical Psychology*, 52, 1028–1038.

Duckworth, D.H. (1986). Psychological problems arising from disaster work. *Stress Medicine*, 2, 315–323.

Dyck, M. J. (1993). A proposal for a conditioning model of eye movement desensitization treatment for posttraumatic stress disorder. *Journal of Behaviour Therapy and Experimental Psychiatry*, 24, 201–210.

Dyregrov, A., & Yule, W. (1995a). Screening measures – the development of the UNICEF screening battery. Paper presented at Symposium on 'Children and War' at Fourth European Conference on Traumatic Stress, Paris, 7–11 May 1995.

Dyregrov, A., & Yule, W. (1995b). Screening measures – the development of the UNICEF screening battery. Paper presented at Symposium on 'War Affected Children in Former Yugoslavia' at Eleventh Annual Meeting of the International Society for Traumatic Stress Studies, Boston, 2–6 November 1995.

Earls, F., Smith, E., Reich, W., et al. (1988). Investigating psychopathological consequences of a disaster in children: A pilot study incorporating a structured diagnostic interview. *Journal of the American Academy Child and Adolescent Psychiatry*, 27, 90–95.

Eisler, R. M., Skidmore, J. R., & Ward, C. H. (1988). Masculine gender-role stress: predictor of anger, anxiety, and health-risk behaviours. *Journal of Personality Assessment*, 52, 133–141.

Eitinger, L. (1959). The incidence of mental disease among refugees in Norway. *Journal of Mental Science*, 105, 326–338.

Ellis, E. M., Atkeson, B. M., & Calhoun, K. S. (1981). An assessment of long-term reaction to rape. *Journal of Abnormal Psychology*, 90, 263–266.

Endicott, J., & Spitzer, R. (1972). What! another rating scale? the Psychiatric Evaluation Form. *Journal of Nervous and Mental Disease*, 154, 88–104.

Endler, N. S., & Parker, J. D. A. (1990). Multidimensional assessment of coping: A critical evaluation. *Journal of Personality and Social Psychology*, 58, 844–854.

Epstein, S. (1994). Integration of the cognitive and the psychodynamic unconscious. *American Psychologist*, 49, 709–724.

Erichsen, J. E. (1866). *On railway and other injuries of the nervous system*. London: Walton & Maberly.

Erikson, K. T. (1976). *Everything in its path*. New York: Simon & Schuster.

Eysenck. J., & Eysenck, S. B. G. (1964). *Manual of the Eysenck Personality Inventory*. London: London University Press.

Fairbank, J. A., & Brown, T. A. (1987). Current behavioral approaches to the treatment of posttraumatic stress disorder. *Behaviour Therapist*, 3, 57–64.

Fairbank, J. A., Gross, R. T., & Keane, T. M. (1983a). Treatment of post-traumatic stress disorder: Evaluating outcome with a behavioural code. *Behaviour Modification*, 7, 557–568.

Fairbank, J. A., & Keane, T. M. (1982). Flooding for combat-related stress disorders: Assessment of anxiety reduction across traumatic memories. *Behaviour Therapy*, 13, 499–510.

Fairbank, J. A., Keane, T. M., & Malloy, P. F. (1983b). Some preliminary data on the psychological characteristics of Vietnam veterans with PTSD. *Journal of Consulting and Clinical Psychology*, 51, 912–919.

Fairbank, J. A., McCaffrey, R. J., & Keane, T. M. (1985). Psychometric detection of fabricated symptoms of post-traumatic stress disorder. *American Journal of Psychiatry*, 142, 501–503.

Fairbank, J. A., & Nicholson, R. A. (1987). Theoretical and empirical issues in the treatment of post-traumatic stress disorder in Vietnam veterans. *Journal of Clinical*

Psychology, **43**, 44–55.

Faschingbauer, T. R., Devaul, R., & Zisook, S. (1977). Development of the Texas Inventory of Grief. *American Journal of Psychiatry*, **134**, 696–698.

Feldman, L. A. (1993). Distinguishing depression and anxiety in self-report: Evidence from confirmatory factor analysis on nonclinical and clinical samples, *Journal of Consulting and Clinical Psychology*, **61**, 631–638.

Figley, C. R. (1978). Psychosocial adjustment among Vietnam veterans. In C. R. Figley (Ed.), *Stress disorders among Vietnam veterans*. New York: Brunner/Mazel.

Finkelhor, D. (1990). Early and long-term effects of child sexual abuse: An update. *Professional Psychology: Research and Practice*, **21**, 325–330.

Finkelhor, D., Hotaling, G., Lewis, I. A., & Smith, C. (1990). Sexual abuse in a national survey of adult men and women: Prevalence, characteristics, and risk factors. *Child Abuse and Neglect*, **14**, 19–28.

Flannery, R. B. (1990). Social support and psychological trauma: A methodological review. *Journal of Traumatic Stress*, **3**, 593–612.

Foa, E. B., Feske, U., Murdock, T. B., Kozac, M. J., & McCarthy, P. R. (1991). Processing of threat-related information in rape victims. *Journal of Abnormal Psychology*, **100**, 156–162.

Foa, E. B., & Kozak, M. J. (1986). Emotional processing of fear: Exposure to corrective information. *Psychological Bulletin*, **99**, 20–35.

Foa, E. B., & Riggs, D. S. (1993). Post-traumatic stress disorder in rape victims. In J. Oldham, M. B. Riba, & A. Tasman (Eds), *American Psychiatric Press Review of Psychiatry*, Vol. 12. Washington, DC: American Psychiatric Press.

Foa, E. B., Steketee, G., & Rothbaum, B. O. (1989). Behavioural/cognitive conceptualizations of post-traumatic stress disorder. *Behaviour Therapy*, **20**, 155–176.

Foa, E. B., Rothbaum B. O., Riggs D. S. & Murdock T. B. (1991) Treatment of posttraumatic stress disorder in rape victims: A comparison between cognitive-behavioural procedures and counselling. *Journal of Consulting and Clinical Psychology*, **59**, 715–723.

Foa, E. B., Zinbarg, R., & Rothbaum, B. O. (1992). Uncontrollability and unpredictability in post-traumatic stress disorder: An animal model. *Psychological Bulletin*, **112**, 218–238.

Folkman, S. (1984). Personal control and stress and coping process: A theoretical analysis. *Journal of Personality and Social Psychology*, **46**, 839–852.

Folkman, S., & Lazarus, R. S. (1980). An analysis of coping in a middle-aged community sample. *Journal of Health and Social Behaviour*, **21**, 219–239.

Folkman, S., & Lazarus, R. S. (1985). If it changes it must be a process: Study of emotion and coping during three stages of a college examination. *Journal of Personality and Social Psychology*, **48**, 150–170.

Folkman, S., & Lazarus, R. S. (1988). Coping as a mediator of emotion. *Journal of Personality and Social Psychology*, **54**, 466–475.

Folkman, S., Lazarus, R. S., Dunkel-Schetter, C., DeLongis, A., & Gruen, R. J. (1986a). The dynamics of a stressful encounter: Cognitive appraisal, coping, and encounter outcomes. *Journal of Personality and Social Psychology*, **50**, 992–1003.

Folkman, S., Lazarus, R.S., Gruen, R.L., & DeLongis, A. (1986b). Appraisal, coping, health status, and psychological symptoms. *Journal of Personality and Social Psychology*, **50**, 571–579.

Fontana, A., & Rosenheck, R. (1994a). Traumatic war stressors and psychiatric symptoms among World War II, Korean, and Vietnam war veterans. *Psychology and Aging*, **9**, 27–33.

Fontana, A., & Rosenheck, R. (1994b). Attempted suicide among Vietnam veterans: A model of etiology in a community sample. *American Journal of Psychiatry*, **152**,

102–109.

Fontana, A., & Rosenheck, R. (1994c). Posttraumatic stress disorder among Vietnam theater veterans: A causal model of etiology in a community sample. *Journal of Nervous and Mental Disease*, 182, 677–684.

Fontana, A., Rosenheck, R., & Brett, E. (1992). War zone traumas and posttraumatic stress disorder symptomatology. *Journal of Nervous and Mental Disease*, 180, 748–755.

Fösterling, F. (1985). Attribution retraining: A review. *Psychological Bulletin*, 98, 495–512.

Foy, D. W., Resnick, H. S., Sipprelle, R. C., & Carroll, E. M. (1987). Premilitary, military, and postmilitary factors in the development of combat-related stress disorders. *The Behaviour Therapist*, 10, 3–9.

Foy, D. W., Sipprelle, R., Rueger, D., & Carroll, E. M. (1984). Etiology of posttraumatic stress disorder in Vietnam veterans: Analysis of premilitary, military, and combat exposure influences. *Journal of Consulting and Clinical Psychology*, 52, 79–87.

Frank, E., & Anderson, B. P. (1987). Psychiatric disorders in rape victims: Past history and current symptomatology. *Comprehensive Psychiatry*, 28, 77–82.

Frank, E., & Stewart, B. D. (1984). Depressive symptoms in rape victims. A revisit. *Journal of Affective Disorders*, 7, 77–85.

Frank, E., Turner, S. M., & Duffy, B. (1979). Depressive symptoms in rape victims. *Journal of Affective Disorders*, 1, 269–277.

Frank, E., Turner, S. M., Stewart, B. D., Jacob, M., & West, D. (1981). Past psychiatric symptoms and the response to sexual assault. *Comprehensive Psychiatry*, 22, 479–487.

Frankl, V. E. (1963). *Man's search for meaning*. New York: Washington Square Press.

Fraser, R. M. (1971). The cost of commotion–analysis of psychiatric sequelae of 1969 Belfast riots. *British Journal of Psychiatry*, 118, 257–264.

Frazier, P. (1990). Victim attributions and postrape trauma. *Journal of Personality and Social Psychology*, 59, 298–304.

Frazier, P., & Schauben, L. (1994). Causal attributions and recovery from rape and other stressful life events. *Journal of Social and Clinical Psychology*, 13, 1–14.

Frederick, C. J. (1985a). Selected foci in the spectrum of posttraumatic stress disorders. In J. Laube & S. A. Murphy (Eds), *Perspectives on disaster recovery* (pp. 110–130). East Norwalk, CT: Appleton-Century-Crofts.

Frederick, C. J. (1985b). Children traumatized by catastrophic situations. In S. Eth & R. Pynoos (Eds), *Post-traumatic stress disorder in children*. Washington, DC: American Psychiatric Press.

Frederick, C. J. (1987). Psychic trauma in victims of crime and terrorism. In G. R. Vandenbos & B. K. Bryant (Eds), *Cataclysms, crisis, and catastrophes: Psychology in action*. Washington, DC: American Psychological Association.

Freedy, J. R., Darlene, L. S., Jarrell, M. P., & Masters, C. R. (1992). Towards an understanding of the psychological impact of natural disasters: An application of the Conservation Resources Stress Model. *Journal of Traumatic Stress*, 5, 441–454.

Freedy, J. R., Kilpatrick, D. G., & Resnick, H. S. (1993). Natural disasters and mental health: Theory, assessment, and intervention. In R. Allen (Ed.), *Handbook of post-disaster interventions*. [Special Issue]. *Journal of Social Behaviour and Personality*, 8, 49–103.

Freud, S. (1894). On the grounds for detaching a particular syndrome from neurasthenia under the description 'anxiety neurosis'. *The Standard Edition of the Complete Psychological Works of Sigmund Freud*, Vol. 3. London: Hogarth Press.

Freud, S. (1919). *Introduction to the psychology of the war neurosis* (*Standard Ed.*, Vol. 18). London: Hogarth Press.

Friedman, M. J., Kolb, L. C., Arnold, A., Baker, R., Falcon, S., Furey, J., Gelsomino, J., Gusman, F., Keane, T., Petty, S., Podkul, T., & Smith, J. R. (1987). *Third Annual*

Report of the Chief Medical Director's Special Committee on Post-Traumatic Stress Disorder. Washington, DC: Veterans Administration.

Friedrich, W. N., Grambsch, P., Damon, C., Hewitt, S., Leonard, T., & Broughton, D. (1992). The Child Sexual Behaviour Inventory: Normative and clinical comparisons. *Psychological Assessment*, **4**, 303–311.

Frye, J., & Stockton, R. A. (1982). Discriminant analysis of posttraumatic stress disorder among a group of Vietnam veterans. *American Journal of Psychiatry*, **139**, 52–56.

Galante, R., & Foa, D. (1986). An epidemiological study of psychic trauma and treatment effectiveness for children after a natural disaster. *Journal of the American Academy of Child Psychiatry*, **25**, 357–363.

Garmezy, N. (1986). Children under severe stress: Critique and comments. *Journal of the American Academy of Child Psychiatry*, **25**, 384–392.

Garmezy, N., & Rutter, M. (1985). Acute reactions to stress. In M. Rutter & L. Hersov (Eds) *Child and adolescent psychiatry: Modern approaches* (2nd edition). Oxford: Blackwell.

Genest, M., Bowen, R. C., Dudley, J., & Keegan, D. (1990). Assessment of strategies for coping with anxiety: Preliminary investigations. *Journal of Anxiety Disorders*, **4**, 1–14.

Gerardi, R., Keane, T. M., & Penk, W. (1989). Utility: Sensitivity and specificity in developing diagnostic tests of combat-related post-traumatic stress disorder (PTSD). *Journal of Clinical Psychology*, **45**, 691–703.

Gersons, B. P. R. (1989). Patterns of PTSD among police officers following shooting incidents: A two-dimensional model and treatment implications. *Journal of Traumatic Stress*, **2**, 247–257.

Gersons, P. R., & Carlier, I. V. E. (1992). Post-traumatic stress disorder: The history of a recent concept. *British Journal of Psychiatry*, **161**, 742–748.

Gibbs, M. S. (1989). Factors in the victim that mediate between disaster and psychopathology: A review. *Journal of Traumatic Stress*, **2**, 489–514.

Gil, T., Calev, A., Greenberg, D., Kugelmass, S., & Lerer, B. (1990). Cognitive functioning in post-traumatic stress disorder. *Journal of Traumatic Stress*, **3**, 29–46.

Glaubman, H., Mikulincer, M., Porat, A., Wasserman, O., & Birger, M. (1990). Sleep of chronic posttraumatic patients. *Journal of Traumatic Stress*, **3**, 255–263.

Gleser, G. C., Green, B. L., & Winget, C. N. (1981). *Prolonged psychosocial effects of disaster.* New York: Academic Press.

Goenjian, A. (1993). A mental health relief programme in Armenia after the 1988 Earthquake: Implementation and clinical observations. *British Journal of Psychiatry*, **163**, 230–239.

Goenjian, A. K., Najarian, L. M., Pynoos, R. S., Steinberg, A. M., Manoukian, G., Tavosian, A., & Fairbanks, L. A. (1994). Posttraumatic stress disorder in elderly and younger adults after the 1988 earthquake in Armenia. *American Journal of Psychiatry*, **151**, 895–901.

Goffman, E. (1968). *Stigma: Notes on the management of a spoiled identity.* Harmondsworth, Middlesex: Penguin books.

Gold, E. R. (1986). Long-term effects of sexual victimization in childhood: An attributional approach. *Journal of Consulting and Clinical Psychology*, **54**, 471–475.

Gold, S. R., Milan, L. D., Mayall, A., & Johnson, A. E. (1994). A cross-validation study of the Trauma Symptom Checklist: The role of mediating variables. *Journal of Interpersonal Violence*, **9**, 12–26.

Goldberg, D. P. (Ed.) (1972). *The detection of psychiatric illness by questionnaire.* London: Oxford University Press.

Goldberg, D. (1978). *Manual of the General Health Questionnaire.* Windsor, England:

NFER Publishing Company.

Golberg, D. P., & Hillier, V. F. (1979). A scaled version of the General Health Questionnaire. *Psychological Medicine*, **9**, 139–145.

Goldberg, D., & Williams, P. (1988). *A user's guide to the General Health Questionnaire.* NFER-NELSON.

Goodman, R. (1994). A modified version of the Rutter Parent Questionnaire including extra items on children's strengths: A research note. *Journal of Child Psychology and Psychiatry*, **35**, 1483–1494.

Gore, S. (1981). Stress buffering functions of social supports: An appraisal and clarification of research models. In B. S. Dohrenwend & B. P. Dohrenwend (Eds), *Stressful life events and their contexts* (pp. 202–222). New York: Prodist.

Green, B. L., Grace, M. C., & Gleser, G. C. (1985a). Identifying survivors at risk: Long-term impairment following the Beverly Hills Supper Club fire. *Journal of Consulting and Clinical Psychology*, **53**, 672–678.

Green, B. L., Grace, M. C., Lindy, J. D., & Gleser, G. C. (1990b). War stressors and symptom persistence in posttraumatic stress disorder. *Journal of Anxiety Disorders*, **4**, 31–39.

Green, B. L., Grace, M. C., Lindy, J. D., Gleser, G. C., Leonard, A. C., & Crummier, T. L. (1990a). Buffalo Creek survivors in the second decade: comparison with unexposed and nonlitigant groups. *Journal of Applied Social Psychology*, **20**, 1033–1050.

Green, B. L., Grace, M. C., Lindy, J. D., Titchener, J. L., & Lindy, J. G. (1983). Levels of functional impairment following a civilian disaster: the Beverly Hills Supper club fire. *Journal of Consulting and Clinical Psychology*, **51**, 573–580.

Green, B. L., Grace, M. C., Vary, M. G., Crummier, T. L., Gleser, G. C., & Leonard, A. C. (1994). Children of disaster in the second decade: A 17-year follow up of Buffalo Creek survivors. *Journal of the American Academy of Child and Adolescent Psychiatry*, **33**, 71–79.

Green, B. L., & Lindy, J. D. (1994). Post-traumatic stress disorder in victims of disaster. *Psychiatric Clinics of North America*, **17**, 301–309.

Green, B.L., Lindy, J.D., & Grace, M.C. (1985b). Posttraumatic stress disorder. Toward DSM-IV. *Journal of Nervous and Mental Disease*, **173**, 406–411.

Green, B. L., Wilson, J., & Lindy. J. (1985c). Conceptualizing post-traumatic stress disorder: A psycho-social framework. In C. Figley (Ed.), *Trauma and its wake* (pp. 53–69). New York: Brunner/Mazel.

Greenberg, J., Pyszczynski, T., Solomon, S., Pinel, E., Simon, L., & Jordan, K. (1993). Effects of self-esteem on vulnerability-denying defensive distortions: Further evidence of an anxiety-buffering function of self-esteem. *Journal of Experimental Social Psychology*, **29**, 229–251.

Greenberg, J., Solomon, S., Pyszczynski, T., Rosenblatt, A., Burling, J., Lyon, D., Simon, L., & Pinel, E. (1992). Why do people need self-esteem? Converging evidence that self-esteem serves an anxiety-buffering function. *Journal of Personality and Social Psychology*, **63**, 913–922.

Greer, S., Morris, T., & Pettingale, K. W. (1979). Psychological response to breast cancer: Effect on outcome. *Lancet*, ii, 785–787.

Grinker, R. R., & Spiegel, J. P. (1943). *War neurosis in North Africa, the Tunisian Campaign, January to May 1943.* New York: Josiah Macy Foundation.

Hadden, W. A., Rutherford, W. H., & Merret, J. D. (1978). The injuries of terrorist bombing: A study of 1,532 consecutive patients. *British Journal of Surgery*, **65**, 525–530.

Hammarberg, M. (1992). Penn Inventory for posttraumatic stress disorder: Psychometric properties. *Psychological Assessment*, **4**, 67–76.

Handford, H. A., Mayes, S. O., Mattison, R. E., Humphrey, F. J., Bagnato, S., Bixler, E. O., & Kales, J. D. (1983). Child and parent reaction to the TMI nuclear accident. *Journal of the American Academy of Child and Adolescent Psychiatry*, **25**, 346–355.

Hansson, R., Jones, W., & Carpenter, B. (1984). Relational competence and social support. In P. Shaver (Ed.), *Review of Personality and Social Psychology* (Vol. 5, pp. 265–284). Beverly Hills, CA: Sage.

Harper, H., Oei, T. P. S., Medalgio, S., & Evans, L. (1990). Dimensionality, validity, and utility of the I-E scale with anxiety disorders. *Journal of Anxiety Disorders*, **4**, 89–98.

Hartsough, D.M., & Myers, D.G. (1985). *Disaster work and mental health: Prevention and control of stress among workers.* Washington, DC: NIMH.

Harvey, J. H., Stein, S. K., Olsen, N., Roberts, R. J., Lutgendorf, S. K., & Ho, J. A. (1995). Narratives of loss and recovery from a natural disaster. *Journal of Social Behaviour and Personality*, **10**, 313–330.

Harvey, J. H., & Weary, G. (1985). *Attribution: Basic issues and applications.* Orlando, FL: Academic.

Hayman, P. M., & Scaturo, D. J. (1993). Psychological debriefing of returning military personnel: a protocol for post-combat intervention. In R. Allen (Ed.), *Handbook of post-disaster interventions* [Special Issue]. *Journal of Social Behaviour and Personality*, **8**, 117–130.

Hefez, A., Metz, L., & Lavie, P. (1987). Long-term effects of extreme situational stress on sleep and dreaming. *American Journal of Psychiatry*, **144**, 344–347.

Heider, F. (1958). *The psychology of interpersonal relations.* New York: Wiley.

Helzer, J. E., Robins, L. N., & McEvoy, L. (1987). Post-traumatic stress disorder in the general population: Findings of the epidemiological catchment area survey. *New England Journal of Medicine*, **317**, 1630–1634.

Henderson, A. S., Byrne, D. G., & Duncan-Jones, P. (1981). *Neurosis and the social environment.* New York and London: Academic Press.

Herman, J. L. (1992a). Complex PTSD: A syndrome in survivors of prolonged and repeated trauma. *Journal of Traumatic Stress*, **5**, 377–392.

Herman, J. L. (1992b). *Trauma and recovery: From domestic abuse to political terror.* London: Pandora.

Hickling, E. J., & Blanchard, E. B. (1992). Post-traumatic stress disorder and motor vehicle accidents. *Journal of Anxiety Disorders*, **6**, 285–291.

Hierholzer, R., Munson, J., Peabody, C., & Rosenberg, J. (1992). Clinical presentation of PTSD in World War II combat veterans. *Hospital and Community Psychiatry*, **43**, 806–820.

Hill, J., & Zautra, A. (1989). Self-blame attributions and unique vulnerability as predictors of postrape demoralization. *Journal of Social and Clinical Psychology*, **8**, 368–375.

Hobfoll, S. E. (1989). Conservation of resources: A new attempt at conceptualizing stress. *American Psychologist*, **44**, 513–524.

Hobfoll, S. E., Lilly, R. S., & Jackson, A. P. (1991). Conservation of social resources and the self. In H. O. F. Veiel & U. Baumann (Eds), *The meaning and measurement of social support: Taking stock of 20 years of research.* Washington, DC: Hemisphere Publishing.

Hodgkinson, P., & Joseph, S. (1995). Factor analysis of the Impact of Event Scale with female bank staff following a raid. *Personality and Individual Differences*, **5**, 773–775.

Hodgkinson, P. E., Joseph, S., Yule, W., & Williams, R. (1993). Viewing human remains following disaster: helpful or harmful? *Medicine, Science, and the Law*, **33**, 197–202.

Hodgkinson, P. E., Joseph, S., Yule, W., & Williams, R. (1995). Measuring grief after sudden violent death: Zeebrugge bereaved at 30 months. *Personality and Individual Differences*, **18**, 805–808.

Hodgkinson, P. E., & Stewart, M. (1991). *Coping with catastrophe: A handbook of disaster management*. London: Routledge.

Holen, A. (1991). A longitudinal study of the occurrence and persistence of post-traumatic health problems in disaster survivors. *Stress Medicine*, 7, 11–17.

Holen, A. (1993). The North Sea oil rig disaster. In J. P. Wilson & B. Raphael (Eds), *International Handbook of Traumatic Stress Syndromes*. New York: Plenum.

Hollon, S. D., & Kendall, P. C. (1980). Cognitive self-statements in depression: Development of an automatic thoughts questionnaire. *Cognitive Therapy and Research*, 4, 383–395.

Hollon, S. D., Shelton, R. C., & Davis, D. D. (1993). Cognitive therapy for depression: Conceptual issues and clinical efficacy. *Journal of Consulting and Clinical Psychology*, **61**, 270–275.

Horowitz, M. J. (1975). Intrusive and repetitive thoughts after stress. *Archives of General Psychiatry*, **32**, 1457–1463.

Horowitz, M. J. (1976). *Stress response syndromes*. New York: Jason Aronson.

Horowitz, M. J. (1979). Psychological response to serious life events. In V. Hamilton and D. M. Warburton (Eds), *Human stress and cognition: An information processing approach*. New York: Wiley.

Horowitz, M. J. (1982). Psychological processes induced by illness, injury, and loss. In T. Millon, C. Green, & R. Meagher (Eds), *Handbook of clinical health psychology* (pp. 53–68). New York: Plenum.

Horowitz, M. J. (1986a). *Stress response syndromes*. Northvale, NJ: Jason Aronson.

Horowitz, M. J. (1986b). Stress–response syndromes: A review of posttraumatic and adjustment disorders. *Hospital and Community Psychiatry*, **37**, 241–249.

Horowitz, M. J., Wilner, N., & Alvarez, W. (1979). Impact of Event Scale: A measure of subjective stress. *Psychosomatic Medicine*, **41**, 209–218.

Hough, R. L., Vega, W. A., Valle, R., Kolody, B., Griswald del Castillo, R., & Tarke, H. (1990). Mental health consequences of the San Ysidro McDonald's massacre: A community study. *Journal of Traumatic Stress*, 3, 71–92.

House, J. S., & Kahn, R. L. (1985). Measuring social support. In S. Cohen & S.L. Syme (Eds), *Social support and health* (pp. 83–108). New York: Academic Press.

Houskamp, B. M., & Foy, D. W. (1991). The assessment of posttraumatic stress disorder in battered women. *Journal of Interpersonal Violence*, **6**, 365–371.

Hovens, J. E., & van der Ploeg, H. M. (1993). Post Traumatic Stress Disorder in Dutch psychiatric in-patients. *Journal of Traumatic Stress*, **6**, 91–101.

Hovens, J. E., van der Ploeg, H. M., Bramsen, I., Klaarenbeek, M. T. A., Schreuder, J. N., & Rivero, V. V. (1994a). The development of the self-rating inventory for posttraumatic stress disorder. *Acta Psychiatric Scandanavia*, **90**, 172–183.

Hovens, J. E., van der Ploeg, H. H., Klaarenbeek, M. T. A., Bramsen, I., Schreuder, J. N., & Rivero, V. V. (1994b). The assessment of posttraumatic stress disorder: with the clinician administered PTSD Scale: Dutch results. *Journal of Clinical Psychology*, **50**, 325–340.

Huerta, F., & Horton, R. (1978). Coping behaviour of elderly flood victims. *The Gerontologist*, **18**, 541–546.

Hughes, C. F., Uhlmann, C., & Pennebaker, J. W. (1994). The body's response to processing emotional trauma: Linking verbal text with autonomic activity. *Journal of Personality*, **62**, 565–585.

Husaini, B. A., & Neff, J. A. (1981). Social class and depressive symptomatology. The role of life change events and locus of control. *Journal of Nervous and Mental Disease*, **169**, 638–647.

Hyer, L., Davis, H., Boudewyns, P., & Woods, M. G. (1991). A short form of the Mississippi Scale for combat related PTSD. *Journal of Clinical Psychology*, 47, 510–518.

Ingram, R, E., Lumrey, A. E., Cruet, D., & Sieber, W. (1987). Attentional processes in depressive disorders. *Cognitive Therapy and Research*, 11, 351–360.

Inman, D. J., Silver, S. M., & Doghramji, K. (1990). Sleep disturbance in post-traumatic stress disorder: A comparison with non-PTSD insomnia. *Journal of Traumatic Stress*, 3, 429–437.

International Federation of Red Cross and Red Crescent Societies World Disaster Report (1993). Dordrecht, The Netherlands: Martinus Nijhoff.

Jacobson, D. E. (1986). Types and timing of social support. *Journal of Health and Social Behaviour*, 27, 250–264.

Janet, P. (1889). *L'automatisme psychologique*. Paris: Alcan.

Janet, P. (1909). *Les Nervoses*. Paris: Flammarion.

Janney, J. G., Masuda, M., & Holmes, T. H. (1977). Impact of a natural catastrophe on life events. *Journal of Human Stress*, 3, 22–34.

Janoff-Bulman, R. (1979). Characterological versus behavioral self-blame: Inquiries into depression and rape. *Journal of Personality and Social Psychology*, 37, 1798–1809.

Janoff-Bulman, R. (1985). The aftermath of victimisation: Rebuilding shattered assumptions. In C. R. Figley (Ed.), *Trauma and its wake*, Vol. 1. New York: Brunner/Mazel.

Janoff-Bulman, R. (1989). Assumptive worlds and the stress of traumatic events: Applications of the schema construct. *Social Cognition*, 7, 113–136.

Janoff-Bulman, R. (1992). *Shattered assumptions: Towards a new psychology of trauma*. New York: The Free Press.

Jelinek, J.M., & Williams, T. (1984). Post-traumatic stress disorder and substance abuse in Vietnam veterans: Treatment problems, strategies and recommendations. *Journal of Substance Abuse and Treatment*, 1, 87–97.

Jensen, J. A. (1994). An investigation of eye movement desensitization and reprocessing (EMD/R) as a treatment for posttraumatic stress disorder (PTSD) symptoms of Vietnam combat veterans. *Behavior Therapy*, 25, 311–325.

Johnson, D. R., Feldman, S. C., Lubin, H., & Southwick, S. M. (1995). The therapeutic use of ritual and ceremony in the treatment of post-traumatic stress disorder. *Journal of Traumatic Stress*, 8, 283–298.

Jones, D. R. (1985). Secondary disaster victims: The emotional effects of recovering and identifying human remains. *American Journal of Psychiatry*, 142, 303–307.

Jones, J. C., & Barlow, D. H. (1990). The etiology of posttraumatic stress disorder. *Clinical Psychology Review*, 10, 299–328.

Joseph, S., Andrews, Williams, R., & Yule, W. (1992a). Crisis support and psychiatric symptomatology in survivors of the Jupiter cruise ship disaster. *British Journal of Clinical Psychology*, 31, 63–73.

Joseph, S., Brewin, C.R., Yule, W., & Williams, R. (1991). Causal attributions and psychiatric symptoms in survivors of the Herald of Free Enterprise disaster. *British Journal of Psychiatry*, 159, 542–546.

Joseph, S., Brewin, C.R., Yule, W., & Williams, R. (1993a). Causal attributions and post-traumatic symptoms in adolescent survivors of disaster. *Journal of Child Psychology and Psychiatry*, 34, 247–253.

Joseph, S., Dalgleish, T., Thrasher, S., Yule, W., Williams, R., & Hodgkinson, P. (1996). Chronic emotional processing in survivors of the Herald of Free Enterprise disaster: The relationship of intrusion and avoidance at 3 years to distress at 5 years. *Behaviour Research and Therapy*, 34, 357–360.

Joseph, S., Dalgleish, T., Williams, R., Thrasher, S., Yule, W., & Hodgkinson, P.

(1997). Attitudes towards emotional expression and post-traumatic stress in survivors of the Herald of Free Enterprise disaster. *British Journal of Clincial Psychology*, **36**, 133–138.

Joseph, S., Hodgkinson, P., Yule, W., & Williams, R. (1993b). Guilt and distress 30 months after the capsize of the Herald of Free Enterprise. *Personality and Individual Differences*, **14**, 271–273.

Joseph, S., Williams, R., & Yule, W. (1993c). Changes in outlook following disaster: The preliminary development of a measure to assess positive and negative responses. *Journal of Traumatic Stress*, **6**, 271–279.

Joseph, S., Williams, R., Yule, W., & Walker, A. (1992b). Factor analysis of the Impact of Event Scale in survivors of two disasters at sea. *Personality and Individual Differences*, **13**, 693–697.

Joseph, S., Yule, W., & Williams, R. (1993d). Post-traumatic stress: attributional aspects. *Journal of Traumatic Stress*, **6**, 501–513.

Joseph, S., Yule, W., & Williams, R. (1994). The Herald of Free Enterprise disaster: The relationship of intrusion and avoidance to subsequent depression and anxiety. *Behaviour Research and Therapy*, **32**, 115–117.

Joseph, S., Yule, W., & Williams, R. (1995a). Emotional processing in survivors of the Jupiter cruise ship disaster. *Behaviour Research and Therapy*, **33**, 187–192.

Joseph, S., Yule, W., Williams, R., & Andrews, B. (1993e). Crisis support in the aftermath of disaster: A longitudinal perspective. *British Journal of Clinical Psychology*, **32**, 177–185.

Joseph, S., Yule, W., Williams, R., & Hodgkinson, P. (1993f). Increased substance use in survivors of the Herald of Free Enterprise disaster. *British Journal of Medical Psychology*, **66**, 185–191.

Joseph, S., Yule, W., Williams, R., & Hodgkinson, P. (1993g). The Herald of Free Enterprise disaster: Measuring post-traumatic symptoms thirty months on. *British Journal of Clinical Psychology*, **32**, 327–332.

Kardiner, A. (1941). *The traumatic neurosis of war*. Psychosomatic Medicine Monograph II–III. New York: Paul B. Hoeber.

Karlehagen, S., Malt, U. F., Hoff, H., Tibell, E., Herrstromer, U., Hildingson, K., & Leymann, H. (1993). The effect of major railway accidents on the psychological health of train drivers—II. A longitudinal study of the one-year outcome after the accident. *Journal of Psychosomatic Research*, **37**, 807–817.

Keane, T. M. (1993). Symptomatology of Vietnam veterans with posttraumatic stress disorder. In J. R. T. & E. B. Foa (Eds), *Posttraumatic stress disorder: DSM-IV and beyond* (pp. 99–112). Washington, DC: American Psychiatric Press.

Keane, T. M., Caddell, J. M., Martin, B., Zimering, R. T., & Fairbank, J. A. (1983). Substance abuse among Vietnam veterans with posttraumatic stress disorders. *Bulletin of Psychologists and Addictive Behaviour*, **2**, 117–122.

Keane, T. M., Caddell, J. M., & Taylor, K, L. (1988). Mississippi scale for combat-related posttraumatic stress disorder: Three studies in reliability and validity. *Journal of Consulting and Clinical Psychology*, **56**, 85–90.

Keane, T. M., & Kaloupek, D.G. (1982). Imaginal flooding in the treatment of post-traumatic stress disorder. *Journal of Consulting and Clinical Psychology*, **50**, 138–140.

Keane, T. M., Malloy, P. P., & Fairbank, J. A. (1984). Empirical development of an MMPI subscale for the assessment of combat-related PTSD. *Journal of Consulting and Clinical Psychology*, **52**, 888–891.

Keane, T. M., Scott, W. O., Chavoya, G. A., Lamparski, D. M., & Fairbank, J. A. (1985a). Social support in Vietnam veterans: A comparative analysis. *Journal of Consulting and Clinical Psychology*, **53**, 95–102.

Keane, T. M., Wolfe, J. A., & Taylor, K. L. (1987). Post-traumatic stress disorder: Evidence for diagnostic validity and methods of psychological assessment. *Journal of Clinical Psychology*, 43, 32–43.

Keane, T. M., Zimering, R. T., & Caddell, J. M. (1985b). A behavioural formulation of post-traumatic stress disorder in Vietnam veterans. *The Behaviour Therapist*, 8, 9–12.

Kee, M., Bell, P., Loughrey, G. C., Roddy, R. J., & Curran, P. S. (1987). Victims of violence: A demographic and clinical study. *Medicine, Science and the Law*, 27, 241.

Kendall, R. E. (1976). Classification of depressions: A review of contemporary confusion. *British Journal of Psychiatry*, 129, 15–28.

Kessler, R. C., McGonagle, K. A., Zhao, S., Nelson, C. B., Hughes, M., Eshleman, S., Wittchen, H., & Kendler, K. S. (1994). Lifetime and 12 month prevalence of DSM-III-R psychiatric disorders in the United States: Results from the National Comorbidity Survey. *Archives of General Psychiatry*, 51, 8–19.

Kilpatrick, D. G., Resick, P. A., & Veronen, L. J. (1981). Effects of a rape experience: A longitudinal study. *Journal of Social Issues*, 37, 105–122.

Kilpatrick, D. G., Saunders, B. E., Amick-McMullan, A., Best, C. L., Veronen, L. J., & Resnick, H. S. (1989). Victim and crime factors associated with the development of crime-related post-traumatic stress disorder. *Behavior Therapy*, 20, 199–214.

Kilpatrick, D. G., Saunders, B. E., Veronen, L. J., Best, C. L., & Von, J. M. (1987). Criminal victimization: Lifetime prevalence reporting to police, and psychological impact. *Crime and Delinquency*, 33, 479–489.

Kilpatrick, D. G., & Veronen, L. J. (1983). Treatment for rape-related problems: crisis intervention is not enough. In L. H. Cohen, W. L. Clauban, & G. A. Specter (Eds), *Crisis Intervention*. New York: Human Sciences Press.

Kilpatrick, D. G., Veronen, L. J., & Best, C. L. (1985). Factors predicting psychological distress among rape victims. In C. R. Figley (Ed.), *Trauma and its wake*. New York: Brunner/Mazel.

Kilpatrick, D. G., Veronen, L. J., & Resick, P. A. (1979). Assessment of the aftermath of rape: Changing patterns of fear. *Journal of Behavioural Assessment*, 1, 133–148.

Kimerling, R., & Calhoun, K. S. (1994). Somatic symptoms, social support, and treatment seeking among sexual assault victims. *Journal of Consulting and Clinical Psychology*, 62, 333–340.

King, D. W., King, L. A., Gudanowski, D. M., & Vreven, D. L. (1995). Alternative representations of war zone stressors: Relationships to posttraumatic stress disorder in male and female Vietnam veterans. *Journal of Abnormal Psychology*, 104, 184–196.

Kinzie, J. D., Sack, W. H., Angell, R. H., et al. (1986). The psychiatric effects of massive trauma on Cambodian children: I. The children. *Journal of the American Academy for Child and Adolescent Psychiatry*, 25, 370–376.

Kiser, L. J., Ackerman, B. J., Brown, E., Edwards, N. B., McColgan, E., Pugh, R., & Pruitt, D. B. (1988). Posttraumatic stress disorder in young children: A reaction to purported sexual abuse. *Journal of the American Academy for Child and Adolescent Psychiatry*, 27, 645–649.

Kluznik, J. C., Speed, N., Van Valkenburg, C., & Magraw, R. (1986). Forty year follow up of United States prisoners of war. *American Journal of Psychiatry*, 143, 1443–1446.

Koss, M. (1993). Detecting the scope of rape: A review of prevalence research methods. *Journal of Interpersonal Violence*, 8, 198–222.

Kolb, L. C. (1987). A neuropsychological hypothesis explaining post-traumatic stress disorders. *American Journal of Psychiatry*, 144, 989–995.

Kovacs, M. (1983). A self-rated depression scale for school-aged youngsters. Unpublished manuscript. University of Pittsburgh School of Medicine, Pittsburgh, PA.

Kraepelin, E. (1886). *Psychiatrie*, Vol. 5. Leipzig: Barth.

Krantz, L. (1992). *What the odds are*. New York: Harper Perennial.

Krause, N. (1987). Exploring the impact of a natural disaster on the health and well being of older adults. *Journal of Human Stress*, Summer, 61–69.

Krystal, H. (1970). Trauma and the stimulus barrier. Paper presented at the Annual General Meeting of the Psychoanalytic Association. San Francisco.

Kubler-Ross, E. (1969). *On death and dying*. New York: Macmillan.

Kuch, J., & Cox, B. J. (1992). Symptoms of PTSD in 124 survivors of the Holocaust. *American Journal of Psychiatry*, **149**, 337–340.

Kulka, R. A., Schlenger, W. E., Fairbank, J. A., Hough, R. L., Jordon, B. K., Marmar, C. R., & Weiss, D. S. (1990). *Trauma and the Vietnam war generation: Report of findings from the National Vietnam Veterans Readjustment Study*. New York: Brunner/Mazel.

Kulka, R. A., Schlenger, W. E., Fairbank, J. A., Jordan, B. K., Hough, R. L., Marmar, C. R., & Weiss, D. S. (1991). Assessment of Posttraumatic Stress Disorder in the community: Prospects and pitfalls from recent studies of Vietnam veterans. Psychological Assessment. *Journal of Consulting and Clinical Psychology*, **3**, 547–560.

Lacoursiere, R. B. (1993). Diverse motives for fictitious post-traumatic stress disorder. *Journal of Traumatic Stress*, **6**, 141–149.

Lacoursiere, R. B., Godfrey, K. E., & Ruby, L. M. (1980). Traumatic neurosis in the etiology of alcoholism: Vietnam combat and other trauma. *American Journal of Psychiatry*, **137**, 966–968.

Lang, P. J. (1977). Imagery in therapy: An information processing analysis of fear. *Behavior Therapy*, **8**, 862–886.

Lang, P. J. (1985). The cognitive psychophysiology of emotion: Fear and anxiety. In A. H. Tuma & J. D. Maser (Eds), *Anxiety and the anxiety disorder* (pp. 131–170). Hillsdale, NJ: Erlbaum.

Langer, E. J., & Rodin, J. (1976). The effects of choice and enhanced personal responsibility for the aged: A field experiment in an institutional setting. *Journal of Personality and Social Psychology*, **34**, 191–198.

Laufer, R. S., Brett, E., & Gallops, M. S. (1985). Dimensions of post-traumatic stress disorder among Vietnam veterans. *Journal of Nervous and Mental Disorder*, **173**, 538–545.

Lavie, P., Hefez, A., Halperin, G., & Enoch, D. (1979). Long-term effects of traumatic war-related events on sleep. *American Journal of Psychiatry*, **136**, 175–178.

Layden, M. A. (1982). Attribution style therapy. In C. Antaki & C. Brewin (Eds), *Attributions and psychological change*. London: Academic Press.

Lazarus, R. S. (1966). *Psychological stress and the coping process*. New York: McGraw-Hill.

Lazarus, R. S., & Folkman, S. (1984). *Stress, appraisal, and coping*. (pp. 378–389). New York: Springer.

Lees-Haley, P. R. (1990). Malingering mental disorder on the Impact of Events Scale. *Journal of Traumatic Stress*, **3**, 315–321.

Lehman, D. R., Davis, C. G., DeLongis, A., Wortman, C. B., Bluck, S., Mandel, D. R., & Ellard, J. H. (1993). Positive and negative life changes following bereavement and their relations to adjustment. *Journal of Social and Clinical Psychology*, **12**, 90–112.

Leopold, R. L., & Dillon, H. (1963). Psychanatomy of a disaster: A long-term study of post-traumatic neurosis in survivors of a marine explosion. *American Journal of Psychiatry*, **119**, 913–921.

Lerner, M. J. (1975). The justice motive in social behaviour: Introduction. *Journal of Social Issues*, **31**, 1–19.

Lerner, M. J. (1980). *The belief in a just world*. New York: Plenum Press.

Lerner, M. J., & Miller, D. T. (1978). Just world research and the attribution process: Looking back and ahead. *Psychological Bulletin*, **85**, 1030–1051.

Lewinsohn, P. M., & Talkington, J. (1979). Studies on the measurement of unpleasant events and relations with others. *Applied Psychological Measurement*, 3, 83–101.

Liese, B. S. (1994). Brief therapy, crisis intervention and the cognitive therapy of substance abuse. *Crisis Intervention*, 1, 11–29.

Lifton, R. J. (1967). *Death in life: Survivors of Hiroshima*. New York: Random House.

Lifton, R. J., & Olson, E. (1976). The human meaning of total disaster: The Buffalo Creek experience. *Psychiatry*, 39, 1–18.

Lima, B. R., Chavez, H., Samaniego, N., Pompe, M. S., Pai, S., Santacruz, H., & Lozano, J. (1989). Disaster severity and emotional disturbance: implications for primary mental health care in developing countries. *Acta Psychiatric Scandanavia*, 79, 74–82.

Lima, B. R., Pai, S., Santacruz, H., & Lozano, J. (1987). Screening for the psychological consequences of a major disaster in a developing country. *Acta Psychiatric Scandanavia*, 76, 561–567.

Lima, B. R., Pai, S., Toledo, V., Caris, L., Haro, J. M., Lozano, J., & Santacruz, H. (1993). Emotional distress in disaster victims: a follow up study. *Journal of Nervous and Mental Disease*, 181, 388–393.

Lima, B.R., Pai, S., Lozano, J., & Santacruz, H. (1991). The stability of emotional symptoms among disaster victims in a developing country. *Journal of Traumatic Stress*, 3, 497–506.

Lisak, D. (1994). The psychological impact of sexual abuse: Content analysis of interviews with male survivors. *Journal of Traumatic Stress*, 7, 525–548.

Lisak, D., & Luster, L. (1994). Educational, occupational, and relationship histories of men who were sexually and/or physically abused as children. *Journal of Traumatic Stress*, 7, 507–524.

Litt, M. D. (1988). Cognitive mediators of stressful experience: Self-efficacy and perceived control. *Cognitive Therapy and Research*, 12, 241–260.

Litz, B. T., & Keane, T. M. (1989). Information processing in anxiety disorders: Application to the understanding of posttraumatic stress disorder. *Clinical Psychology Review*, 9, 243–257.

Litz, B. T., Penk, W. E., Gerardi, R. J., & Keane, T. M. (1992). In P. A. Saigh (Ed.), *Posttraumatic stress disorder: A behavioral approach to assessment and treatment*. Boston: Allyn & Bacon.

Lloyd, C. (1980). Life events and depressive disorder reviewed. *Archives of General Psychiatry*, 37, 529–541.

Logue, J.N., Hansen, H., & Struening, E. (1979). Emotional and physical distress following Hurricane Agnes in Wyoming Valley of Pennsylvania. *Public Health Reports*, 4, 495–502.

Lopez-Ibor, J.J., Soria. J., Canas, F., & Rodrigues-Gamazo, M. (1985). Psychopathological aspects of the toxic oil syndrome catastrophe. *British Journal of Psychiatry*, 147, 352–365.

Loughrey, G. C., Bell, P., Kee, M., Roddy, R. J., & Curran, P. S. (1988). Posttraumatic stress disorder and civil violence in Northern Ireland. *British Journal of Psychiatry*, 153, 554–560.

Lund, M., Foy, D., Sipprelle, C., & Strachan, A. (1984). The combat exposure scale: A systematic assessment of trauma in the Vietnam war. *Journal of Clinical Psychology*, 40, 1323–1328.

Lyons, H. A. (1974). Terrorist bombing and the psychological sequelae. *Journal of the Irish Medical Association*, 67, 15.

Lyons, J. A. (1991). Strategies for assessing the potential for positive adjustment following trauma. *Journal of Traumatic Stress*, 4, 93–112.

Lyons, J.A., & Keane, T.M. (1989). Implosive therapy for the treatment of combat related PTSD. *Journal of Traumatic Stress*, 2, 137–152.

Lyons, J. A., & Keane, T. M. (1992). Keane PTSD scale: MMPI and MMPI-2 update. *Journal of Traumatic Stress*, 5, 111–117.

MacLeod, A. K., & Tarbuck, A. F. (1994). Explaining why negative events will happen to oneself: Parasuicides are pessimistic because they can't see any reason not to be. *British Journal of Clinical Psychology*, 33, 317–326.

Madakasira, S., & O'Brien, K. F. (1987). Acute posttraumatic stress disorder in victims of a natural disaster. *Journal of Nervous and Mental Disease*, 175, 286–290.

Maida, C. A., Gordon, N. S., Steinberg, A., & Gordon, G. (1989). Psychosocial impact of disasters: Victims of the Baldwin fire. *Journal of Traumatic Stress*, 2, 37–48.

Maj, M., Starace, F., Crepet, P., Lobrace, S., Veltro, F., DeMarco, F., & Kemali, D. (1989). Prevalence of psychiatric disorders among subjects exposed to a natural disaster. *Acta Psychiatric Scandanavia*, 79, 544–549.

Malloy, P. F., Fairbank, J. A., & Keane, T. M. (1983). Validation of a multimethod assessment of post-traumatic stress disorders in Vietnam veterans. *Journal of Consulting and Clinical Psychology*, 51, 488–494.

Malmquist, C. P. (1986). Children who witness parental murder: Post-traumatic aspects. *Journal of the American Academy of Child Psychiatry*, 25, 320–325.

Malt, U. F., Karlehagen, S., Hoff, H., Herrstromer, U., Hildingson, K., Tibell, E., & Leymann, H. (1993). The effect of major railway accidents on the psychological health of train drivers—I. Acute psychological responses to accident. *Journal of Psychosomatic Research*, 37, 793–805.

Manton, M., & Talbot, A. (1991). Crisis intervention after an armed hold-up: Guidelines for counsellors. *Journal of Traumatic Stress*, 3, 507–522.

March, J. S. (1990). The nosology of posttraumatic stress disorder. *Journal of Anxiety Disorders*, 4, 61–82.

March, J. S. (1993). What constitutes a stressor? The criterion A issue. In J. R. T. Davidson & E. B. Foa (Eds), *Posttraumatic stress disorder: DSM-IV and beyond*. Washington, DC: The American Psychiatric Press.

Marcus, B. F. (1989). Incest and the borderline syndrome: The mediating role of identity. *Psychoanalytic Psychology*, 6, 199–215.

Markowitz, J. S., & Gutterman, E. (1986). Predictors of psychological distress in the community following two toxic chemical incidents. In A. H. Lebovits., A. Baum., & J. E. Singer (Eds), *Advances in environmental psychology. Vol. 6: Exposure to hazardous substances: Psychological parameters* (pp. 89–107). Hillsdale, NJ: Erlbaum.

Marks, I. M. (1969). *Fears and phobias*, London: Heinemann.

Marks, I. M. (1981). *Cure and care of neurosis: Theory and practice of behavioural psychotherapy*. New York: Wiley.

Marks, I. M., & Nesse, R. M. (1994). Fear and fitness: An evolutionary analysis of anxiety disorders. *Ethology and Sociobiology*, 15, 247–261.

Marmar, C. R., Weiss, D. S., Schlenger, W. E., Fairbank, J. A., Jordan, B. K., Kulka, R. A., & Hough, R. L. (1994). Peritraumatic dissociation and posttraumatic stress in male Vietnam theatre veterans. *American Journal of Psychiatry*, 151, 902–907.

Marquis, J. (1991). A report on seventy-eight cases treated by eye movement desensitization. *Journal of Behaviour Therapy and Experimental Psychiatry*, 22, 187–192.

Marshall, J. R. (1975). The treatment of night terrors associated with the posttraumatic syndrome. *American Journal of Psychiatry*, 132, 293–295.

Martini, D. R., Ryan, C., Nakayama, D., et al. (1990). Psychiatric sequelae after traumatic injury: the Pittsburgh Regatta accident. *Journal of the American Academy for Child and Adolescent Psychiatry*, 29, 70–75.

Matheny, K. B., Curlette, W. L., Aycock, D. W., Pugh, J. L., & Taylor, H. F. (1987). *The Coping Resources Inventory for Stress*. Atlanta, GA: Health Prisms.

Matheny, K. B., Aycock, D. W., Curlette, W. L., & Junker, G. N. (1993). The coping resources inventory for stress: A measure of perceived resourcefulness. *Journal of Clinical Psychology*, **49**, 815–830.

Mayou, R. A., Bryant, B. M., & Duthie, R. (1993). Psychiatric consequences of road traffic accidents. *British Medical Journal*, **307**, 647–651.

McCaffrey, R. J., Hickling, E. J., & Marrazo, M. J. (1989). Civilian-related posttraumatic stress disorder: Assessment-related issues. *Journal of Clinical Psychology*, **45**, 72–76.

McCann, I. L., & Pearlman, L. A. (1990). *Psychological trauma and the adult survivor: Theory, therapy, and transformation.* New York: Brunner/Mazel.

McCauley, R., & Troy, M. (1983). The impact of urban conflict and violence on children referred to a child guidance clinic. In J. Harbison (Ed.), *Children of the troubles: Children in Northern Ireland.* Belfast: Stranmillis College Learning Resources Unit.

McCormick, R. A., Taber, J. I., & Kruedelbach, N. (1989). The relationship between attributional style and post traumatic stress disorder in addicted patients. *Journal of Traumatic Stress*, **2**, 477–487.

McFall, M. E., Smith, D. E., Mackay, P. W., & Tarver, D. J (1990a). Reliability and validity of Mississipi scale for combat-related posttraumatic stress disorder. *Psychological Assessment*, **2**, 114–121.

McFall, M. E., Smith, D. E, Roszell, D. K., Tarver, D. J., & Malas, K. L. (1990b). Convergent validity of measures of PTSD in Vietnam combat veterans. *American Journal of Psychiatry*, **147**, 645–648.

McFarlane, A.C. (1985). The effects of stressful life events and disasters: Research and theoretical issues. *Australian and New Zealand Journal of Psychiatry*, **19**, 409–421.

McFarlane, A. C. (1986a). Chronic posttraumatic morbidity of a natural disaster: Implications for disaster planners and emergency services. *Medical Journal of Australia*, **145**, 561–563.

McFarlane, A. C. (1986b). Post-traumatic morbidity of a disaster: A study of cases presenting for psychiatric treatment. *Journal of Nervous and Mental Disease*, **174**, 4–14.

McFarlane, A. C. (1987). Family functioning and overprotection following a natural disaster: The longitudinal effects of post-traumatic morbidity. *Australian and New Zealand Journal of Psychiatry*, **21**, 210–218.

McFarlane, A. C. (1988a). The aetiology of post-traumatic stress disorders following a natural disaster. *British Journal of Psychiatry*, **152**, 116–121.

McFarlane, A. C. (1988b). The longitudinal course of posttraumatic morbidity: The range of outcomes and their predictors. *Journal of Nervous and Mental Disease*, **176**, 22–29.

McFarlane, A. (1989). The aetiology of post-traumatic morbidity: Predisposing, precipitating and perpetuating factors. *British Journal of Psychiatry*, **154**, 221–228.

McFarlane, A. C. (1992a). Avoidance and intrusion in posttraumatic stress disorder. *Journal of Nervous and Mental Disease*, **180**, 439–445.

McFarlane, A. C. (1992b). Commentary. Posttraumatic stress disorder among injured survivors of a terrorist attack: Predictive value of early intrusion and avoidance symptoms. *Journal of Nervous and Mental Disease*, **180**, 599–600.

McFarlane, A. C. (1994). Individual psychotherapy for post-traumatic stress disorder. *Psychiatric Clinics of North America*, **17**, 393–408.

McFarlane, A. C., & Papay, P. (1992). Multiple diagnoses in posttraumatic stress disorder in the victims of a natural disaster. *Journal of Nervous and Mental Disease*, **180**, 498–504.

McFarlane, A. C., Atchison, M., Rafalowicz, E., & Papay, P. (1994). Physical symptoms in post-traumatic stress disorder. *Journal of Psychosomatic Research*, **38**, 715–726.

McFarlane, A. C., Policansky, S., & Irwin, C. P. (1987). A longitudinal study of the psychological morbidity in children due to a natural disaster. *Psychological Medicine*, 17, 727–738.

McNally, R. J. (1991). Assessment of posttraumatic stress disorder in children. *Psychological Assessment*, 3, 531–537.

McNally, R. J. (1993). Stressors that produce posttraumatic stress disorder in children. In J. R. T. Davidson & E. B. Foa (Eds), *Posttraumatic stress disorder: DSM-IV and beyond*. Washington, DC: American Psychiatric Press.

McNally, R. J., English, G. E., & Lipke, H. J. (1993). Assessment of intrusive cognition in PTSD: Use of the modified Stroop paradigm. *Journal of Traumatic Stress*, 6, 33–41.

McNally, R. J., Lasko, N. B., Macklin, M. L., & Pitman, R. K. (1995). Autobiographical memory disturbance in combat-related posttraumatic stress disorder. *Behaviour Research and Therapy*, 33, 619–630.

McLeer, S. V., Deblinger, E., Atkins, M. S., Foa, E. B., & Ralphe, D. L. (1988). Post-traumatic stress disorder in sexually abused children: A prospective study. *Journal of the American Academy of Child and Adolescent Psychiatry*, 27, 650–654.

Mechanic, D. (1977). Illness behaviour, social adaptation, and the management of illness. *Journal of Nervous and Mental Disease*, 2, 79–87.

Meichenbaum, D. (1993). Stress inoculation training: A 20-year update. In P. M. Lehrer & R. L. Woolfolk (Eds), *Principles and practice of stress management* (2nd edn.). New York: Guilford.

Melick, M. E. (1978). Life change and illness: Illness behavior of males in the recovery period of a natural disaster. *Journal of Health and Social Behavior*, 19, 335–342.

Mellman, T. A., Kulick-Bell, R., Ashlock, L. E., & Nolan, B. (1995). Sleep events among veterans with combat-related posttraumatic stress disorder. *American Journal of Psychiatry*, 152, 110–115.

Meyer, C., & Taylor, S. (1986). Adjustment to rape. *Journal of Personality and Social Psychology*, 50, 1226–1234.

Mikulincer, M., & Solomon, Z. (1988). Attributional style and combat-related post-traumatic stress disorder. *Journal of Abnormal Psychology*, 97, 308–313.

Mikulincer, M., Solomon, Z., & Benbenishty, R. (1988). Battle events, acute combat stress reaction and long-term psychological sequelae of war. *Journal of Anxiety Disorders*, 2, 121–133.

Milgram, N. A. (1986). Attributional analysis of war-related stress: Models of coping and helping. In N. A. Milgram (Ed.), *Generalizations from the Israeli experience*. New York: Brunner/Mazel.

Miranda, J. (1992). Dysfunctional thinking is activated by stressful life events. *Cognitive Therapy and Research*, 16, 473–483.

Mitchell, J. T. (1983). When disaster strikes. . . . The critical incident stress debriefing process. *Journal of Emergency Medical Services*, 8, 36–39.

Moody, D. R., & Kish, G. B. (1989). Clinical meaning of the Keane PTSD scale. *Journal of Clinical Psychology*, 45, 542–546.

Mott, F. W. (1919). *War neuroses and shell shock*. London: Oxford University Press.

Mullen, P. E., Martin, J. L., Anderson, J. C., Romans, S. E., & Herbison, G. P. (1994). The effect of child sexual abuse on social, interpersonal and sexual function in adult life. *British Journal of Psychiatry*, 165, 35–47.

Muris, P., van Zuuren, F. J., de Jong, P. J., de Beurs, E., & Hanewald, G. (1994). Monitoring and blunting coping styles: The Miller Behavioural Style Scale and its correlates, and the development of an alternative questionnaire. *Personality and Individual Differences*, 17, 9–19.

Murphy, S. A. (1986). Status of natural disaster victims' health and recovery 1 and 3 years later. *Research in Nursing and Health*, 9, 331–340.

Murphy, S. A. (1988). Mediating effects of intrapersonal and social support on mental health 1 and 3 years after a natural disaster. *Journal of Traumatic Stress*, 2, 155–172.

Nader, K., Pynoos, R. S., Fairbanks, L., & Frederick, C. (1990). Childhood PTSD reactions one year after a sniper attack at their school. *American Journal of Psychiatry*, 147, 1526–1530.

National Victims Center (1992). *Rape in America: a report to the nation*. National Victims Center.

Nezu, A. M., & Carnevale, G. J. (1987). Interpersonal problem solving and coping reactions of Vietnam veterans with post-traumatic stress disorder. *Journal of Abnormal Psychology*, 96, 155–157.

Norris, F. H. (1992). Epidemiology of trauma: Frequency and impact of different potentially traumatic events on different demographic groups. *Journal of Consulting and Clinical Psychology*, 60, 409–418.

North, C. S., Smith, E. M., McCool, R. E., & Shea, J. M. (1989). Short-term psychopathology in eye witnesses to mass murder. *Hospital and Community Psychiatry*, 40, 1293–1295.

North, C. S., Smith, E. M., & Spitznagel, E. L. (1994). Posttraumatic stress disorder in survivors of a mass shooting. *American Journal of Psychiatry*, 151, 82–88.

O'Brien, L. S., & Hughes, S. J. (1991). Symptoms of post-traumatic stress disorder in Falklands veterans five years after the conflict. *British Journal of Psychiatry*, 159, 135–141.

O'Donahue, W., & Elliot, A. (1992). The current status of post-traumatic stress disorder as a diagnostic category: Problems and proposals. *Journal of Traumatic Stress*, 5, 421–439.

Oei, T. P. S., Lim, B., & Hennessy, B. (1990). Psychological dysfunction in battle: Combat stress reactions and post-traumatic stress disorder. *Clinical Psychology Review*, 10, 355–388.

Ollendick, D., & Hoffman, M. (1982). Assessment of psychological reactions in disaster victims. *Journal of Community Psychology*, 10, 157–167.

Ollendick, T. H. (1983). Reliability and validity of the revised fear survey schedule for children (FSSC-R). *Behaviour Research and Therapy*, 21, 685–692.

Oppenheim, H. (1892). *Die Traumatischen Neurosen*. Berlin: August Hirschwald.

Orlando, J. A., & Koss, M. P. (1983). Effects of sexual victimization on sexual satisfaction: A study of the negative association hypothesis. *Journal of Abnormal Psychology*, 92, 104–106.

Orley, J., & Kuyken, W. (Eds) (1994). *Quality of life assessment: International perspectives*. Berlin: Springer-Verlag.

Orner, R. J., Lynch, T., & Seed, P. (1993). Long-term traumatic stress reactions in British Falklands war veterans. *British Journal of Clinical Psychology*, 32, 457–459.

Orr, S. P., Claiborn, J. M., Altman, B., Forgue, D. F., de Jong, J. B., & Pitman, R. K. (1990). Psychometric profile of posttraumatic stress disorder, anxious, and healthy Vietnam veterans: Correlations with psychophysiological responses. *Journal of Consulting and Clinical Psychology*, 58, 329–335.

Overmier, J. B., & Seligman, M. E. P. (1967). Effects of inescapable shock upon subsequent escape and avoidance learning. *Journal of Comparative Physiological Psychology*, 63, 23–33.

Page, H. (1885). *Injuries of the spine and spinal cord without apparent mechanical lesion*. London: Churchill.

Parker, G. (1977). Cyclone Tracy and Darwin Evacuees: On the restoration of the species. *British Journal of Psychiatry*, 130, 548–555.

Parry-Jones, B., & Parry-Jones, W. L. L. (1994). Post-traumatic stress disorder: Supportive evidence from an eighteenth century natural disaster. *Psychological Medicine*,

24, 15–27.
Patrick, V., & Patrick, W. K. (1981). Cyclone 78 in Sri Lanka: The mental health trail. *British Journal of Psychiatry*, **138**, 210–216.
Paykel, E. S. (1983). Methodological aspects of life events research. *Journal of Psychosomatic Research*, 27, 341–352.
Pearlin, L. I., & Schooler, C. (1978). The structure of coping. *Journal of Health and Social Behaviour*, **19**, 2–21.
Penk, W. E., Robinowitz, R., Roberts, W. R., Patterson, E. T., Dolan, M. P., & Atkins, H. G. (1981). Adjustment differences among male substance abusers varying in degree of combat experience in Vietnam. *Journal of Consulting and Clinical Psychology*, 49, 426–437.
Pennebaker, J. W. (1985). Traumatic experience and psychosomatic disease: Exploring the roles of behavioural inhibition, obsession, and confiding. *Canadian Psychology*, 26, 82–95.
Pennebaker, J. W. (1993). Putting stress into words: Health, linguistic, and therapeutic implications. *Behaviour Research and Therapy*, 31, 539–548.
Pennebaker, J. W., & Beall, S. (1986). Confronting a traumatic event: Toward an understanding of inhibition and disease. *Journal of Abnormal Psychology*, 95, 274–281.
Pennebaker, J. W., & Chew, C. H. (1985). Deception, electrodermal activity, and the inhibition of behavior. *Journal of Personality and Social Psychology*, 49, 1427–1433.
Pennebaker, J. W., Hughes, C. F., & O'Heeron, R. C. (1987). The psychophysiology of confession: Linking inhibitory and psychosomatic processes. *Journal of Personality and Social Psychology*, 52, 781–793.
Pennebaker, J. W., Kiecolt-Glaser, J., & Glaser, R. (1988). Disclosure of traumas and immune function: Health implications for psychotherapy. *Journal of Consulting and Clinical Psychology*, 56, 239–245.
Pennebaker, J. W., & O'Heeron, R. C. (1984). Confiding in others and illness rate among spouses of suicide and accidental death victims. *Journal of Abnormal Psychology*, 93, 473–476.
Perconte, S. T. (1988). Stability of positive outcome and symptom relapse in posttraumatic stress disorder. *Journal of Traumatic Stress*, 2, 127–135.
Perloff, L. S. (1983). Perceptions of vulnerability to victimization. *Journal of Social Issues*, 39, 41–61.
Perry, S., Difede, J., Musngi, G., Frances, A. J., & Jacobsberg, L. (1992). Predictors of posttraumatic stress disorder after burn injury. *American Journal of Psychiatry*, 149, 931–935.
Peterson, C., Semmel, A., von Baeyer, C., Abramson, L. Y., Metalsky, G. I., & Seligman, M. E. P. (1982). The attributional style questionnaire. *Cognitive Therapy and Research*, 6, 287–300.
Phifer, J., & Norris, F. (1989). Psychological symptoms in older adults following natural disaster: Nature, timing, duration, and course. *Journal of Gerontology: Social Science*, 44, 207–217.
Pitman, R. K., Altman, B., Greenwald, E., Longpre, R. E., Macklin, M. M., Poire, R. E. & Steketee, G. S. (1991) Psychiatric complications during flooding therapy for posttraumatic stress disorder. *Journal of Clinical Psychiatry*, 52, 17–20.
Popovic, M., & Petrovic, D. (1964). After the earthquake. *Lancet*, 2, 1169–1171.
Powell, B. J., & Penick, E. C. (1983). Psychological distress following a natural disaster: A one year follow up of 98 flood victims. *Journal of Community Psychology*, 11, 269–276.
Power, M. J. (1988). Stress-buffering effects of social support: A longitudinal study. *Motivation and Emotion*, 12, 197–204.
Price, J. (1978). Some age-related effects of the 1974 Brisbane floods. *Australian and*

New Zealand Journal of Psychiatry, **12,** 55–58.

Puk, G. (1991). Treating traumatic memories: A case report on the eye movement desensitization procedure. *Journal of Behaviour Therapy and Experimental Psychiatry,* **22,** 149–151.

Pynoos, R. S., & Eth, S. (1986). Witness to violence: The child interview. *Journal of the American Academy of Child Psychiatry,* **25,** 3, 306–319.

Pynoos, R. S., Frederick, C., Nader, K., Arroyo, W., Steinberg, A., Eth, S., Nuner, F., & Fairbanks, C. (1987). Life threat and post traumatic stress in school-age children. *Archives of General Psychiatry,* **44,** 1057–1063.

Pynoos, R. S., Goenjian, A., Tashjian, M., Karakashian, M., Manjikian, R., Manoukian, G., Steinberg, A. M., & Fairbanks, L. A. (1993). Post-traumatic stress reactions in children after the 1988 Armenian Earthquake. *British Journal of Psychiatry,* **163,** 239–247.

Pynoos, R. S., & Nader, K. (1988). Psychological first aid and treatment approach for children exposed to community violence: research implications. *Journal of Traumatic Stress,* **1,** 243–267.

Quarantelli, E. L. (1985a). What is disaster? The need for clarification in definition and conceptualization in research. In B. J. Sowder (Ed.,), *Disasters and mental health: Selected contemporary perspectives.* Rockville, MD: US Department of Health and Human Services.

Quarantelli, E. L. (1985b). An assessment of conflicting views on mental health: the consequences of traumatic events. In C. R. Figley (Ed.,), *Trauma and its wake.* New York: Brunner/Mazel.

Quay, H. C., & Peterson, D. R. (1979). Manual of the Behaviour Problem Checklist (Unpublished): cited in Yule, W., & Williams, R. (1990). Post-traumatic stress reactions in children. *Journal of Traumatic Stress,* **3,** 279–296.

Rabkin, J. G., & Struening, E. L. (1976). Life-events, stress, and illness. *Science,* **194,** 1013–1020.

Rachman, S. (1968). *Phobias: Their nature and control.* Springfield, IL: Thomas.

Rachman, S. (1980). Emotional processing. *Behaviour Research and Therapy,* **18,** 51–60.

Rado, S. (1942). Pathodynamics and treatment of traumatic war neurosis (traumatophobia). *Psychosomatic Medicine,* **42,** 363–368.

Raphael, B. (1986). *When disaster strikes.* London: Hutchinson.

Realmuto, G. M., Wagner, N., & Bartholow, J. (1991). The Williams Pipeline disaster: A controlled study of a technological accident. *Journal of Traumatic Stress,* **4,** 469–479.

Renfry, G., & Spates, C. R. (1994). Eye movement desensitisation and reprocessing: A partial dismantling procedure. *Journal of Behaviour Therapy and Experimental Psychiatry,* **25,** 231–239.

Resick, P. A., Calhoun, K. S., Atkeson, B. M., & Ellis, E. M. (1982). Social adjustment in victims of sexual assault. *Journal of Consulting and Clinical Psychology,* **49,** 705–712.

Resick, P. A., & Schnicke, M. K. (1992). Cognitive processing therapy for sexual assault victims. *Journal of Consulting and Clinical Psychology,* **60,** 748–756.

Resnick, H. S., Kilpatrick, D. G., Best, C. L., & Crummier, T. L. (1992). Vulnerability-stress factors in development of post-traumatic stress disorder. *Journal of Nervous and Mental Disease,* **180,** 424–430.

Resnick, H. S., Kilpatrick, D. G., Dansky, B. S., Saunders, B. E., & Best, C. L. (1993). Prevalence of civilian trauma and posttraumatic stress disorder in a representative national sample of women. *Journal of Consulting and Clinical Psychology,* **61,** 984–991.

Resnick, H. S., Veronen, L. J., Saunders, B. E., Kilpatrick, D. G., & Cornelison, V. (1989). Assessment of PTSD in a subset of rape victims at 12 to 36 months post-assault. Unpublished manuscript cited in Rothbaum, B. O., Foa, E. B., Riggs, D. S.,

Murdock, T., & Walsh, W. (1992). A prospective examination of post-traumatic stress disorder in rape victims. *Journal of Traumatic Stress*, 5, 455–475.

Reynolds, C. R., & Richmond, B. O. (1978). What I think and feel: A revised measure of children's manifest anxiety. *Journal of Abnormal Child Psychology*, 6, 271–282.

Richards, D. A., & Rose, J. S. (1991). Exposure therapy for post-traumatic stress disorder. *British Journal of Psychiatry*, 58, 836–840.

Richards, D. A., Lovell K., & Marks I. M. (1994) Post-traumatic stress disorder: Evaluation of a treatment program. *Journal of Traumatic Stress*, 7, 669–680.

Riggs, D. S., Dancu, C. V., Gershuny, B. S., Greenberg, D., & Foa, E. B. (1992). Anger and post-traumatic stress disorder in female crime victims. *Journal of Traumatic Stress*, 5, 613–625.

Roberts, W. R., Penk, W. E., Robinowitz, R., & Patterson, E. (1982). Interpersonal problems of Vietnam veterans with symptoms of PTSD. *Journal of Abnormal Psychology*, 91, 444–450.

Robins, L. N., & Helzer, J. E. (1985). Diagnostic Interview Schedule (DIS) Version III-A. St. Louis, MO: Washington University.

Rosen, J., Fields, R. B., Hand, A. M., Falsettie, G., & Van Kammen, D. P. (1989). Concurrent posttraumatic stress disorder in psychogeriatric patients. *Journal of Geriatric Psychiatry and Neurology*, 2, 65–69.

Rosen, J., Reynolds, C. F., Yeager, A. L., Houck, P. R., & Hurwitz, L. F. (1991). Sleep disturbances in survivors of the Nazi Holocaust. *American Journal of Psychiatry*, 148, 62–66.

Rosenheck, R., & Fontana, A. (1994). A model of homelessness among male veterans of the Vietnam war generation. *American Journal of Psychiatry*, 151, 421–427.

Ross, R. J., Ball, W. A., Sullivan, K. A., & Caroff, S. N. (1989). Sleep disturbance as the hallmark of posttraumatic stress disorder. *American Journal of Psychiatry*, 146, 697–707.

Roth, L. M. (1986). Substance use and mental health among Vietnam veterans. In G. Boulanger & C. Kadushin (Eds), *The Vietnam veteran redefined* (pp. 61–78). Hillsdale, NJ: Erlbaum.

Roth, S., Wayland, K., & Woolsey, M. (1990). Victimization history and victim–assailant relationships as factors in recovery from sexual assault. *Journal of Traumatic Stress*, 3, 169–180.

Rothbaum, B. O., & Foa, E. B. (1992). Cognitive-behavioral treatment of posttraumatic stress disorder. In P. A. Saigh (Ed.), *Posttraumatic stress disorder: A behavioral approach to assessment and treatment*. Boston: Allyn & Bacon.

Rothbaum, B. O., Foa, E. B., Riggs, D. S., Murdock, T., & Walsh, W. (1992). A prospective examination of post-traumatic stress disorder in rape victims. *Journal of Traumatic Stress*, 5, 455–476.

Rotter, J. B. (Ed.) (1966). Generalized expectancies for internal vs. external control of reinforcement. *Psychological Monograph*, 80 (1, Whole No. 609).

Rowan, A. B., Foy, D. W., Rodriguez, N., & Ryan, S. (1993). Posttraumatic stress disorder in a clinical sample of adults sexually abused as children. *Child Abuse and Neglect*, 18, 51–61.

Roy, M. P., & Steptoe, A. (1994). Daily stressors and social support availability as predictors of depressed mood in male firefighters. *Work and Stress*, 8, 210–219.

Rubonis, A. V., & Bickman, L. (1991). Psychological impairment in the wake of disaster: The disaster–psychopathology relationship. *Psychological Bulletin*, 109, 384–399.

Ruch, L. O., Chandler, S. M., & Harter, R. A. (1980). Life change and rape impact. *Journal of Health and Social Behaviour*, 21, 248–260.

Russel, C. K. (1919). War neurosis: Some views on diagnosis and treatment. *Archives of*

Neurological Psychiatry, **25**, 25–38.

Rutter, M. (1967). A children's behaviour questionnaire for completion by teachers: Preliminary findings. *Journal of Child Psychology and Psychiatry*, **8**, 1–11.

Rychtarik, R. G., Silverman, W. K., & Van Landingham, W. P. (1984). Treatment of an incest victims with implosive therapy: A case study. *Behavior Therapy*, **15**, 410–420.

Saigh, P. A. (1987). In vitro flooding of an adolescent post-traumatic stress disorder. *Journal of Clinical Child Psychology*, **16**, 147–150.

Saigh, P. A. (1989). The development and validation of the Children's Posttraumatic Stress Disorder Inventory. *International Journal of Special Education*, **4**, 75–84.

Saigh, P. A., Yule, W., & Inamdar, S. C. (1996). Imaginal flooding of traumatized children and adolescents. *Journal of School Psychology*.

Salkovskis, P. M. (1985). Obsessional-compulsive problems: A cognitive-behavioural analysis. *Behaviour Research and Therapy*, **27**, 677–682.

Sarason, I. G., Johnson, J. H., & Siegal, J. M. (1978). Assessing the impact of life changes: development of the life-experiences survey. *Journal of Consulting and Clinical Psychology*, **46**, 932–946.

Sarason, I. G., Levine., H. M., Basham, R. B., & Sarason, B. R. (1983). Assessing social support: The social support questionnaire. *Journal of Personality and Social Psychology*, **44**, 127–139.

Sarason, B. R., Sarason, I. G., Hacker, T. A., & Basham, R. B. (1985). Concomitants of social support: Social skills, physical attractiveness, and gender. *Journal of Personality and Social Psychology*, **49**, 469–480.

Sarason, B. R., Sarason, I. G., & Pierce, G. R. (1990). Traditional views of social support and their impact on assessment. In B. R. Sarason, I. G. Sarason and G. R. Pierce (Eds), *Social support: An interactional view*. New York: Wiley.

Sarason, I. G., Sarason, B. R., & Shearin, E. N. (1986) Social support as an individual difference variable: Its stability, origins, and relational aspects. *Journal of Personality and Social Psychology*, **4**, 845–855.

Sarason, B. R., Shearin, E. N., Pierce, G. R., & Sarason, I. G. (1987). Interrelations of social support measures: Theoretical and practical implications. *Journal of Personality and Social Psychology*, **52**, 813–832.

Schaefer, C., Coyne, J. C., & Lazarus, R. S. (1981). The health related functions of social support. *Journal of Behavioural Medicine*, **4**, 381–406.

Scheeringa, M. S., Zeanah, C. H., Drell, M. J., & Larrieu, J. A. (1995). Two approaches to the diagnosis of posttraumatic stress disorder in infancy and early childhood. *Journal of the American Academy for Child and Adolescent Psychiatry*, **34**, 191–200.

Schlenger, W. E., & Kulka, R. A. (1989). *PTSD scale development for the MMPI-2*. Research Triangle Park, NC: Research Triangle Institute.

Schlenger, W. E., Kulka, R. A., Fairbank, J. A., Hough, R. L., Jordan, B. K., Marmar, C. R., & Weiss, D. S. (1992). The prevalence of post-traumatic stress disorder in the Vietnam generation: A multimethod, multiscore assessment of psychiatric disorder. *Journal of Traumatic Stress*, **5**, 333–364.

Schulte, J. G., Dinwiddie, S. H., Pribor, E. F., & Yutzy, S. H. (1995). Psychiatric diagnoses of adult male victims of childhood sexual abuse. *Journal of Nervous and Mental Disease*, **183**, 111–113.

Schwarz, E. D., & Kowalski, J. M. (1991). Posttraumatic stress disorder after a school shooting: Effects of symptom threshold selection and diagnosis by DSM-III, DSM-III-R, or proposed DSM-IV. *American Journal of Psychiatry*, **148**, 592–597.

Schwarzwald, J., Solomon, Z., Weisenberg, M., & Mikulincer, M. (1987). Validation of the impact of event scale for psychological sequelae of combat. *Journal of Consulting and Clinical Psychology*, **55**, 251–256.

Schulman, P., Castellan, C., & Seligman, M. E. P. (1989). Assessing explanatory style:

The content analysis of verbatim explanations and the attributional style questionnaire. *Behaviour Research and Therapy*, 27, 505–512.

Seligman, M. E. P. (1975). *Helplessness: On depression, development, and death*. San Francisco: Freeman.

Seligman, M. E. P., Abramson, L. Y., Semmel, A., & von Baeyer, C. (1979). Depressive attributional style. *Journal of Abnormal Psychology*, 88, 242–247.

Seligman. M. E. P., & Maier, S. F. (1967). Failure to escape traumatic shock. *Journal of Experimental Psychology*, 74, 1–9.

Shalev, A. Y. (1992). Posttraumatic stress disorder among injured survivors of a terrorist attack. *Journal of Nervous and Mental Disease*, 180, 505–509.

Shapiro, F. (1989a). Efficacy of the eye movement desensitization procedure in the treatment of traumatic memories. *Journal of Traumatic Stress*, 2, 199–223.

Shapiro, F. (1989b). Eye movement desensitization: A new treatment for Post-Traumatic Stress Disorder. *Journal of Behaviour Therapy and Experimental Psychiatry*, 20, 211–217.

Shapiro, F. (1995). *Eye movement desensitization and reprocessing: Basic principles, protocols and procedures*. New York: Guilford Press.

Shaver, K. G., & Drown, D. (1986). On causality, responsibility, and self blame: A theoretical note. *Journal of Personality and Social Psychology*, 50, 697–702.

Shore, J. H., Tatum, E. L., & Vollmer, W. M. (1986). Psychiatric reactions to disaster: The Mount St Helens experience. *American Journal of Psychiatry*, 143, 590–595.

Silver, R. L., Boon, C., & Stones, M. H. (1983). Searching for meaning in misfortune: Making sense of incest. *Journal of Social Issues*, 39, 81–101.

Silver, R., Wortman, C. B., & Crofton, A. (1990). The role of coping in support provision: The self-presentational dilemma of victims of life crisis. In B. R. Sarason, I. G. Sarason, & G. R. Pierce (Eds), *Social support: An interactional view* (pp. 397–426). New York: Wiley.

Silver, S. M. (1984). An inpatient program for post-traumatic stress disorder: Context as treatment. In C. R. Figley (Ed.), *Trauma and its wake*, Vol. II: *Traumatic stress theory, research, and intervention*. New York: Brunner/Mazel.

Silver, S. M., & Iacono, C. U. (1984). Factor-analytic support for DSM-III's post-traumatic stress disorder for Vietnam veterans. *Journal of Clinical Psychology*, 40, 5–14.

Silver, S. M., & Salamone-Genovese, L. (1991). A study of the MMPI Clinical and Research Scales for Post-Traumatic Stress Disorder Diagnostic Utility. *Journal of Traumatic Stress*, 4, 533–548.

Singh, B., & Raphael, B. (1981). Postdisaster morbidity of the bereaved: A possible role for preventative psychiatry? *Journal of Nervous and Mental Disease*, 169, 203–212.

Smith, T. W. (1992). A life-events approach to developing an index of societal well being. *Social Science Research*, 21, 353–379.

Smith, E. M., Robins, L. N., Pryzbeck, T. R., Goldring, E., & Solomon, S. D. (1986). Psychosocial consequences of a disaster. In J. Shore (Ed.), *Disaster stress studies: New methods and findings* (pp. 49–76). Washington, DC: American Psychiatric Press.

Smith, P., & Yule, W. (1997). Eye movement desensitization and reprocessing. Chapter to appear in W. Yule (Ed.), *Post traumatic stress disorder*. Chichester: Wiley.

Smucker, M. R., Dancu, C., Foa, E. B., & Niederee, J. L. (1995) Imagery rescripting: A new treatment for survivors of childhood sexual abuse suffering from posttraumatic stress. *Journal of Cognitive Psychotherapy*, 9, 3–17.

Solkoff, N., Gray, P., & Keill, S. (1986). Which Vietnam veterans develop posttraumatic stress disorders? *Journal of Clinical Psychology*, 42, 687–698.

Solomon, R. M., & Horn, J. M. (1986). Post shooting traumatic reactions: A pilot study. In J. Reese & H. Goldstein (Eds), *Psychological Services for Law Enforcement* (pp. 383–393), Washington, DC: United States Government Printing Office.

Solomon, S. (1986). Mobilizing social support networks in times of disaster. In C. Figley (Ed.), *Trauma and its Wake*. Vol. 2: *Traumatic stress theory, research, and intervention* (pp. 232–263). New York: Brunner/Mazel.

Solomon, S., & Canino, G. (1990). Appropriateness of the DSM-III-R criteria for post-traumatic stress disorder. *Comprehensive Psychiatry*, **31**, 227–237.

Solomon, S. D., Smith, E. M., Robins, L. N., & Fischbach, R. L. (1987a). Social involvement as a mediator of disaster induced stress. *Journal of Applied Social Psychology*, **17**, 1092–1112.

Solomon, Z. (1993). Immediate and long-term effects of traumatic combat stress among Israeli veterans of the Lebanon war. In J. P. Wilson & B. Raphael (Eds), *International handbook of traumatic stress syndromes* (pp. 321–332). New York: Plenum Press.

Solomon, Z., Avitzur, M., & Mikulincer, M. (1989a). Coping resources and social functioning following combat stress reactions: A longitudinal study. *Journal of Social and Clinical Psychology*, **8**, 87–96.

Solomon, Z., Benbenishty, R., & Mikulincer, M. (1988a). A follow-up of Israeli casualties of combat stress reaction ('battle shock') in the 1982 Lebanon war. *British Journal of Clinical Psychology*, **27**, 125–135.

Solomon, Z., Benbenishty, R., Neria, Y., Abramowitz, M., Ginzburg, K., & Ohry, A. (1993a). Assessment of PTSD: Validation of the Revised PTSD Inventory. *Israel Journal of Psychiatry and Related Sciences*, **30**, 110–115.

Solomon, Z., Laor, N., Weiler, D., Muller, U. F., Hadar, O., Waysman, M., Koslowsky, M., Yakar, M. B., & Bleich, A. (1993b). The psychological impact of the Gulf war: a study of acute stress in Israeli evacuees. *Archives of General Psychiatry*, **50**, 320–321.

Solomon, Z., & Mikulincer, M. (1992). Aftermaths of combat stress reactions: A three year study. *British Journal of Clinical Psychology*, **31**, 21–32.

Solomon, Z., Mikulincer, M., & Avitzur, E. (1988b). Coping, locus of control, social support, and combat related posttraumatic stress disorder: A prospective study. *Journal of Personality and Social Psychology*, **55**, 279–285.

Solomon, Z., Mikulincer, M., & Benbenishty, R. (1989b). Locus of control and combat-related post-traumatic stress disorder: The intervening role of battle intensity, threat appraisal and coping. *British Journal of Clinical Psychology*, **28**, 131–144.

Solomon, Z., Mikulincer, M., & Flum, H. (1988c). Negative life events, coping responses, and combat-related psychopathology: A prospective study. *Journal of Abnormal Psychology*, **97**, 302–307.

Solomon, Z., Mikulincer, M., & Kotler, M. (1987b). A two year follow-up of somatic complaints among Israeli combat stress reaction casualties. *Journal of Psychosomatic Research*, **31**, 463–469.

Solomon, Z., Weisenberg, M., Schwarzwald, J., & Mikulincer, M. (1987c). Posttraumatic stress disorder among frontline soldiers with combat stress reaction: The 1982 Israeli experience. *American Journal of Psychiatry*, **144**, 448–454.

Sorenson, S. B., & Golding, J. M. (1990). Depressive sequelae of recent criminal victimization. *Journal of Traumatic Stress*, **3**, 337–350.

Southward, E. E. (1919). *Shell shock and neuropsychiatric problems*. Boston: Leonard.

Speed, N., Engdahl, B., Schwartz, J., & Eberly, R. (1989). Post-traumatic stress disorder as a consequence of the POW experience. *Journal of Nervous and Mental Disease*, **177**, 147–153.

Spiegel, D. (1988). Dissociation and hypnosis in post-traumatic stress. *Journal of Traumatic Stress*, **1**, 17–34.

Spielberger, C. D., Gorsuch, R. L., & Lushene, R. E. (1970). *STAI Manual for the state-trait anxiety inventory*. Palo Alto, CA: Consulting Psychologists Press.

Spiro, A., Schnurr, P. P., & Aldwin, C. M. (1994). Combat-related posttraumatic stress disorder symptoms in older men. *Psychology and Aging*, **9**, 17–26.

Spitzer, R. L., Williams, J. B. W., & Gibbon, M. (1987). *Structured Clinical Interview for DSM-III-R, Version NP-V*. New York: New York State Psychiatric Institute, Biometrics Research Department.

Spitzer, R. L., Williams, J. B. W., Gibbon, M., & First, M. (1992). The Structured Clinical Interview for DSM-III-R (SCID): History, rationale, and description. *Archives of General Psychiatry*, **49**, 624–629.

Stallard, P., & Law, F. (1993). Screening and psychological debriefing of adolescent survivors of life-threatening events. *British Journal of Psychiatry*, **163**, 660–665.

Stampfl, T. G., & Levis, D. J. (1967). Essentials of implosive therapy: A learning theory-based psychodynamic behavioural therapy. *Journal of Abnormal Psychology*, **72**, 157–163.

Steele, C. M. (1988). The psychology of self-affirmation: Sustaining the integrity of the self. In L. Berkowitz (Ed.), *Advances in experimental social psychology* (pp. 261–302), vol. 21. San Diego, CA: Academic Press.

Stein, J. H. (1977). *Better services for crime victims: A perspective package LGAA Grant Report*. Blackstone Institute.

Steinglass, P., & Gerrity, E. (1990). Natural disasters and post-traumatic stress disorder: Short-versus long-term recovery in two disaster-affected communities. *Journal of Applied Social Psychology*, **20**, 1746–1765.

Steketee, G., & Foa, E. B. (1987). Rape victims: Post-traumatic stress responses and their treatment: A review of the literature. *Journal of Anxiety Disorders*, **1**, 69–86.

Stratton, P., Heard, D., Hanks, H. G. I., Munton, A. G., Brewin, C. R., & Davidson, C. (1986). Coding causal beliefs in natural discourse. *British Journal of Social Psychology*, **25**, 299–313.

Stretch, R. (1985). PTSD among US army reserve Vietnam and Vietnam-era veterans. *Journal of Consulting and Clinical Psychology*, **55**, 272–275.

Stretch, R. H., Vail, J. D., & Maloney, J. P. (1985). Posttraumatic stress disorder among army nurse corps Vietnam veterans. *Journal of Consulting and Clinical Psychology*, **53**, 704–708.

Suls, J., & Fletcher, B. (1985). The relative efficacy of avoidant and nonavoidant coping strategies: A meta analysis. *Health Psychology*, **4**, 249–288.

Summerfield, D. (1993). War and posttraumatic stress disorder: The question of social context. *Journal of Nervous and Mental Disease*, **181**, 522.

Sutherland, S. M., & Davidson, J. R. T. (1994). Pharmacotherapy for post-traumatic stress disorder. *Psychiatric Clinics of North America*, **17**, 409–423.

Sweeney, P. D., Anderson, K., & Bailey, S. (1986). Attributional style in depression: A meta-analytic review. *Journal of Personality and Social Psychology*, **50**, 974–991.

Takuma, T. (1978). Human behaviour in the event of earthquakes. In E. L. Quarantelli (Ed.), *Disasters: Theory and Research*. Beverly Hills, CA: Sage.

Tangney, J. P., Wagner, P., & Gramzow, R. (1992). Proneness to shame, proneness to guilt, and psychopathology. *Journal of Abnormal Psychology*, **101**, 469–478.

Tatum, E., Vollmer, W., & Shore. J. H. (1985). High-risk groups of the Mount St. Helen's disaster. Paper presented at 138th Annual General Meeting of the American Psychiatric Association, Dallas, Texas, 18–24 May, 1985.

Taylor, A. J. W., & Frazer, A. G. (1982). The stress of post-disaster body handling and victim identification. *Journal of Human Stress*, **8**, 4–12.

Taylor, P., Abrahams, D., & Hewstone, M. (1988). Cancer, stress and personality: A correlational investigation of life-events, repression-sensitization and locus of control. *British Journal of Medical Psychology*, **61**, 179–183.

Taylor, S. (1981). The interface of cognitive and social psychology. In J. H. Harvey (Ed.), *Cognition, social behaviour, and the environment*. Hillsdale, NJ: Erlbaum.

Taylor, S. (1983). Adjustment to threatening life events: A theory of cognitive adaptation. *American Psychologist*, **38**, 1161–1173.

Taylor, S. E. (1984). Issues in the study of coping: A commentary. *Cancer*, **53**, 2313–2315.

Taylor, S. E., Lichtman, R. R., & Wood, J. V. (1984). Attributions, beliefs about control, and adjustment to breast cancer. *Journal of Personality and Social Psychology*, **46**, 489–502.

Taylor, V. A., Ross, G. A., & Quarantelli, E. L. (1976). *Delivery of mental health services in disasters: The Xenia tornado and some implications*. (Book and Monograph Series II.) Disaster Research Center, The Ohio State University, Colombus.

Teasdale, J. D. (1988). Cognitive vulnerability to persistent depression. *Cognition and Emotion*, **2**, 247–274.

Teasdale, J. D., & Barnard, P. J. (1993). *Affect, cognition and change: Remodelling depressive thought*. Hillsdale, NJ: Laurence Erlbaum.

Tennen, H., & Affleck, G. (1990). Blaming others for threatening events. *Psychological Bulletin*, **108**, 209–232.

Tennant, C. (1977). The General Health Questionnaire: A valid index of psychological impairment in Australian populations. *Medical Journal of Australia*, **2**, 392–394.

Tennant, C., & Andrews, G. (1978). The pathogenic quality of life event stress in neurotic impairment. *Archives of General Psychiatry*, **35**, 859–863.

Terr, L. C. (1985). Children traumatized in small groups. In S. Eth & R. Pynoos (Eds), *Posttraumatic stress disorder in children* (pp. 45–70). Washington, DC: American Psychiatric Association.

Terr, L. C. (1991). Childhood traumas: An outline and overview. *American Journal of Psychiatry*, **148**, 10–20.

Tesser, A., & Campbell, J. (1980). Self-definition and self-evaluation maintenance. In J. Suls & A. G. Greenwald (Eds), *Psychological perspective on the self* (vol. 2). Hillsdale, NJ: Erlbaum.

Thoits, P. A. (1982). Conceptual, methodological and theoretical problems in studying social support as a buffer against life event stress. *Journal of Health and Social Behaviour*, **23**, 145–159.

Thompson, J. A., Charlton, P. F. C., Kerry, R., Lee, D., & Turner, S. W. (1995). An open trial of exposure therapy based on de-conditioning for post-traumatic stress disorder. *British Journal of Clinical Psychology*, **34**, 407–416.

Thornton, B., Ryckman, R., Kirchner, G., Jacobs, J., Kaczor, L., & Kuehnel, R. (1988). Reaction to self-attributed victim responsibility: A comparative analysis of rape crisis counsellors and lay observers. *Journal of Applied Social Psychology*, **18**, 409–422.

Tierney, K. J. (1985). Report on the Coalinga earthquake of May 2, 1983: Report SSC 85–01. Sacramento, State of California Seismic Safety Commission, September 1985.

Tobin, D. L., Holroyd, K. A., Reynolds, R. V., & Wigal, J. K. (1989). The hierarchical factor structure of the coping strategies inventory. *Cognitive Therapy and Research*, **13**, 343–361.

Trimble, M. R. (1981). *Post-traumatic neurosis: From railway spine to the whiplash*. New York: Wiley.

True, W. R., Rice, J., Eisen, S. A., Heath, A. C., Goldberg, J., Lyons, M. J., & Nowak, J. (1993). A twin study of genetic and environmental contributions to liability for posttraumatic stress symptoms. *Archives of General Psychiatry*, **50**, 257–264.

Turner, R. J. (1981). Social support as a contingency in psychological well being. *Journal of Health and Social Behaviour*, **22**, 357–367.

Turnquist, D. C., Harvey, J. H., & Anderson, B. L. (1988). Attributions and adjustment to life-threatening illness. *British Journal of Clinical Psychology*, **27**, 55–65.

Tversky, A., & Kahneman, D. (1974). Judgement under uncertainty: Heuristics and biases in judgements reveal some heuristics of thinking under uncertainty. *Science*, **185**, 1124–1131.

Vaillant, G. E. (1971). Theoretical hierarchy of adaptive ego mechanisms. *Archives of General Psychiatry*, **24**, 107–118.

Vaillant, G. E. (1977). *Adaption to life*. Boston: Little, Brown.

van der Kolk, B. A. (1983). Psychopharmacological issues in post-traumatic stress disorder. *Hospital and Community Psychiatry*, **34**, 683–691.

van der Kolk, B. A. (1987). *Psychological trauma*. Washington, DC: American Psychiatric Press.

van der Kolk, B. A., Blitz, R., Burr, W., Sherry, S., & Hartmann, E. (1984a). Nightmares and trauma: A comparison of nightmares after combat with lifelong nightmares in veterans. *American Journal of Psychiatry*, **141**, 187–190.

van der Kolk, B.A., Boyd, H., Krystal, J., & Greenberg, M. (1984b). Post-traumatic stress disorder as a biologically based disorder: Implications of the animal model of inescapable shock. In B. A. van der Kolk (Ed.), *Post-traumatic stress disorder: Psychological and biological sequelae* (pp. 124–134). Washington, DC: American Psychiatric Press.

van der Ploeg, H. M., & Kleijn, W. C. (1988). Being held hostage in the Netherlands: A study of long-term aftereffects. *Journal of Traumatic Stress*, **2**, 153–169.

Vaughan, K., Wiese, M., Gold, R., & Tarrier, N. (1994). Eye-movement desensitisation: Symptom change in post-traumatic stress disorder. *British Journal of Psychiatry*, **164**, 533–541.

Vogel, J. M., & Vernberg, E. M. (1993). Children's psychological responses to disasters. *Journal of Clinical Child Psychology*, **22**, 464–484.

Wakefield, J. C. (1992). The concept of mental disorder: On the boundary between biological facts and social values. *American Psychologist*, **47**, 373–388.

Warr, P. B., & Jackson, P. R. (1984). Self-esteem and employment among young workers. *Le Travail Humain*, **46**, 355–366.

Watson, C. G. (1990). Psychometric posttraumatic stress disorder measurement techniques: A review. *Psychological Assessment*, **2**, 460–469.

Watson, C. G., Juba, M. P., Manifold, V., Kucala, T., & Anderson, P. E. D. (1991d). The PTSD interview: Rationale, description, reliability, and concurrent validity of a DSM-III based technique. *Journal of Clinical Psychology*, **47**, 179–214.

Watson, C. G., Kucala, T., Juba, M., Manifold, V., & Anderson, P. E. D. (1991b). A factor analysis of the DSM-III post-traumatic stress disorder criteria. *Journal of Clinical Psychology*, **47**, 205–214.

Watson, D., & Clark, L. A. (1984). Negative affectivity: The predisposition to experience aversive emotional states. *Psychological Bulletin*, **96**, 465–490.

Watson, D., Clark, L. A., Weber, K., Assenheimer, J. S., Strauss, M. E., & McCormick, R. A. (1995a). Testing a tripartite model. II: Exploring the symptom structure of anxiety and depression in student, adult, and patient samples. *Journal of Abnormal Psychology*, **104**, 15–25.

Watson, D., Weber, K., Assenheimer, J. S., Clark, L. A., Strauss, M. E., & McCormick, R. A. (1995b). Testing a tripartite model. I: Evaluating the convergent and discriminant validity of anxiety and depression symptom scales. *Journal of Abnormal Psychology*, **104**, 3–14.

Watson, P. B. (1987). Post-traumatic stress disorder in Australia and New Zealand: A critical review of the consequences of inescapable horror. *Medical Journal of Australia*, **147**, 443–446.

Watts, F. N. (1982). Attributional aspects of medicine. In C. Antaki & C. Brewin (Eds), *Attributions and psychological change* (pp. 135–155). London: Academic Press.

Wayland, K., Roth, S., & Lochman, J. E. (1991). The relation between physical assault and psychological functioning in a sample of university women, and the relative effects of physical and sexual assault. *Journal of Traumatic Stress*, 4, 495–514.

Wegner, D. M., Shortt, J. W., Blake, A. W., & Page, M. S. (1990). The suppression of exciting thoughts. *Journal of Personality and Social Psychology*, 58, 409–418.

Wegner, D. M., & Zanakos, S. (1994). Chronic thought suppression. *Journal of Personality*, 62, 615–640.

Weighill, V. E. (1983). Compensation neurosis: A review of the literature. *Journal of Psychosomatic Research*, 27, 97–104.

Weiner, B. (1972). *Theories of motivation: From mechanism to cognition.* Chicago: Rand McNally.

Weiner, B. (1979). A theory of motivation for some classroom experiences. *Journal of Educational Psychology*, 71, 3–25.

Weiner, B. (1983). Some methodological pitfalls in attributional research. *Journal of Educational Psychology*, 75, 530–543.

Weiner, B. (1985). Spontaneous causal thinking. *Psychological Bulletin*, 97, 74–84.

Weiner, B. (1986). *An attributional theory of motivation and emotion.* New York: Springer Verlag.

Weinstein, N. D., & Lachendro, E. (1982). Egocentrism as a source of unrealistic optimism. *Personality and Social Psychology Bulletin*, 8, 195–200.

Weisaeth, L. (1983). The study of a factory fire. Doctoral dissertation, University of Oslo.

Weisaeth, L. (1989). Research on long term outcome of disasters. Paper presented at the discussion meeting—Post-traumatic stress disorder; prospects for inter-disciplinary investigation. CIBA Foundation, London, UK.

Weisenberg, M., Solomon, Z., Schwarzwald, J., & Mikulincer, M. (1987). Assessing the severity of posttraumatic stress disorder: Relation between dichotomous and continuous measures. *Journal of Consulting and Clinical Psychology*, 55, 432–434.

Weiss, D. S. (1993a). Structured clinical interview techniques. In J. P. Wilson & B. Raphael (Eds), *International handbook of traumatic stress syndromes* (pp. 179–187). New York: Plenum Press.

Weiss, D. S. (1993b). Psychological processes in traumatic stress. In R. Allen (Ed.), *Handbook of post-disaster interventions* [Special Issue]. *Journal of Social Behaviour and Personality*, 8, 3–28.

Weiss, R. (1974). The provisions of social relationships. In Z. Rubin (Ed.), *Doing onto others.* Englewood Cliffs, NJ: Prentice Hall.

Weiss, R. (1976). Transition states and other stressful situations: Their nature and programs for their management. In G. Caplan and M. Killilea (Eds), *Support systems and mutual help: Multidisciplinary explorations.* New York: Grune & Stratton.

Wells, A., & Matthews, G. (1994). *Attention and emotion: A clinical perspective.* Hillsdale, NJ: Laurence Erlbaum.

Westermeyer, J. (1989). Cross-cultural care for PTSD: Research, training, and service needs for the future. *Journal of Traumatic Stress*, 2, 515–536.

Westermeyer, J., Vang, T. F., & Neider, J. (1983). Migration and mental health among refugees: Association of pre- and post-migration factors with self-rating scales. *Journal of Nervous and Mental Disease*, 171, 92–96.

Western, J. S., & Milne, G. (1979). Some social effects of a natural hazard: Darwin residents and cyclone Tracy. In R. L. Heathcote & B. G. Thom (Eds), *Natural hazards in Australia.* Canberra: Australian Academy of Science.

Wethington, E., & Kessler, R. C. (1986). Perceived support, received support, and adjustment to stressful life events. *Journal of Health and Social Behaviour*, **27**, 78–89.

Whittington, R., & Wykes, T. (1991). Coping strategies used by staff following assault by a patient: An exploratory study. *Work and Stress*, **5**, 37–48.

Wilkinson, C.B. (1983). Aftermath of a disaster: The collapse of the Hyatt Regency Hotel Skywalk. *American Journal of Psychiatry*, **140**, 1134–1139.

Williams, J. B. W., Gibbon, M., First, M. B., Spitzer, R. L., Davies, M., Borus, J., Howes, M., Kane, J., Pope, H. G., Rounsaville, B., & Wittchen, H. U. (1992). The Structured Clinical Interview for DSM-III-R (SCID): Multisite test-retest reliability. *Archives of General Psychiatry*, **49**, 630–636.

Williams, R. M. (1989). Towards a cognitive model of PTSD. Paper presented at the discussion meeting—Post-traumatic stress disorder; prospects for inter-disciplinary investigation. CIBA Foundation, London, UK.

Williams, R. M., Hodgkinson, P., Joseph, S., & Yule, W. (1995). Attitudes to emotion, crisis support and distress 30 months after the capsize of a passenger ferry. *Crisis Intervention*, **1**, 209–214.

Williams, R., Joseph, S., & Yule, W. (1993). Disaster and mental health. In D. Bhugra & J. Leff (Eds), *Principles of social psychiatry*. Oxford: Blackwell Scientific Publications.

Williams, R. M., Joseph, S., & Yule, W. (1994). The role of avoidance in coping with disasters: A study of survivors of the capsize of the *Herald of Free Enterprise*. *Clinical Psychology and Psychotherapy*, **1**, 97–94.

Wilson, J. P., & Krause, G. (1985). Predicting PTSD among Vietnam veterans. In W. Kelly (Ed.), *Post-traumatic stress disorder and the war veteran patient* (pp. 102–148). New York: Brunner/Mazel.

Wolfe, D. A., Sas, L., & Wekerle, C. (1994). Factors associated with the development of posttraumatic stress disorder among child victims of sexual abuse. *Child Abuse and Neglect*, **18**, 37–50.

Wolfe, J., Brown, P. J., & Buscela, M. L. (1992). Symptom responses of female Vietnam veterans to Operation Desert Storm. *American Journal of Psychiatry*, **149**, 676–679.

Wolfe, J., & Charney, D. S. (1991). Use of neuropsychological assessment in posttraumatic stress disorder. *Psychological Assessment*, **3**, 573–580.

Wolfe, J., & Keane, T. M. (1993). New perspectives in the assessment and diagnosis of combat-related posttraumatic stress disorder. In J. P. Wilson & B. Raphael (Eds), *International handbook of traumatic stress syndromes* (pp. 165–177). New York: Plenum Press.

Wolfe, V. V., Gentile, C., Michienzi, T. et al. (1991). The Children's Impact of Traumatic Events Scale: A measure of post-sexual abuse PTSD symptoms. *Behaviour Assessment*, **13**, 359–383.

Wolfe, V. V., Gentile, C., & Wolfe, D. A. (1989). The impact of sexual abuse on children: A PTSD formulation. *Behavior Therapy*, **20**, 215–228.

Wolfe, V. V., & Wolfe, D. A. (1986). The sexual abuse fear evaluation (SAFE): A subscale for the fear survey schedule for children—revised. Unpublished questionnaire. University of Western Ontario, London, Canada.

Wolfe, V. V., Wolfe, D. A., Gentile, C., & LaRose, L. (1986). The children's impact of traumatic events scale (CITES). Available from V. Wolfe, Dept. of Paediatric Psychology, Children's Hospital of Western Ontario, London, Canada.

Wolfenstein, M. (1957). *Disaster: A psychological essay*. Glencoe, IL: Free Press.

Wong, P. T. P., & Weiner, B. (1981). When people ask 'why' questions, and the heuristics of attributional search. *Journal of Personality and Social Psychology*, **40**, 650–663.

Wolpe, J., & Abrams, J. (1991). Post-Traumatic Stress Disorder overcome by eye-movement desensitization: A case report. *Journal of Behaviour Therapy and Experimen-*

tal Psychiatry, **22**, 39–43.

World Health Organisation (1978). *Mental disorders: Glossary and guide to their classification in accordance with the ninth revision of the international classification of diseases.* Geneva: WHO.

World Health Organisation (1993). *Mental disorders: Glossary and guide to their classification in accordance with the tenth revision of the international classification of diseases.* Geneva: WHO.

Worthington, E. R. (1977). Pre-service adjustment and Vietnam era veterans. *Military Medicine*, **142**, 865–866.

Wright, D., & Gaskell, G. (1992). The construction and function of vivid memories. In M. A, Conway, D. C. Rubin, H. Spinnler, & W. A. Wagenaar (Eds), *Theoretical perspectives on autiobiographical memory* (pp. 275–292). Dordrecht, Netherlands: Kluwer Academic Publishers.

Wright, K. M., Ursano, R. J., Bartone, P. T., & Ingraham, L. H. (1990). The shared experience of catastrophe: An expanded classification of disaster community. *American Journal of Orthopsychiatry*, **60**, 35–42.

Yeary, J. (1982). Incest and chemical dependency. *Journal of Psychoactive Drugs*, **14**, 133–135.

Yehuda, R., Southwick, S. M., & Giller, E. L. (1992). Exposure to atrocities and severity of chronic posttraumatic stress disorder in Vietnam combat veterans. *American Journal of Psychiatry*, **149**, 333–336.

Yule, W. (1990). Post traumatic stress in children who survived the *Jupiter* cruise ship disaster. Paper presented at the 1990 American Psychological Association Conference.

Yule, W. (1991). Children in shipping disasters. *Journal of the Royal Society of Medicine*, **84**, 12–15.

Yule, W., & Gold, A. (1993). *Wise before the event: Coping with crises in school.* London: Calouste Gulbenkian Foundation.

Yule, W., Hodgkinson, P., Joseph, S., Parkes, C. M., & Williams, R. (1990a). The *Herald of Free Enterprise*: 30 months follow-up. Paper presented at the second European Conference on Traumatic Stress, Netherlands, 23–27 September 1990.

Yule, W., & Udwin, O. (1991). Screening child survivors for post-traumatic stress disorders: Experiences from the 'Jupiter sinking'. *British Journal of Clinical Psychology*, **30**, 131–138.

Yule, W., Udwin, O. & Murdoch, K. (1990b). The 'Jupiter' sinking: Effects on children's fears, depression and anxiety. *Journal of Child Psychology and Psychiatry*, **31**, 1051–1061.

Yule, W., & Williams, R. A. (1990). Post-traumatic stress reactions in children. *Journal of Traumatic Stress*, **3**, 279–295.

Yule, W., Ten Bruggencate, S., & Joseph, S. (1994). Principal components analysis of the impact of event scale in adolescents who survived a shipping disaster. *Personality and Individual Differences*, **16**, 685–691.

Zeidner, M., & Ben-Zur, H. (1994). Individual differences in anxiety, coping, and post-traumatic stress in the aftermath of the Persian Gulf war. *Personality and Individual Differences*, **16**, 459–476.

Zeiss, R., & Dickman, H. (1989). PTSD 40 years later: Incidence and person-situation correlates in former POW's. *Journal of Clinical Psychology*, **45**, 80–87.

Zeller, R. A., & Carmines, E. G. (1980). *Measurement in the social sciences. The link between theory and data.* Cambridge: Cambridge University Press.

Zilberg, N. J., Weiss, D. S., & Horowitz, M. J. (1982). Impact of Event Scale: A cross-validation study and some empirical evidence supporting a conceptual model of stress response syndromes. *Journal of Consulting and Clinical Psychology*, **50**, 407–414.

Zuckerman, M. (1979). Attribution of success and failure revisited, or: The motivational bias is alive and well in attribution theory. *Journal of Personality*, 47, 245–287.

Zuckerman, L. A., Oliver, J. M., Hollingsworth, H. H., & Austrin, H. R. (1986). A comparison of life events scoring methods as predictors of psychological symptomatology. *Journal of Human Stress*, 12, 64–70.

SUBJECT INDEX